REAL PROPERTY

IN A NUTSHELL

THIRD EDITION

By

ROGER BERNHARDT
Professor of Law
Golden Gate University, School of Law

ST. PAUL, MINN.
WEST PUBLISHING CO.
1993

COPYRIGHT © 1975, 1981 WEST PUBLISHING CO.
COPYRIGHT © 1993 By WEST PUBLISHING CO.

>620 Opperman Drive
>P.O. Box 64526
>St. Paul, MN 55164–0526
>1–800–328–9352

Library of Congress Cataloging-in-Publication Data
Bernhardt, Roger.
    Real property in a nutshell / by Roger Bernhardt. — 3rd ed.
      p.   cm. — (Nutshell series)
    Includes index.
    ISBN 0–314–02436–0
    1. Real property—United States. I. Title. II. Series.
KF570.Z9B47   1993
346.7304'3—dc20
[347.30643]
                                                  93–24677
                                                    CIP

ISBN 0–314–02436–0

Bernhardt, Real Prop. 3rd NS
1st Reprint–1996

INTRODUCTION

No other course in the first year of law school seems to involve as many rules as does Real Property. This feature too often makes the course terrifying to students and grim to professors. Students suffer under the sheer number of rules thrown at them, and professors chafe at the monstrous amount of class time consumed in the brute articulation of all of these rules. This book is an attempt to remedy that a little. For the students it offers a brief compilation of all or most of the rules which are covered in the standard casebooks on the subject, organized so as to minimize their seeming randomness and arbitrariness. For the professors it offers an opportunity to free up class time for an exploration of how the rules came to be, how they operate (or how to operate around them), and whether they work. My goal is to make the mechanical statement of the rules the beginning rather than the end of the study of Property in law school.

Anyone who finds this book helpful should also thank Jo Walker whose editorial assistance converted a lot of random notes into a coherent text.

*

OUTLINE

OUTLINE

OUTLINE

PART THREE. MISCELLANEOUS PROPERTY DOCTRINES

OUTLINE

*

TABLE OF CASES

References are to Pages

XLIX

TABLE OF CASES

TABLE OF CASES

REAL PROPERTY

IN A NUTSHELL

THIRD EDITION

*

PART ONE

INTERESTS IN LAND

CHAPTER ONE

ADVERSE POSSESSION

I. POSSESSION AND OWNERSHIP

A. POSSESSION APART FROM OWNERSHIP

While it is often the case that a person in possession of land is the owner of it or is in possession by virtue of the owner's consent (e.g., a tenant), it may also happen that a possessor of land is there without either being the owner or having the owner's consent. (In all of the illustrations in this section "Olga" will refer to the record owner of the property, and "Paul" will refer to a possessor of that property who is not the owner of it.)

Illustration: Paul received a deed to lot 1, but mistakenly moved onto lot 2 instead. Here Paul owns lot 1, but possesses (without owning or having the consent of the owner) lot 2.

Illustration: Paul received a deed to lot 1, and took possession of lot 1, but in fact the deed to Paul was defectively executed (or alternatively, an earlier deed in the chain of title was defectively executed) so that he is not the owner of lot 1, although he is in possession of it.

Illustration: Paul received a valid deed to lot 1 and took possession of lot 1. However, by mistake, Paul built a fence which encroached 5 feet over into lot 2 and then built his house up to the fence line. Here, Paul possesses but does not own the 5 foot strip.

Illustration: Paul is a squatter, knowing that he does not own the property being occupied, but hoping that the real owner will not do anything about it, and intending to stay until evicted.

B. CONSEQUENCES OF POSSESSION UNCONNECTED TO OWNERSHIP

Possession has always been an important concept in our legal system. The old doctrine of seisin had more to do with possession than with ownership. (On seisin, see Chapter 2, p. 30) A possessor has a legal status in the common law even when he or she is not an owner. Both rights and liabilities attach to possession.

1. Liabilities of a Possessor—Ejectment

If a possessor is not the owner, and if the owner does appear, the owner may bring ejectment to recover both possession and damages in an action of ejectment against the possessor. Ejectment is an action designed to restore possession to the person entitled to it. Not only must the plaintiff establish a right to possession in himself, but he must also show that the defendant is in (wrongful) possession, i.e. dispossessing the plaintiff. If the defendant has not possessed the property, but has only occasionally trespassed on it, an action for trespass (damages) may lie, but not ejectment.

2. Rights of a Possessor

Even though a possessor does not own the property and is subject to ejectment by the owner, nevertheless as against the rest of the world the possessor is entitled to maintain that possession. ("Possession is nine points"). If a stranger appears and dispossesses him, he may bring ejectment against the stranger to be restored to possession. And it is no defense for the stranger to show that the former possessor was not in fact the owner (unless the stranger can also show that he himself is the owner or claims through the owner).

Illustration: Paul entered onto lot 1 under a deed he believed to be valid. Paul was then ousted from possession by Rachel and brought ejectment against her. At the trial Paul discovers that his deed is defective and that it did not in fact convey any title to lot 1 to him. Nevertheless he may prevail against Rachel by virtue of having been in peaceable possession of the lot prior to her entry. Paul prevails, not because he is a wrongful possessor (as against Olga), but because he is a prior possessor as against Rachel.

3. Possession as Both Rightful and Wrongful

Since a nonowning possessor may defend that possession against all of the world (except the owner) and yet is at the same time subject to ejectment by the owner, such possession is both "rightful" and "wrongful". To the degree that ownership is usually taken as the ability to exclude others, the possessor is already a 99% owner in that he or she can exclude everyone else in the world from the property except the owner.

C. THE DURATION OF POSSESSION

There is no required length of possession that a plaintiff in ejectment must show in order to claim as a prior possessor. Time is relevant in that the plaintiff prior possessor must have been there first, but it does not matter how long he was there beforehand (so long as he was still there at the time of the defendant's entry). But time is relevant with regard to the question of how long a defendant possessor has been in possession of the property, because in this case the statute of limitations comes into play. A cause of action in ejectment arises in favor of the owner or a prior possessor the moment someone else wrongfully takes possession of the property. And like all causes of action, except where the government owns the property, it expires after a certain lapse of time. Thus if a person has been in possession long enough, persons who previously were entitled to eject him will now lose their rights to do so.

Illustration: Paul possessed lot 1 and then was dispossessed by Rachel. That was 11 years ago and the statute of limitations on ejectment actions is 10 years. Paul can now no longer recover in ejectment against Rachel. This would be true even if Paul's prior possession had itself endured 15 years.

Illustration: Paul was in possession of lot 1 for 2 years before Rachel dispossessed him. That was 5 years ago, and the statute of limitations is 10 years for ejectment actions.

Paul may still bring ejectment against Rachel. A comparison of durations is irrelevant.

Illustration: Paul has been in possession of lot 1 for 11 years and the statute of limitations in ejectment is 10 years. As a result Olga, the owner, cannot now eject Paul.

II. ADVERSE POSSESSION

A. DURATION AND ADVERSE POSSESSION

It has already been said that a nonowning possessor of property may protect that possession against everyone but the owner. The last illustration shows that such possession extended long enough immunizes the possessor from even the claims of the owner. The possessor's 99% rights thus become 100%. If there is no one in the world who can eject him, and if he can bring ejectment against anyone else in the world who intrudes, then for all practical purposes he is now the owner of the property. He might as well be said to have title to the property, since he now has all of the rights which title is considered to give to the person having it. The possessor is now a successful adverse possessor. Adverse possession does not transfer the former owner's title to the possessor; rather, by eliminating the one defect which previously existed in the possessory title it operates to create a new and complete title in the possessor.

1. How Long Must the Possession Continue

Statutes dealing with adverse possession vary from an upper limit of 20 years to a lower one of 5 years, with even more extreme time periods covering certain special cases. There may be different periods of time even within a single state, depending on whether or not the adverse possessor has color of title and/or whether or not taxes have been paid. In some cases a longer possession is required against public entities than against individuals. (In all of the following illustrations, it will be assumed that a 10 year statute is in effect.)

2. Tacking

Even though the possessor has not personally possessed the property for the requisite period of time it may be possible to "tack" on time that predecessors possessed the property so as to accumulate enough years to satisfy the statute.

Illustration: Paul possessed the property from 1960 to 1966 and then purported to convey the property to Rachel who possessed it from 1966 to 1971. Under a 10 year statute of limitations, Rachel prevails against Olga, since she may tack Paul's 6 years to her own 5 years and claim 11 years of possession.

a. Privity

Tacking will not be allowed unless there is privity between the possessor and his or her predecessor. This means that the possessor must be connected with the predecessor in such a way that the two possessions may be viewed as related.

Illustration: Paul possessed the property for 6 years and then died leaving Rachel as his heir who possessed the property for 5 years thereafter. The two periods may be tacked together because there is privity between ancestor and heir.

Illustration: Paul possessed for 6 years and sold the property to Rachel who possessed for 5 years. There is privity between a grantor and grantee, and so the periods may be tacked together. (Paul had no "title" to convey to Rachel, but he had a transferable possessory interest, which is what Rachel purchased from him).

Illustration: Paul possessed for 6 years and was then ousted by Rachel, who possessed for 5 years. Tacking will not be permitted here since Rachel's possession is in no way related to Paul's earlier possession. Rachel will not gain title by adverse possession until she has possessed for at least 5 more years. (Theoretically, on Paul's ouster, Olga's constructive possession was reinstated momentarily, so that Olga acquired a whole new cause of action against Rachel which would be good for 10 years from the date of the ouster.)

b.   Tacking When There Is No Color of Title

If the privity claimed comes from a deed between the possessor and his predecessor, but that deed does not cover the property in question, the more common view is that there is privity anyway, so long as both possessor and predecessor actually possess the property.

Illustration: For 6 years Paul possessed lot 1 under a deed describing (and perhaps actually conveying to him) lot 2. Paul then executed a deed to Rachel using the same description, and Rachel entered lot 1 under it and continued possessing lot 1 for 5 more years. Rachel should be allowed to tack on Paul's prior possession of lot 1, even though Rachel and Paul are connected by a deed referring to lot 2. They were still in privity as to possession of lot 1. The same tacking will be allowed where Paul possessed lot

1 and a part of lot 2 under a deed which described only lot 1, and then executed a deed to Rachel containing the same description. Rachel will acquire good title to lot 1 and will also be able to tack Paul's possession on lot 2 to her own.

B. ACTS OF POSSESSION REQUIRED—STANDARDS

In some states, by statute, a person may qualify as an adverse possessor only if certain acts were performed during the running of the statute of limitations, e.g., cultivating, enclosing, or residing on the property. However, in most states there is no such requirement and any acts of possession, if they have the correct quality, may justify a finding of adverse possession. Any acts by a person during the prescriptive period which establish that in fact he or she has been in possession of the property for the requisite period of time may suffice.

There is no set rule as to what sorts of activities are or are not possessory. A standard sometimes applied is to ask whether the activities of the possessor in the past were of such a sort as to support an action of ejectment by the owner. Occasional trespasses in the past would justify an action in trespass, but not ejectment, and therefore the presence of only those acts, for the statutory period would not make the trespasser an adverse possessor. However, most courts prefer a less circular requirement and use phrases such as "acts which publicly indicate a control consistent with the character of the land", or "acts such as an average owner of similar property would undertake."

1. Payment of Taxes

In some states by statute no person can become an adverse possessor unless he or she also pays taxes on the property being possessed. In other states the time required for adverse possession may be shortened by the payment of taxes (usually when it is coupled with a color of title in the possessor). One justification offered for this requirement is that by being able to check the tax records an owner can discover whether there is any risk of potential adverse possession. Or, possibly the requirement is based upon an attitude that squatters ought not be able to acquire land by adverse possession, and that nonsquatting possessors who really believe themselves to be owners will pay taxes anyway. In this light, payment of taxes is just another appropriate act of possession.

a. *When Both Parties Pay Taxes*

When the payment of taxes is required, it is a requirement that the adverse possessor must meet; it is not a requirement of an owner desiring to eliminate threats of adverse possession. As long as the adverse possessor is paying taxes, this test is met, even though the owner may also be making tax payments at the same time (although in some states the issue turns on who paid the taxes first).

b. Boundary Disputes

The tax requirement can cause particular trouble in boundary line cases when the disputed strip has not been separately taxed, and both neighbors have been paying all of the taxes billed to them by the assessor. Probably no one involved, including the assessor, knows to which party the disputed strip has been assessed. The most sensible result in this case is to ignore the tax question entirely.

C. THE REQUIRED QUALITIES OF POSSESSION

Although rarely mentioned in statutes, every court in the country requires that the possession be "open, notorious, visible, actual, adverse, exclusive, continuous, uninterrupted, hostile and under claim of right", or at least some of these adjectives. The burden of proof is usually placed upon the alleged adverse possessor to establish that the possession has complied with all of the adjectives required in that jurisdiction. From a strictly technical point of view, any possession which subjected the possessor to liability in ejectment during the prescriptive period should perhaps lead to a holding of adverse possession at the end of the period. Under that analysis, none of the adjectives mentioned should be required unless they are only ways of saying that the possession had to be real (i.e., actionable) possession, or at least that the possession had to be such as would have supported a claim of prior possession had the possessor ever needed to bring ejectment against subsequent intruders. In fact, in most cases that is all that many of the adjectives do.

1. Open—Visible

Usually the requirement of open or visible possession is just another way of saying that there has to be real possession by a person in order to become an adverse possessor. The furtive possessor is really not a possessor at all. It is doubtful whether one could ever sustain a claim to have been a prior possessor in an ejectment action brought against a subsequent intruder by proof of nothing more than previous clandestine entries upon the land. A real possessor generally treats the property as a true owner would and leaves physical evidence of his possession there; thus some cases state that his possession must be "appropriate" or that there must be permanent signs of his possession.

2. Notorious

"Notorious" is rarely mentioned separately from open, but it may serve a slightly different function. There is no requirement that the owner actually know of the adverse possession, and ignorance by the owner does not extend the time allotted to sue. The omission of such a requirement can be justified by the presence of notoriety as an element of adverse possession. If a person is in notorious possession, i.e., acting so that all who are interested will know about it, then the possessor has done all that can be expected. Like as not, the possessor believes himself to own the property he is possessing, so that he can hardly be expected to notify an owner of whom he has never heard. Instead, it becomes the owner's obligation to check out the property periodically.

Illustration: Paul resides in a house on Lot 1, which is in fact owned by Olga, but Paul believes himself to be the owner of the house. Everyone in the neighborhood knows that Paul lives there, but Olga resides elsewhere and does not know this. Paul will become an adverse possessor after the statutory period, since it is Olga's fault for failing to check on her property rather than Paul's fault for not telling Olga.

Illustration: Paul's house encroaches onto Olga's property, but Olga does not realize it. Paul can still be an adverse possessor even though Olga does not have a survey taken until it is too late.

(*Subjacent Possession*) A person may adversely possess property underneath another's land (i.e., below the surface) even though the owner cannot see it. The possession is quite open and notorious where it is, and the only problem is that the owner does not know that the possession is below the surface of his or her land. But this is basically no different from when an owner does not realize that a neighbor's building is encroaching over the lot line.

Illustration: Paul operates a cave (or a coal mine) which tunnels under Olga's property, but Paul makes no secret about his activities. The fact that Olga does not realize that the tunnel runs under her property is irrelevant, and Paul may gain adverse possession of the cave.

3. Actual (and Constructive)

"Actual" as a requirement of adverse possession, means no more than real possession. Its main function is as a counterpart to constructive possession. Constructive possession is the absence of real possession. By itself constructive possession never ripens into adverse possession. Ejectment lies only against real possessors.

Illustration: For 20 years Paul has claimed that he owns Olga's lot, but has never actually set foot on it. No statute of limitations will run against Olga since she has never had a cause of action against Paul for ejectment. Only if Paul actually takes possession of her land can she bring ejectment; claiming land is not the same as possessing it. (Olga might bring an action of quiet title against Paul's claim, but that is not a possessory action).

a. Constructive Possession and Color of Title

An adverse possessor may ultimately be given title to more property than was ever actually adversely possessed, if there was actual adverse possession of a part of that property and an entry onto that part under a deed giving color of title to an area larger than, and including the property actually possessed.

Illustration: Paul has a void deed to a five acre parcel. He enters onto the parcel and lives on one acre, doing nothing as to other four acres. At the end of 10 years Paul will acquire adverse possession to all five acres. The boundaries in Paul's deed serve as a sort of substitute for a fence built by Paul (which probably would have made Paul an actual possessor of the five acres had one been built). In some states it is required that Paul have a good faith belief in the validity of his deed for this doctrine to operate. Other states require that the deed be recorded to work as color of title.

b. Constructive Possession and Prior Possession

The same enlargement of the area conferred by a color of title operates in favor of a prior possessor.

13

n actually possessing only one acre un-
f title to five acres should be able to eject
.t intruders from any of the five acres.

Limitations on Constructive Possession

The doctrine does not apply when that part of the property which is only constructively possessed is separately owned, or when the part actually possessed is not adversely possessed, or where the color of title does not cover the property in dispute.

Illustration: Paul has a void deed to lots 1 and 2, which are in fact owned by Olga and Owen respectively. Paul enters and occupies only lot 1. Paul will never become an adverse possessor of lot 2, since at no time has Owen ever had a cause of action in ejectment against Paul.

Illustration: Paul has a deed to lots 1 and 2, which is valid as to lot 1 and invalid as to lot 2 (because his grantor owned only lot 1, but believed that he also owned lot 2, and intended to convey both to Paul). Paul actually possessed only lot 1. Paul cannot claim adverse possession of lot 2, because he has not adversely possessed anything at all. His possession of lot 1 was not adverse, since he really owned it; and he never possessed lot 2.

Illustration: Paul has a deed to lot 1 but entered by mistake onto lot 2 and possessed some part of it only. Paul can make no claim to constructive possession to any other part of lot 2, since his deed refers only to lot 1, and affords no color of title to lot 2. Paul gains adverse possession of only that part of lot 2 that he actually occupied. (It is irrelevant here whether the deed is valid or invalid as to lot 1, since it is lot 2 which is in question). The same is true for cases where Paul claims strips of land outside the boundaries of his deed.

d. *Conflicting Constructive Possessions*

Real title also gives constructive possession and without the need for being accompanied by any actual possession. Thus an absentee owner is able to eject wrongful possessors because his or her own constructive possession has been breached. Sometimes the constructive possession claims of various parties may conflict. How these conflicts are resolved is demonstrated in the following illustrations:

Illustration: Olga is absent from her 40 acres and Paul enters under a color of title to all 40 acres, but actually possesses only 1 acre. Paul will acquire all 40 acres by adverse possession because his constructive possession of 39 acres coupled with his actual possession of the 1 acre prevails over Olga's constructive possession.

Illustration: Olga is actually occupying only 1 of her 40 acres and Paul enters under a color of title to the 40 acres and actually possesses 1 acre (a different acre from the acre Olga possesses). Paul will acquire adverse possession to only 1 acre because his claim of constructive possession to the other 39 acres here is defeated by Olga's constructive possession of 38 of them plus her actual possession of 1 acre. Olga's claim of constructive possession, supported by both title and some actual possession is superior to Paul's claim which is supported only by some actual possession.

Illustration: Olga is absent from her 40 acres and Paul enters under a color of title to all 40 acres, actually possessing only 1 acre. Subsequently Rachel enters onto the same 40 acres under a color of title to all 40 acres and actually possesses 1 different acre herself. Paul now can only acquire adverse possession to 39 acres (the 1 acre he actually possesses and the 38 acres no one actually possesses), but he cannot acquire title to the acre where Rachel is, since her actual possession defeats Paul's claim to constructive possession of it. If Rachel remains long enough, she can acquire adverse possession of the 1 acre she is on, but she cannot claim constructive possession of any of the rest because Paul's claim of constructive possession, being prior in time, is superior to her.

4. Color of Title

"Color of title," in the context of adverse possession, refers to a document which purports but fails to convey actual title, typically a void deed. If the deed is valid, then the grantee under it takes real title and may claim rights as an owner. Since the adverse possessor is always someone who is not an owner of the property in dispute, any deed he or she claims under is by definition void. Possession of a void deed, however, may have important consequences, discussed in the following sections.

a. *Color of Title as an Absolute Requirement of Adverse Possession*

In a few states there can be no adverse possession at all except under color of title. The actual possessor of property who has no document supporting the possession gets nothing.

b. *Color of Title as Affecting the Acts Required*

In a few states color of title enables an ordinary use of the property to qualify as an adverse possession, whereas more significant possessory acts (e.g., fencing or cultivating) are necessary when there is no color of title.

c. *Color of Title as Affecting the Time Period*

In a few states a possessor with a color of title needs fewer years of possession to become an adverse possessor than does a possessor without any color of title.

d.　Color of Title and Hostility

In some states a possessor with color of title is presumed to be hostile to the owner whereas otherwise independent proof of hostility is needed.

5.　Continuous—Uninterrupted

These words have no constant meaning, are often used interchangeably, and are sometimes entirely devoid of content, signifying no more than real possession. "Continuous" does not mean constant. There is no requirement that the possessor possess every minute of the day. Many successful adverse possessors have been persons who have merely made a seasonal use of the land (e.g., grazing or hunting). In these situations continuous means only that the activity be carried on regularly (i.e., the grazer must graze every year during the grazing season). If the acts are too irregular, they will be viewed as a series of unconnected trespasses not amounting to a dispossession of the owner. Also, a possessor who abandoned the property (i.e., with no intent to return) and then returned did not continuously possess the property and the statute of limitations starts anew from his reentry.

The most common meaning of "uninterrupted" is that no one other than the possessor has possessed the land during the statutory period without the possessor's consent.

Illustration: Rachel intruded onto Paul's possession after Paul had been there 9 years and remained there for a year. Paul cannot claim adverse possession under a 10 year statute because his possession was interrupted after 9 years. This same result can be explained by saying that Paul was not exclusive (*q.v.*) for 10 years, or merely by saying that Paul was not in actual possession for 10 years.

Illustration: Paul was in possession for 5 years and was then ousted by Rachel. Paul (as prior possessor) brought a successful ejectment action against Rachel and Paul was thus restored to possession one year after his initial dispossession, and has since been in possession a second time for 3 years. Most authorities agree that Paul should not have to start all over again (which would mean 7 more years under a 10 year statute), but do not agree as to whether Paul can count in Rachel's time. If Paul can include Rachel's year, then Paul needs only 1 more year; if Paul cannot, then he needs 2 more years. The result depends on whether or not Olga's cause of action is viewed as continuing to run against Paul during the year that Rachel had possession.

(*Interruptions by the Owner*) A successful ejectment action (followed up by an execution of the judgment) interrupts an adverse possession by revesting possession in the owner, and a successful judgment will relate back to the date of filing the complaint, so that the action need merely be filed in time. But a complaint which is not followed up in court will not interrupt an adverse possession.

Any act by the owner which amounts to a resumption of possession is an interruption. But a furtive entry, or an accidental entry, or an entry under the possessor's consent has no such effect because these are not really possessory acts. To interrupt another's possession the owner must actually become a possessor, i.e., commit such acts as would entitle the possessor to bring ejectment were the owner someone else.

Illustration: Paul's deed was to lot 1 but he mistakenly possessed lot 2. Olga, who owns lot 2 possessed lot 3 under a similar mistake. During the statutory time period Olga frequently visited Paul on lot 2, and even slept over occasionally. None of these acts by Olga interrupted Paul's possession, since they were all committed with (and as a result of) Paul's permission.

6. Exclusive

"Exclusive" does not mean that no one other than the possessor is ever on the property. It is generally used to require that no one else is ever there without the possessor's consent. (It comes from the notion that possession is usually treated as involving an intent to exclude). Consequently, an adverse possession which fails for want of exclusivity is probably lacking other requirements as well.

Illustration: During his 10 years on the property others frequently intrude and are not ousted by Paul. Paul will not become an adverse possessor because he was not exclusive. This result can also be explained by saying that there was no actual possession at all, since a "real" possessor does not tolerate intruders.

Illustration: During the past 10 years Paul has sometimes possessed it himself, but at other times he has brought friends with him or has leased it out to third persons. Paul is an adverse possessor; the other activities were all done under Paul's auspices which enables Paul to count them as his own possessory acts.

7. Hostile—Claim of Right—Adverse

Although these adjectives are almost everywhere used, there is a great disagreement as to their meaning and significance. All agree that a person possessing property under the permission of the owner is not adversely possessing. Under an objective view of adverse possession, lack of permission is all that these adjectives signify; but under a subjective view, more is required.

a. The Subjective Standard

The subjective view requires that a person not only possess the property but that he also have a certain state of mind throughout the time of his possession. An adverse possessor is someone who does not in fact own the land he is possessing and it may be said generally that he either knows or does not know this fact. The courts requiring a mental element do not agree as to which state of mind is the "correct" one.

(1) The Mentality of Thievery

If the possessor knows that he does not own the property, some jurisdictions hold that he cannot become an adverse possessor. (He has a "claim of wrong" rather than a "claim of right"; or he is not in "good faith" as some courts require an adverse possessor to be). If he intends to stay only until he is evicted by the owner he is held to lack true hostility. This rule is designed to keep squatters from acquiring title to land.

(2) The Mentality of Mistake

If the possessor believes that he is the owner, some other states hold he cannot become an adverse possessor. The rationale is that one must "claim" the property and if the possessor testifies that he only intended to claim what he owned (and would not have claimed the property if he had known the truth), then his actual nonownership of it means that he did not claim it. In these states, only the "thief" can become an adverse possessor.

b. The Objective Standard

Most states now do not permit the possessor to be psychoanalyzed, holding that state of mind is irrelevant if in fact the person acted as a possessor for the requisite time. "Hostility" enters in only to defeat the possessor who publicly disclaims any intent to acquire title by adverse possession during the time of possession. (This result could also be explained as an application of the doctrine of estoppel).

c. Permissive Possession

A tenant under a lease is not adverse to the landlord, because the lease has transferred the possessory right from the landlord to the tenant. Nor is the possession of a tenant in common or joint tenant adverse to the other cotenants, because each co-owner has a right to possess the entire property, and no cotenant, therefore, is entitled to demand that the other not possess the property. In each of these cases the possession is permissive, i.e., not generating a cause of action in ejectment in the (other) owner.

Consequently, such possession never ripens into adverse possession, no matter how long continued.

(1) Ouster

A permissive possessor can become adverse to the owner if he repudiates the owner's title and asserts his own independent possessory right and if he makes this claim known to the owner or is appropriately notorious about it. This is an ouster of the owner, generating a cause of action which will expire after enough years.

Illustration: Paul has been in possession for 3 years as a tenant under a lease from Olga; now he announces that since he had learned (erroneously) that Olga is not the owner he will no longer pay rent to her. Paul can become an adverse possessor after a sufficient number of years following the disclaimer, but he cannot include his first three years, since those were years of permissive possession. (Many states, however, have a special statute dealing with adverse possession by tenants).

Illustration: Paul and Olga are joint tenants, but Paul has been in sole possession for the past three years. Now Paul announces to Olga that he no longer will allow Olga to share in the ownership, profits or possession of the property. Paul's possession will ripen into a full title after enough years, but again the first three years cannot be counted.

(*What Constitutes an Ouster*) Any act which serves to give notice to the owner that his or her title to the property is no longer recognized by the possessor should serve as an ouster. In the case of cotenants this can consist of a refusal to permit the other cotenant to enter, or a refusal to account for the profits, or sometimes merely a statement that the possessor regards himself as the sole owner. In the landlord-tenant situation the refusal to pay rent constitutes the clearest kind of ouster.

d.　*Other Cases of Permissive Possession*

A mortgagor's possession is not hostile to the mortgagee and does not become so until there is a repudiation of the mortgage (or a foreclosure followed by the retention of possession by the mortgagor). A mortgagee in possession is not hostile to the mortgagor until the mortgagee refuses to account for the profits from the land. A grantor under a valid deed who retains possession is usually not considered hostile to the grantee unless the deed is repudiated. But a grantee taking possession under a void deed is considered hostile to the grantor. In general, possession by a member of the family is not deemed hostile to the rest of the family.

D.　EXTERNAL FACTORS THAT PROLONG THE STATUTE OF LIMITATIONS

1.　Disabilities

Generally the statute of limitations is tolled if a plaintiff is under some legal disability, such as infancy, insanity, imprisonment or military service at the time the cause of action arises. This is also true in adverse possession cases, and either the entire statutory period, or else some special shorter period is allotted to the owner for suit after the disability ends. Further refinements of this principle are shown in the following illustrations, all of which presuppose a 10 year statute of limitations which is entirely suspended during the disability.

Illustration: Paul entered in 1960, while Olga was insane. Olga recovered her sanity in 1963. Paul did not gain title by adverse possession until 1973, 10 years after Olga's disability ended.

Illustration: Paul entered in 1960, when Olga was 12 years old and insane (and the age of majority is 18). Olga recovered her sanity in 1963. Paul gained title by adverse possession only in 1976, 10 years after Olga reached majority. If Olga remained insane until she were 20 years old (1968), then Paul would have had to wait until 1978, since whenever there are two disabilities existing at the start, both must be eliminated.

Illustration: Paul entered in 1960, and Olga went insane in 1963. Paul became a successful adverse possessor in 1970, since subsequently arising disabilities generally have no effect on the running of the statute.

Illustration: Paul entered in 1960 and Olga died in 1963, leaving a 15 year old daughter as her heir. Paul gained title in 1970, since this was not a disability existing in the person who had the cause of action at the time that it first accrued. However, some statutes refer to the time when "the adverse possession commences or the title first descends", and these can be read as giving the heir in this case until 10 years after she reaches majority (thus until 1976). But even in states with statutes such as this the other result is often reached, with the disability in the daughter being rejected.

2. Future Interests

It is generally the case that the holder of a future interest in property is not entitled to bring ejectment against a wrongful possessor because the future interest gives no present possessory right. Therefore, it is also generally held that the statute of limitations does not begin to run against the holder of the future interest until that interest becomes possessory.

Illustration: In 1969 Olga died, leaving land to her husband for life and thereafter to her daughter. In 1970 Paul entered. In 1980, assuming Olga's husband was still alive, Paul gained only a life estate from his adverse possession (measured by the husband's life). Paul does not acquire the entire fee by adverse possession until he is there for at least 10 years after the death of Olga's husband when her daughter acquires her own cause of action against him.

Illustration: Olga rented her property to Tom for a 20 year term, ending in 1980. Paul entered in 1965. In 1975 Paul became a successful adverse possessor against Tom, but that only gave Paul the balance of Tom's term. For Paul to become a successful adverse possessor against Olga, he must possess until 1990, 10 years after Olga's reversion has become possessory. (This result makes sense only if Olga has no problem with rent during the adverse possession, e.g., if Tom has prepaid the rent for the entire term. If rent is regularly due and is not paid, Olga's right and time to sue may be accelerated).

Illustration: Paul entered onto Olga's property in 1965; in 1970 Olga signed a lease on the property to Tom for 15 years. In 1975 Paul gained a complete title by adverse possession. Since the adverse possession commenced first, Olga was capable only of leasing adversely possessed land. The same would be true if Olga had conveyed the property to Tom after Paul had entered. She is only transferring to Tom her cause of action against Paul, and the time Paul needs to perfect his claim to adverse possession is not thereby extended.

3. The Effect of Adverse Possession on Nonpossessory Interests

Easements and restrictive covenants held by third parties are not automatically extinguished by adverse possession of the property. Those claims are not dependent on the owner's title and therefore do not fail merely because that title fails nor are they necessarily affected by the acts of adverse possession on the property. But if during the period of possession the possessor has interfered with the rights of the easement and covenant holders, thereby generating causes of action in them, then they too may be barred by the running of the statute of limitations upon their own independent claims.

Illustration: Paul adversely possesses Olga's property by, among other acts, fencing it off. One effect of this fence is to block off a right of way which Olga had formerly granted to Sam. If Sam fails to sue Paul to recover access, he will ultimately lose his easement over the property. But if Paul's possessory acts do not interfere with Sam, then even though Paul later acquires a title by adverse possession, it will nevertheless be a title subject to Sam's easement.

Illustration: Olga owns property subject to a restrictive covenant limiting any building to 2 stories. Paul adversely possesses the land, but never builds a building over 2 stories. At the end of the limitations period Paul will have title by adverse possession but it will be subject to the covenant since at no time have the beneficiaries of the covenant ever had a cause of action against Paul for breach.

III. THE CONSEQUENCES OF HAVING BEEN AN ADVERSE POSSESSOR

Whenever all of the requirements are met, two significant changes occur in the adverse possessor's status. On the one hand, he is no longer liable in ejectment or trespass for his former possession; the statute of limitations eliminates yesterday's as well as last year's liability. On the other hand, he acquires an original title to the property, by virtue of no longer being subject to ejectment by the former owner. Thereafter, whether he knows it or not, the adverse possessor has title. From then on he is freed not only from all liability for his previous possession, but from all the earlier requirements of adverse possession; he need no longer be exclusive, continuous, etc. The property is his, and he may do with it as he pleases. He may find it necessary to obtain a quiet title decree in order to have a marketable title (i.e., one which he can force a prospective purchaser to accept), but the decree itself only confirms the title he has already acquired. That title arose at the moment that the former owner lost the right to bring ejectment.

Illustration: Paul possessed for the requisite number of years. Thereafter Paul failed to pay the taxes. Even if taxes are a requirement of adverse possession in the jurisdiction Paul will still prevail against Olga. Possession plus taxes during the limitations period made Paul an owner and the failure to pay them thereafter did not work to transfer title back to Olga.

CHAPTER TWO

COMMON LAW ESTATES

I. PRESENT (POSSESSORY) ESTATES IN LAND

A. KINDS OF ESTATES

Under the common law system, a person is regarded as holding or owning an estate in land rather than land itself. Such estates are classified according to duration.*

1. The Fee Simple

This estate comprises the greatest extent of ownership of an interest in property recognized by the law; today we would call it absolute ownership. The owner can dispose of the land as he or she pleases, and on death it will descend to the owner's heir. In other words, this estate will last until the owner dies without heirs.

* To make the common law estate system more intelligible, I have somewhat oversimplified matters in this Chapter. I have, furthermore, made some small and, I believe, harmless distortions so as to give the topic a logic which can more easily be mastered. Where Estates is treated as a major component of the Property course, a more specialized treatise should be consulted. Despite the frequent use of the present tense in the text, most of the rules and many of the estates described here are of historical significance only, and are no longer used in modern estates.

2. The Fee Tail

This estate lasts until its holder dies without issue (children) surviving; it cannot be inherited by collateral heirs. By statute in most states, this estate has been abolished.

3. The Life Estate

This estate is not inheritable; it lasts only so long as its owner is alive, or as long as whatever measuring life is used continues.

4. The Estate for Years (Also Known as Tenancy for a Term)

This estate lasts for a definite period, from 999 years or more down to a single day. Technically, it is not inheritable, but upon the death of the owner of the estate, it passes to the next of kin as personalty.

5. The Periodic Estate (Also Known as Tenancy From Period to Period)

This estate lasts for a certain term, and unless seasonably terminated before the end of the term, repeats for another like term. The term may be for any length of time, e.g. a year or longer, or a week or less.

6. The Tenancy at Will and the Tenancy at Sufferance

The tenancy at will and the tenancy at sufferance are also sometimes called estates in land, but their significance is so slight that they will not be discussed here; they are covered, along with the other nonfreehold estates in Landlord and Tenant (Chapter 4, p. 109.)

B. FREEHOLD v. NONFREEHOLD ESTATES—SEISIN

The fee simple, fee tail, and life estate are called freehold estates; the tenancy for years and the periodic tenancy are nonfreehold estates. Nonfreehold estates terminate on or before an ascertainable date, whereas the termination of freehold estates cannot be so reckoned, since death (with or without heirs) is always the terminating event.

The need for distinguishing between freehold and nonfreehold estates derived from the concept of seisin. One in possession of a freehold estate had seisin (i.e. is seised of the land), whereas one in possession of a nonfreehold estate had possession but not seisin. In England, all titles to land came from the king, either directly to the possessor or by way of intermediate lords. And to the overlord, the holder of the freehold estate owed certain services, somewhat equivalent to modern rent or property taxes. The lord collected these services from the person seised of the land, and so it was important to the lord to know whether the person on the land had seisin or mere possession.

Illustration: Bob held a fee simple of Al (i.e., Al was Bob's lord); Bob by appropriate steps conveyed (transferred) his fee simple to Carl. This passed seisin from Bob to Carl. Carl has the seisin, and must render whatever services to Al as are required by the nature of their relationship. (The estate system developed during a time when women were generally disabled from owning land. Consequently characters in all of the illustrations, and pronouns generally, will be masculine throughout this chapter).

Illustration: Bob held a fee simple of Al; by appropriate steps Bob conveyed a term of years to Carl. It is Bob who must render the services required to Al, for Bob is still seised of the land. Carl has possession but not seisin, since he does not hold a freehold. Someone must have seisin, so that the lord will know who to look to when the services are due. In this case, Bob is seised through the possession of the tenant Carl.

C. THE CREATION OF ESTATES (CREATING WORDS)

1. The Fee Simple—"To Bob and His Heirs"

At common law the only language which could create a fee simple was a grant to the transferee "and his heirs". "And his heirs" was the grantor's way of indicating that the estate was inheritable by the heirs of the grantee. Nothing is given directly to the heirs in this conveyance; they do not share the estate with the ancestor and have no interest of their own from this conveyance. Thus these are "words of limitation" (showing that this is an inheritable estate) rather than "words of purchase" (designating a taker). Today, the requirement of such special words of limitation has been generally abolished.

2. The Fee Tail—"To Bob and the Heirs of His Body"

The estate is again inheritable (because of the use of "heirs" as words of limitation) but it is inheritable only by lineal (and not collateral) descendants. Another common way of creating a fee tail was: "To Bob and heirs, but if he die without issue (or without issue surviving), then * * *" At common law there was a constructional preference for "indefinite failure of issue", i.e. not merely must the first grantee (Bob) have a lineal descendant, but also his son was subject to a similar restriction; thus the estate ended whenever the line ran out.

a. Special Forms of Fee Tail

The fee tail may be a fee tail general, as described above, or it may be a fee tail special: "To Al and the heirs of his body and the body of his wife Jane." There may also be a fee tail male: "To Al and the male heirs of his body" or a fee tail female. It is possible to have a fee tail special male or female.

b. The Earlier Fee Simple Conditional

Before 1285, a conveyance to a person and the heirs of his body gave him a fee simple conditional, i.e., an estate which would become a fee simple as soon as issue were born alive. Since this result did not conform to what grantors desired, the Statute De Donis (1285) declared that a conveyance to a person and the heirs of his body created an estate descendible only to the issue, and the birth of issue did not enlarge the estate into a fee simple. This became the fee tail. If the grantee conveyed this estate to another, then upon his death either his issue (if there were issue) or the original grantor (if there were no issue) could recover back the estate.

c. Disentailing Conveyances—the Common Recovery and the Fine

Certain collusive lawsuits, known as common recovery and fine, made it possible, despite De Donis, for the holder of an estate in fee tail to enlarge his estate into a fee simple without recourse from either his issue or his grantor.

3. The Life Estate—"To Bob for His Life", or Merely "To Bob"

If the phrase "and his heirs" is not included in the grant, the common law limited the duration of the estate to the grantee's life and made it noninheritable. This was called a "conventional" life estate, as distinguished from a legal life estate.

a. The Life Estate Per Autre Vie—"To Bob for the Life of Carl"

This is a life estate per autre vie. It also arises when the life tenant, owning a life estate himself, conveys it to a third person, who then has an estate measured by another life. When the holder of a life estate per autre vie dies before the measuring life ends, no person is eligible to hold the estate: not the heirs of the grantee (because the estate is not inheritable), nor the grantor or any persons with future interest (because they must wait until the measuring life ceases). So the land is open to a general occupant: the first person who comes upon it, and who cannot be dispossessed until the measuring life terminates.

b. The Legal Life Estate

A life estate may result not by virtue of the terms of the gift but from the legal consequences attaching to events concerning other estates.

(1) The Fee Tail Special With Possibility of Issue Extinct

"To Bob and the heirs of his body and the body of his wife Jane" gives Bob a life estate once Jane dies without issue, since there is no longer any possibility of this estate passing on to Bob's designated issue.

(2) Marital Estates

The spouse of the person seised may have dower or curtesy in the estate upon the death of the other. See p. 80.

4. The Estate for Years—"To Bob for 10 Years"

There is no need to add "heirs" to the grant of a non-freehold since the estate is not inheritable, but passes as personalty to the next of kin (rather than to the heirs) upon the death of the grantee.

5. The Estate From Period to Period—"To Bob From Month to Month", or "To Bob for $10 Per Month"

The grant either states that the term is periodic, or else fixes a periodic rent without setting a termination date. This creates a periodic tenancy. The length of the period is usually the measuring time of the rent. Other forms of periodic tenancy are covered in Landlord and Tenant. See Chapter 4.

D. THE QUALITY OF ESTATES—
ABSOLUTE OR UNQUALIFIED

All of the estates described so far differ "quantitatively", i.e., according to their duration and the events which lead to their natural termination. The fees are naturally terminated when there are no appropriate heirs to take; the life estate naturally ends when the measuring life expires; and the non-freeholds naturally end when the designated time interval passes. However all of these estates may be made subject to premature termination if the grant specifies that they are also subject to some other condition or limitation. When and if that condition occurs an estate subject to it will terminate even though this occurs before the event which would naturally terminate the estate. An estate which is made subject to some additional condition is called a "qualified" or "base" estate, while an estate which is subject to no terminating condition (other than the condition which naturally terminates it based on the very nature of the estate) is called an "absolute" or "unqualified" estate. If an estate is a qualified estate, it is either "determinable" or "subject to a condition subsequent."

1. The Determinable Estate (Also Called the Estate Subject to Special Limitation)

This estate lasts only as long as the condition described in it continues to exist. Once the limitation ceases, the estate automatically and naturally ends.

Illustration: "To Bob and his heirs so long as the land is farmed". This creates a fee simple determinable. The moment Bob (or his heirs) stop farming, the estate ends.

Illustration: "To Bob and the heirs of his body so long as the land is farmed". This creates a fee tail determinable. The estate ends if Bob or his lineal heirs stop farming, or if there are no lineal heirs.

Illustration: "To Bob for life so long as the land is farmed." Bob has a determinable life estate, which will end when he dies or stops farming.

Illustration: "To Bob for 10 years so long as the land is farmed." Bob's determinable term of years will end in 10 years or sooner if Bob stops farming.

2. The Estate Subject to Condition Subsequent

Like determinable estates, these estates can end when the condition occurs. However, termination is not automatic, but is at the election of the person with the appropriate future interest.

Illustration: "To Bob and his heirs, but if the land is used for a farm, then the grantor may reenter and repossess." This creates a fee simple subject to a condition subsequent.

Illustration: "To Bob and the heirs of his body, but if the land is used for a farm, then the grantor may reenter and repossess." This creates a fee tail subject to a condition subsequent.

Illustration: "To Bob for life, but if the land is used for a farm, then the grantor may reenter and repossess." This creates a life estate subject to condition subsequent.

Illustration: "To Bob for 10 years, but if the land is used for a farm, then the grantor may reenter and repossess." This creates a term of years subject to condition subsequent.

II. FUTURE INTERESTS

Every estate in land is either present (entitling its owner to an immediate right in the land) or future (entitling its owner to a right at some future time).

A. THE REVERSION

If the owner of land grants away a present estate (or estates) legally smaller than the estate he had, i.e. one which will not endure as long as his own estate, he has a reversion to make up the difference.

Illustration: Al, holding in fee simple, conveyed "to Bob and the heirs of his body." The fee tail conveyed to Bob is legally smaller than the fee simple Al had. Al now has a reversion in fee simple, i.e. he or his heirs will take the land when there is a failure of lineal descendants in Bob's line, and when it returns to Al or his heirs, it will be held by them in fee simple.

Illustration: Al, holding a fee simple, conveyed "to Bob for life". Al has a reversion in fee simple, which will give Al and his heirs the land when Bob dies and his life estate ends.

Illustration: Al, holding a fee tail conveyed "To Bob for life". Al has a reversion in fee tail. When Bob dies, the land will revert to Al, but Al will hold only a fee tail because that is all he ever held. (Someone else holds a future interest upon Al's fee tail making up the rest of fee simple.)

Illustration: Al, holding a life estate for his own life, conveyed "to Bob for Bob's life". Bob's life estate will end on either his death or Al's death (because Al cannot grant an estate greater than his own life). Bob's estate is smaller than Al's, since either one of 2 deaths will end Bob's estate, whereas Al's estate is affected only by one death, and Al therefore has a reversion in a life estate, i.e. he will recover his original life estate when Bob dies, if Bob dies first. Al's reversion will last only for the rest of Al's life, however. Someone else holds a future interest upon Al's life estate.

Illustration: Al, holding a fee or a life estate, conveyed "to Bob for 10 years". Today, it is generally said that Al has a reversion (either in fee or for life) after Bob's term of years. However, it was earlier said that Al held a fee (or life estate) subject to a term of years. Al's interest was not characterized as reversionary since seisin had not passed to Bob (because Bob did not have a freehold estate).

1. Creating Words

No words are necessary to create a reversion in the grantor. He has a reversion by virtue of the fact that he has not given away his entire estate, but has given out an estate or estate legally smaller than what he had.

Illustration: Al, holding in fee simple, conveyed to "Bob for life, then to Carl for life, then to Don and the heirs of his body." Al has a reversion; the two life estates and the fee tail do not add up to a fee simple (no number of lesser estates ever do add up to a fee simple), and so Al has a reversion in fee simple, to take when the prior estates all terminate.

2. Reversion as an Interest Only in the Grantor

A reversion is always an interest left in the grantor. If such an interest is created in someone else, it will have a different name.

3. Other Future Interests in the Grantor Which Are Not Reversions

The reversion arises when the grantor creates in the grantee estates which are legally smaller than his own original estate. Determinable estates and estates subject to condition subsequent are not "smaller" than absolute estates of the same rank, and so there is no reversion in the grantor. Rather he has a different sort of future interest depending on what sort of qualified estate he has given away.

B. THE POSSIBILITY OF REVERTER AND POWER OF TERMINATION

If the grantor conveys a determinable estate, he has left a possibility of reverter, i.e. a possibility that the estate will come back to him or to his heirs if the limitation occurs.

Illustration: Al, holding in fee simple, conveyed "To Bob and his heirs so long as the land is used as a farm." Bob has a fee simple determinable, and Al has a possibility of reverter. Al or his heirs will get the land back automatically if Bob or his heirs ever stop farming.

Illustration: Al, holding in fee simple, conveyed "To Bob for life so long as the land is used as a farm." Bob has a determinable life estate. Al has both a reversion (since his fee simple was larger than Bob's life estate), and a possibility of reverter incident to that reversion (because the land may revert to him even before Bob dies.)

If a grantor conveys an estate subject to condition subsequent, he has left a power of termination (originally called a right of reentry), i.e. the power to declare that the grantee's estate is forfeited because of the breach of condition.

Illustration: Al, holding in fee simple, conveyed "To Bob and his heirs, but if liquor is ever sold on the land, then the grantor may reenter and repossess." Bob has a fee simple subject to condition subsequent, and Al has a power of termination.

Illustration: Al, holding in fee simple, conveyed "To Bob for life, but if liquor is ever sold on the land, then the grantor may reenter and repossess." Bob has a life estate subject to condition subsequent. Al has both a reversion and a power of termination incident to a reversion.

The possibility of reverter gives the grantor or his heirs the estate automatically once the limitation ends (or occurs), but the power of termination merely gives him the option to terminate the previous estate. The holder of a power of termination may elect not to exercise it when entitled to and thereby waive it. Until the power of termination is exercised, the grantee continues with his estate.

A grantor may have either of these interests after a nonfreehold as well as a freehold: e.g., "To Bob for 10 years so long as he farms the land", or "To Bob for 10 years, but if he sells liquor on the land, then the grantor may reenter and repossess."

C. THE REMAINDER

Whenever grantor would have a reversion in himself by virtue of his conveyance of a particular estate smaller than his own, he may create a future interest in another person, comparable in size to or smaller than his reversion. Such a future interest in the third person is then called a remainder. It will be a remainder in fee simple, in fee tail, or in life estate, depending on what the grantor had and what he conveyed. (In all the following illustrations, it is assumed that Al, the grantor, began with a fee simple.)

Illustration: "To Bob and the heirs of his body, and then to Carl and his heirs." Without the gift to Carl, Al would have a reversion in fee simple after Bob's legally smaller fee tail. When instead he creates this in Carl, Carl has a remainder in fee simple.

Illustration: "To Bob for life, and then to Carl and his heirs." Bob has a life estate; Carl has a remainder in fee simple.

Illustration: "To Bob for life, and then to Carl and the heirs of his body." Bob has a life estate; Carl has a remainder in fee tail; Al has a reversion in fee simple, because the combined interests of Bob and Carl do not equal the fee simple Al originally had.

Illustration: "To Bob for life, and then to Carl and the heirs of his body, and then to Don and his heirs." Bob has a life estate, Carl has a remainder in fee tail; Don has a remainder in fee simple. Al has no reversion, because there is nothing left—the entire fee simple has been given.

Illustration: "To Bob for life, and then to Carl for life, and then to Don and his heirs." Bob has a life estate; Carl has a remainder in life estate; Don has a remainder in fee simple; Al has nothing left.

Illustration: "To Bob for 10 years and then to Carl and his heirs." It would probably be said that Bob had a term of years and that Carl had a remainder in fee simple after a term of years. Or it could also be said that Carl has a fee simple absolute subject to a term of years (since seisin is in Carl rather than in Bob).

1. What Is Not a Remainder

A remainder exists in a third person only where the same interest would be a reversion in the grantor if it had not been conveyed out. Thus there is no remainder after a determinable estate or one subject to condition subsequent, because in these cases the grantor would not have a reversion, but would have some other kind of future interest.

Illustration: "To Bob and his heirs so long as used for a farm, and then to Carl and his heirs". Carl does not have a remainder, because the equivalent interest in the grantor would be a possibility of reverter, not a reversion. (What Carl has will be discussed below).

Illustration: "To Bob and his heirs, but if liquor is ever sold on the land, then Carl and his heirs may enter and repossess the land". Carl does not have a remainder, because this would be a power of termination in the grantor, not a reversion. (What this gives Carl will be discussed below).

2. The Remainder Versus the Power of Termination

Like a reversion, a remainder always waits until the prior estate naturally ends (death of life tenant, or failure of line of tenant in tail) before it takes. It does not take before the prior estate naturally ends, and thus is unlike the power of termination.

D. THE CONTINGENT REMAINDER

A remainder is called a contingent remainder when: (1) the remainderman (the person holding the remainder) is either unborn or unascertained; or (2) some condition precedent (other than the termination of the prior estate) must occur before the remainderman is entitled to take; or (3) both.

Illustration: "To Bob for life, remainder to the children who survive him." Bob's children have a contingent remainder, since which of them will survive him is unknown, and so the remaindermen are unascertained.

Illustration: "To Bob for life, remainder to Carl's heirs." No living person has heirs and so they cannot now be ascertained. Thus, so long as Carl is alive, the remainder is contingent. A gift to the widow of a living person is similarly contingent.

Illustration: "To Bob for life, and then to Carl and his heirs if Carl has reached the age of 21 before Bob dies". Carl's remainder will be contingent by virtue of this condition precedent of his attaining a majority. Once he reaches 21, it will no longer be a contingent remainder.

Illustration: "To Bob for life, remainder to Carl and his heirs if Carl is 21 when Bob dies, and if not then to Don and his heirs". Carl has a contingent remainder, and so does Don. The condition precedent for Don is Carl's not becoming 21. These are alternative contingent remainders.

Illustration: "To Bob for life, and then to Carl for life". Carl's remainder is not contingent, since there is no condition precedent except the natural termination of Bob's estate. Of course, Carl will never take possession if he dies first, but throughout his life he has had his remainder, which merely ended with his death in the same way that Bob's estate ended with his death.

Illustration: "To Bob for life, remainder to Carl for life if he is 21 when Bob dies, remainder to Don and his heirs". Carl has a contingent remainder in a life estate. It is contingent because of the condition precedent that Carl become 21 in time. Don's remainder in fee simple is not contingent.

E. THE VESTED REMAINDER

If a remainder is not in a person unborn or unascertained, and if there is no condition precedent involved, (other than termination of the prior estates), then it is a vested remainder.

Illustration: "To Bob for life, then to Carl and his heirs." If Carl is a living person, then he has a vested remainder. Carl is ascertained and his estate is subject to no condition precedent.

Illustration: "To Bob for life, then to Carl for life". As stated before, this remainder is not contingent. Survival is not a condition precedent for it. It is merely another way of referring to termination of the prior estate. Carl's vested remainder in a life estate ends on his death, the same as a possessory life estate ends upon the death of its life tenant. It is vested in interest even though it may never become vested in possession.

Illustration: "To Bob and the heirs of his body, and then to Carl and his heirs". Carl has a vested remainder in fee simple. It is uncertain whether or not Bob's line will ever run out, but since this condition is merely the termination of the prior estate, the remainder is still vested.

1. The Remainder Vested Subject to Total Divestment

The fact that a remainder is vested does not mean that it can never be lost. It can be subject to divestment, i.e. by a condition subsequent.

Illustration: "To Bob for life, remainder to Carl and his heirs, but if Carl ever sells liquor on the land, then Al may reenter and repossess." Carl has a vested remainder in fee simple subject to divestment, i.e. subject to a condition subsequent. (Al has a power of termination).

2. The Remainder Vested Subject to Partial Divestment (Subject to Open)

Partial divestment occurs when the holder of an estate is compelled to share it with others.

Illustration: "To Bob for life, remainder to his children;" Bob has one daughter. Since the child is ascertained, and there is no condition precedent involved, she has a vested remainder in fee simple. But when and if other children are born to Bob, they will share the remainder in fee simple with her, thereby reducing her share. She has a vested remainder in fee simple subject to partial divestment.

3. "Divestible" Contingent Remainders

Contingent remainders can be made subject to conditions which may subsequently defeat or dilute them in the same manner as occurs for vested remainders.

F. REVERSION FOLLOWING REMAINDER

If the last estate granted is a contingent remainder, then there is a reversion in the grantor, which will take if the contingency fails. Thus reversions are always vested rather than contingent. If a contingent remainder does become vested, one consequence is that the reversion is thereby divested. The condition precedent for the contingent remainder is a condition subsequent for the reversion.

Illustration: "To Bob for life and then to Carl if Carl is 21 when Bob dies." Bob has a life estate and Carl has a contingent remainder if he is not yet 21. This means that the grantor has a reversion. Once Carl becomes 21, his remainder vests and the grantor's reversion is thereby divested.

III. THE TRANSFER OF ESTATES
A. METHODS OF TRANSFER

Since the holder of a freehold must be seised, it is necessary that the seisin have passed to him from the previously seised holder of a freehold. The ancient ceremony by which seisin passed—livery of seisin—involved the 2 parties going on or near the land and the grantor (feoffor) symbolically handing over some soil to the grantee (feoffee) thereby making livery of seisin to him. This was known as a feoffment, and operated to immediately transfer the seisin to the feoffee. There was no need for a writing.

Where seisin was not involved, as in the case of an estate for years or other non-freehold estate, there was no need for livery. The transfer of a non-freehold estate could therefore be made without going on the land. Similarly the transfer of a non-possessory future interest was accomplished by grant or deed rather than livery. Today all interests are generally transferred by a deed.

Illustration: Bob, who has a remainder in fee simple wishes to convey it to Carl. He gives Carl a deed of grant. Carl now becomes the remainderman.

Illustration: Al, who has a reversion in fee simple, wishes to convey it to Carl. He gives Carl a deed of grant. Carl now has the reversion. (This reversion does not become a remainder in Carl. A remainder is an interest created in a third person; this interest was created in the grantor and has merely been transferred to a third person.)

1. Release Deeds

The word to describe the conveyance of a future interest by the person holding that interest to the person holding the prior possessory estate is release. Thus a reversioner "releases" his reversion to the holder of the particular freehold below; so does a remainderman.

2. Surrender Deeds

If the conveyance goes in the opposite direction, it is called a surrender: a life tenant "surrenders" his tenancy to his reversioner or remainderman.

B. THE TRANSFERABILITY OF INTERESTS

Vested interests were generally transferable at common law. The holder of a possessory estate or a vested remainder could convey or devise it to whom he pleased. When a future interest was conveyed, the consent of the holder of the present possessory estate was often required (attornment). Partly because of their similarity to choses in action, nonvested future interests were initially not transferable or alienable at common law except to the owner of possessory estate or to a vested remainderman. Thus a contingent remainder, or possibility of reverter, or power of termination could not be conveyed or devised. In the case of the power of termination, an attempted conveyance was not only ineffective, but was held to be destructive of the power itself.

C. THE INHERITABILITY OF INTERESTS

Any estate greater than a life estate was inheritable, even though it was contingent, unless the terms of the contingency made inheritability impossible (as where the contingency involved a timely marriage by that particular remainderman). In all of the following illustrations, assume that Al, the grantor, held in fee simple absolute:

Illustration: Al conveyed "To Bob for life." Al died, then Bob died. On Bob's death the estate goes to Al's heir. Al's reversion descended to his heir, who held it until it was ready to vest in possession, and then took the possessory estate.

Illustration: Al conveyed "To Bob for life, remainder to Carl and his heirs." Carl died; then Bob died. The estate now goes to Carl's heir. The vested remainder descended to Carl's heir, who now takes possession of a fee simple under it.

Illustration: Al conveyed to "Bob and the heirs of his body, then to Carl and his heirs." Carl died before Bob's line ran out. The estate will go to Carl's heirs whenever

Bob's line ends, no matter how many generations are involved.

IV. RULES REGULATING COMMON LAW ESTATES

A. SEISIN CAN NEVER BE IN ABEYANCE

Someone always must be seised of the land, so that the lord may look to that person for rendition of the services required from the land (e.g., sending up knights to help the lord in war time).

B. SEISIN PASSES OUT OF THE GRANTOR ONLY BY LIVERY

Seisin can sometimes go from one grantee (purchaser) to another without a livery, but for it to come out of the grantor, a livery of seisin is necessary.

C. NO SPRINGING INTERESTS (NO FREEHOLD TO COMMENCE IN THE FUTURE)

Since seisin can pass from a grantor to a grantee only by a livery, it is impossible for a grantor to give his grantee an unsupported freehold estate which will begin at some future time and which is not supported by some present estate in a third person. Either the grantee gets the seisin by livery now, in which event he must have a present rather than a future estate, or else he must get the seisin from the grantor at a later time, in which case the livery of seisin will have to be made then, and nothing can be done now in its stead.

Illustration: Al conveys "To Bob and his heirs one year from now". Bob has nothing. Al must have the seisin for this year (or else it would be in abeyance) and Bob can get seisin only if Al makes a livery next year. Bob has no estate in land now; only a hope that Al will make a livery of seisin to him in a year. If Bob did have an interest now, it would be because an estate were somehow allowed to "spring" up out of Al's estate next year; thus this is called the rule against springing interests.

1. A Remainder Cannot Spring

Illustration: Al conveys "To myself for life, and then to Bob and his heirs." The gift to Bob is no good; as a remainder it is springing, which is not allowed. For Bob to take, it would have to be by way of livery of seisin from Al which cannot be made now (since Al has a freehold in possession and is himself seised until he dies), and it cannot be made in the future. (Al cannot make a livery of seisin to Bob once he is dead).

Illustration: Al conveyed "To Bob for life, and one year later to Carl and his heirs." The gift to Carl fails. Bob received seisin but upon his death it would revert to Al, since Carl could not be seised until a year later (and since the seisin could not be in abeyance). Seisin in Al, the grantor, can be transferred to another only by a livery, which clearly cannot be made now to Carl. If Carl's remainder took, it would take by springing up out of Al's reversion without a livery. But a remainder cannot spring, and so Carl gets nothing.

2. A Remainder Must Be Created in the Same Document as the Estate Supporting It

The holder of the particular possessory estate is deemed to accept seisin for both himself and his remainderman, so that when the first estate terminates it goes directly to the remainderman without reverting back to the grantor in between, but this means the remainderman must be designated in the same instrument for this presumption to be indulged.

Illustration: Al conveyed "To Bob for life and then to Carl and his heirs". Carl's vested remainder in fee simple is valid. The seisin passed immediately from Al to Bob, who holds it both for himself and for his remainderman Carl. When Bob dies the seisin will pass from Bob to Carl. Since the grantor is no longer involved, the seisin may pass at a later time without a livery. The rule barring transfers without a livery refers only to transfers from the grantor. Bob is not a grantor in relation to Carl.

Illustration: Al conveyed "To Bob for life" (one document), and "To Carl and his heirs when Bob dies" (another document). Carl's interest is no good, because it is a springing remainder. Bob cannot be said to hold the seisin for Carl, because Carl was not mentioned in the conveyance to Bob. So Carl must get seisin from Al, if from anyone. But that would involve a transfer of seisin from the grantor in the future without a livery, and so is impossible. (Al could have transferred his reversion to Carl by deed of grant, making Carl a reversioner instead of a remainderman.)

(*Application to Nonfreeholds: Illustration*) The same principle applies to nonfreeholds. Al conveys "to Bob for 10 years, and then to Carl and his heirs". Carl has a valid estate. Livery of seisin can be made presently either to Carl himself (since Bob as a nonfreeholder does not have seisin) or to Bob as Carl's agent. In this case, while it is permissible to characterize Carl's estate as a remainder in fee simple after Bob's term, it was more descriptive and accurate at common law to say that Carl had fee simple subject to Bob's term, thereby indicating that Carl had the seisin.

3. No Contingent Remainder After a Term of Years

Illustration: Al conveys "to Bob for 10 years, and then to Carl's heirs". If Carl is alive at the time of the conveyance, the gift to his heirs fails for it is a gift of a contingent remainder (to unascertained persons). A contingent remainderman cannot be seised—the lord can expect feudal services only from a person ascertained and certain to take. Thus seisin cannot be in Carl's heirs. Nor can Bob hold seisin: he cannot hold seisin as agent for the heirs, since they could not hold seisin themselves; he is also unable to hold seisin for himself since he has a nonfreehold. The seisin therefore remains in Al. For Carl's heirs to take, even if they are subsequently ascertained prior to Bob's death, they would have to receive seisin from Al, which requires a livery of seisin which cannot be made now. The heirs would take by a springing remainder if they took. Therefore, "no contingent remainder can be supported by a term of years", is another way of saying no springing remainders.

D. NO SHIFTING INTERESTS—NO CONDITION IN A STRANGER

Illustration: Al conveyed "To Bob and his heirs, but if Bob ever sells liquor on the land, then to Carl and his heirs." Carl's estate fails, because he can never properly get seisin. Bob cannot hold the seisin for Carl, because Carl is not a remainderman. The holder of a present estate can accept seisin for himself and for his remainderman, because a remainder waits patiently until the prior estate naturally terminates in death before it takes possession. But in this case Carl's interest will cut off or cut short Bob's interest. Seisin cannot pass from Bob to Carl, so when Bob's estate ends the seisin must revert to Al. Were it then to go next to Carl, this would be an impermissible springing interest, unless Al actually made livery of seisin to Carl then. Thus there can be "no condition in a stranger."

E. THE DESTRUCTIBILITY OF CONTINGENT REMAINDERS

At common law a contingent remainder must become a vested remainder on or before the time it is due to take possession or else it is destroyed.

Illustration: Al conveyed "To Bob for life, remainder to Carl's heirs." Bob dies before Carl. The gift to the heirs now fails, because it would not become a vested remainder until after it was time for the remaindermen to take possession. The rule is a corollary of the rule against springing remainders. In the above example, Bob has the seisin during his life. If the heirs of Carl are ascertained before Bob's death (i.e. if their remainder becomes vested), then seisin passes from Bob to Carl's heir upon Bob's death. But if there is no ascertained heir when Bob dies, the seisin must return to Al, for it cannot be in abeyance. To permit the seisin to then go from Al to Carl's heir upon ascertainment would be tolerating a springing remainder, since it would spring out of Al's reversion without a livery from Al.

Illustration: Al conveyed "To Bob for life, then to Carl and his heirs, if Carl is then 21." If Bob dies before Carl becomes 21, Carl's contingent remainder is destroyed. Seisin goes back to the grantor and will not later spring out in favor of Carl when he turns 21.

Illustration: Al conveyed "To Bob for life, then to Carl for life, then to Don and his heirs if Don is 21." Bob dies before Don is 21. Don's contingent remainder is still good and not yet destroyed. Don's remainder need not become vested until the time for it to take possession, i.e. when both Bob and Carl have died. The same result would obtain if Carl died before Don became 21, but Bob were still alive.

1.   Reversions Are Not Subject to the Rule

Since reversions are vested interests, they are not destructible. In fact, a reversion always takes when the prior contingent remainder is destroyed.

Illustration: Al conveyed "To Bob for life and then to Carl and his heirs if Carl is 21." Bob dies before Carl is 21. The remainder fails and the property now goes to Al, who takes by virtue of his reversion. Had Carl been 21 in time, he would have taken the fee simple, which would have had the effect of divesting (but not "destroying") Al's reversion.

2.   How Prior Estates Terminate

Contingent remainders are destroyed if they have not become vested remainders by the time the prior estates are terminated whether those prior estates terminate naturally or prematurely.

3.   Premature Termination of Estates—Merger

A life tenant may terminate his estate before his death by renunciation or by tortious conveyance (attempting to convey more than he has). Any contingent remainders not yet ready to take at that time are destroyed.

Illustration: "To Bob for life and then to Carl and his heirs if Carl is 21 before Bob dies, or to Don and his heirs if

Carl is not 21 before Bob dies." Carl and Don have alternative contingent remainders in fee simple. But if Bob re-
nounces his estate before he dies and before Carl is 21,
neither remainder will take. Carl cannot take because he
is not 21 and Don cannot take because it is not certain that
Carl will not be 21 before Bob dies. Thus both contingent
remainders are destroyed. The estate therefore vests in Al
by virtue of his reversion. There is always a reversion
after alternative contingent remainders.

A life estate is also destroyed by being merged into
the next vested estate. Whenever two consecutive
vested estates come into the same person, the lesser is
"merged" into the greater and thereby destroyed.

4. The Effect of Merger Upon Contingent Remainders

Since merger destroys the lesser present estate, any
contingent remainders supported by that estate will
also be destroyed unless they have previously become
vested:

Illustration: "To Bob for life, remainder to his eldest
child who survives him for life, remainder to Carl and his
heirs." Carl releases his remainder to Bob. This will
cause Bob's children to lose their contingent remainder.
Carl's release to Bob means that Bob has a life estate and
the vested remainder next to it, producing a merger and
destroying Bob's lesser life estate. But the contingent
remainder in the children cannot vest until Bob dies, and
being unable therefore to vest in time, it is destroyed. Bob
has the fee simple absolute as a result.

5. Exception to the Doctrine of Merger

If a merger would destroy contingent remainders,
there will be no merger when the two next vested

estates are created in the same person by the same instrument.

Illustration: "To Bob for life, remainder to Bob's children who survive him for their lives, remainder to Bob and his heirs." Bob has a life estate and a vested remainder in fee simple; his children have a contingent remainder. But there is no merger here, leading to a destruction of the contingent remainder since Bob took both of his estates by the same instrument.

Illustration: "To Bob for life, remainder to Bob and his heirs." Bob has a fee simple absolute. Although both estates were given to him simultaneously, there are no contingent remainders to be destroyed here, there is no bar to merger.

6. Exception to the Exception

Although merger is barred by the simultaneous creation of the estates in the grantee, the grantee may later convey both estates to a third person, and a merger will then occur, even though he conveys both simultaneously. This becomes important when the rule in Shelley's case is applied (See p. 71).

V. EQUITABLE INTERESTS IN LAND—USES

Seisin passes only by livery at common law, and so unless livery of seisin is made directly to the grantee or his agent, he has no legal interest in the land. But courts of equity recognized certain situations where a person was in fact the owner of the land even though seisin had never been transferred to him by way of livery.

A. EQUITABLE CONVEYANCES

Certain forms of conveyancing permitted courts of equity to treat a person as having a *use* (an equity) of the land, even though seisin was in someone else.

1. Conveyance for Use

Illustration: Al conveyed by livery "to Bob and his heirs for the use of Carl and his heirs". (Read this today as a conveyance to Bob in trust for Carl). Bob is seised, but equity would regard Carl as having the use of the land in fee simple, even though Carl did not have the title. That is to say equity would compel Bob to put the land to Carl's use.

2. Covenant to Stand Seised

Illustration: Al covenanted "to stand seised to the use of my brother Bob and his heirs." Without a livery, Bob is not seised, but since there is a covenant, and since Bob, the cestui que use (i.e. the beneficiary) is a relative, equity says Bob has the use in fee simple.

3. Bargain and Sale Deed

Illustration: Al gave a bargain and sale deed of the land to Bob and his heirs. Such a deed recited a valuable consideration, which is a conclusive presumption. Without a livery, Bob cannot have seisin, but since consideration has been given, Bob is the equitable owner, and so has a use in fee simple.

4. Resulting Use

Illustration: Al conveyed by livery to Bob but no consideration passed from Bob. Bob has the seisin but, since no consideration was paid, equity finds a resulting use in Al.

(*Uses Compared to Common Law Estates*) Uses can be possessory or nonpossessory (future interests); they can be life estates, fee tails, or fee simples; reversions or remainders, vested or contingent. All of the legal rules relating to remainders apply to equitable remainders.

Illustration: Al "To Bob and his heirs for the use of Carl for life, and then for the use of Don and his heirs if Don survives Carl, or if Don does not survive Carl, then to the use of Earl and his heirs." Bob has the legal fee simple. Carl has an equitable life estate; Don has an equitable contingent remainder in fee simple; Earl has an (alternative) equitable contingent remainder in fee simple; since no vested remainder has been given, Al has an equitable reversion in fee simple and may take if both contingent remainders are destroyed. This is exactly the way the estate would look at common law without the uses.

B. NEW EQUITABLE ESTATES (EXECUTORY INTERESTS)

Considerations of seisin mean that remainders cannot spring or shift. But since seisin is in someone else when a use is involved, there is no reason in equity to bar springing and shifting uses. Therefore, equity recognized these interests, which were called executory interests.

1. The Springing Use

A springing use springs up out of the grantor's estate at a later time.

Illustration: Al bargains and sells "to Bob for life and one year after Bob's death to Carl and his heirs." Carl has a springing executory interest, or springing use. This could not be a remainder, because by nature a remainder is incapable of springing (it must take immediately upon the termination of the prior estate). The interest here springs out of the reversion in the grantor. Title is: life estate in Bob; reversion in fee simple in Al subject to springing use in Carl. All of these estates are equitable; legal title is in Al.

Illustration: Al bargains and sells "to Bob for 10 years and then to Carl's heirs" while Carl is alive. The gift to Carl's heirs is an executory interest. It cannot be a remainder, for it would be a contingent remainder which cannot be supported by a term of years (see p. 52). Title is: term of years in Bob; fee simple in Al subject to Bob's term, and subject to springing use in Carl's heirs; springing use in fee simple in Carl's heirs. All of these estates are equitable; Al has the legal title.

2. The Shifting Use

A shifting use always shifts the title from the previous holder to the person holding the executory interest, by divesting the person previously holding the estate. It is much like a power of termination in a third person, although the conveyance may provide for automatic termination of the prior estate.

Illustration: Al bargains and sells "to Bob and his heirs, but if liquor is ever sold on the land, then to Carl and his heirs." Carl has a shifting executory interest. This cannot be a remainder because it would take in derogation of the prior estate, and would take before that estate is naturally terminated by death. The use here shifts the fee simple from Bob to Carl. So the estate is: fee simple subject to shifting executory interest in Bob (sometimes called a fee simple subject to an executory limitation); shifting executory interest in fee simple in Carl. Both estates are equitable; legal title is in Al.

Illustration: Al bargains and sells "to Bob and his heirs so long as liquor is never sold on the land, then to Carl and his heirs". Although technically Carl's interest does not divest Bob's, but rather waits for it to naturally terminate, it nevertheless is called an executory interest based on the principle that there can be no remainder following a fee simple.

Illustration: Al bargains and sells "to Bob for life and then to Carl and his heirs." Carl has a remainder, not an executory interest. Executory interests only appear when a remainder is impossible. A remainder always takes immediately after the termination of the prior estate (and not sooner or later); executory interests always take either before the prior estate would terminate in death (shifting interest) or remotely after it terminates (springing interest). The estate in this illustration takes as soon as Bob's freehold ends, and so it is a remainder, just as it would be if there had been a common law livery to Bob; however, because there has been no livery it is an equitable remainder.

C. THE INDESTRUCTIBILITY OF USES

The doctrine of the destructibility of contingent remainders was a corollary of the rule of no springing remainders. But since uses are permitted spring, executory interests therefore become indestructible.

Illustration: Al bargains and sells "to Bob for 10 years and then to Carl's heirs." The executory interest in Carl's heirs is indestructible, i.e., it will take even if Carl is not dead when Bob's term ends. The estate is: term of years in Bob; reversion in Al in fee simple subject to springing use; springing use in Carl's heirs (all equitable interests). Whenever Carl dies, his heir gets the equitable fee simple. If that occurs before Bob's term ends, then his heir has a fee simple subject to Bob's term; if that occurs after Bob's term ends, then, in the meantime, Al has his reversion.

Illustration: Al bargains and sells "to Bob for life, and then to Carl and his heirs if Carl is 21." Bob dies before Carl is 21. Carl has nothing. The gift was that of an equitable contingent remainder, not an executory interest. Contingent remainders are still destructible, even in equity. This remainder was destroyed by its failure to vest in time.

D. THE STATUTE OF USES (1536)

The Statute of Uses said: "Where any person be seised of lands to the use or trust of any other person, [then] such person that shall have the use or trust in fee simple, fee-tail, for term or life or for years, shall from henceforth be deemed in lawful seisin and possession in such like estates as [he] had in use [or] trust." (many words omitted). The Statute "executed" uses, i.e., it transferred the seisin from the trustee to the cestui (beneficiary).

Illustration: Al makes livery "to Bob and his heirs for the use of Carl and his heirs". Bob was seised to the use of Carl; but the Statute executes the use and gives the seisin to Carl. Instead of having legal fee simple in Bob, and equitable fee simple in Carl, legal fee simple is now in Carl.

Illustration: Al bargains and sells "to Bob and his heirs". Before the Statute, legal fee simple was in Al, and equitable fee simple was in Bob. Now, legal fee simple is in Bob.

Illustration: Al makes livery "to Bob and his heirs for the use of Carl for 10 years". Carl's equitable use for a term becomes a legal term of years. The Statute does not require that the cestui have a freehold. (Here there is a resulting use in Al for the "reversion" following the term unless Bob can show consideration was paid. The Statute would execute this resulting use as well, giving Al the legal fee simple subject to Carl's term).

Illustration: Al conveys "to Bob for 10 years for the use of Carl for 10 years." The Statute does not apply here; Bob is not seised to the use of Carl. The trustee must have a freehold, even though the cestui need not.

1. Effect of the Statute on Future Interests

a. Executory Interests

Springing and shifting uses now became valid legal interests.

Illustration: Al bargains and sells "to Bob for life and 1 year after to Carl and his heirs". The Statute gives a legal life estate; it gives Al a legal reversion subject to a springing executory interest; and Carl has a springing executory interest in fee simple.

Illustration: Al bargains and sells "to Bob and his heirs but if liquor is ever sold on the land, then to Carl and his heirs." Bob now has legal fee simple subject to shifting executory interest; Carl has shifting executory interest in fee simple. Al has nothing.

The executory interest became a valid legal interest only in situations where it would have been a valid equitable use before the Statute.

Illustration: Al makes livery "to Bob for life and 1 year after to Carl and his heirs." Carl's interest fails even after the Statute of Uses because at common law, this would be a springing remainder. This arrangement would work if done by a bargain and sale deed because that would first create a valid equitable use, which the Statute could then execute into a valid legal executory interest. But here the livery created no equitable uses, so there is nothing to execute, and the Statute has no effect. If before the Statute, an equitable conveyance created a valid use, then under the Statute the same conveyance will create a valid legal interest. But if before the Statute, a legal conveyance was unable to create a valid future interest, then the same legal conveyance after the Statute is still ineffective.

b. Contingent Remainders

Contingent remainders are unaffected by the Statute; i.e., they are still destructible.

Illustration: Al bargains and sells "to Bob for life, and then to Carl and his heirs if Carl is 21." Bob dies before Carl is 21. Carl has nothing. His equitable contingent remainder is executed by the Statute into a legal contingent remainder. But the Statute does not make it indestructible, for it is still a remainder and must abide by the rules of remainders. Only executory interests are indestructible, and this is not an executory interest.

c. Remainder or Executory Interest?

An executory interest appears only where a remainder is impossible; therefore whenever an interest is limited so that it can take effect as a remainder it is a remainder, even though it also could take as an executory interest. (This is the rule of Puerefoy v. Rogers).

Illustration: Al bargains and sells "to Bob for life, and then to Carl and his heirs, if Carl is 21". If Carl becomes 21 after Bob dies, Carl would take by way of executory interest. But if Carl becomes 21 before Bob dies, then he would take by way of remainder. Since the interest can operate as remainder or as executory interest, it will be treated as a remainder, and not as an executory interest. Thus it is destructible. If Carl is not 21 before Bob dies, his interest fails.

Illustration: Al bargains and sells "to Bob for life, and then to his first son who becomes 21." This too is a gift which can take effect either as remainder (for any son over 21 when Bob dies) or as executory interest (where no son becomes 21 until after Bob dies) and will therefore be treated like a remainder, so that unless Bob has a son over 21 when he dies, the remainder fails.

Illustration: Al bargains and sells "to Bob for life, remainder to his first son over 21 at Bob's death, or if there is no son over 21 at Bob's death, then to the first son who becomes 21 after Bob's death upon his reaching that age". Rather than setting up one gift which can take either as a remainder or executory interest, the grantor here has separated it into two different gifts. Now there is a gift of a remainder to any adult son, and a gift of an executory interest to any minor son. Since the executory interest here cannot possibly take by way of remainder (a gift to a minor to take effect only when he reaches majority must be a springing interest), it is indestructible.

E. UNEXECUTED USES

Not every use becomes a legal estate by virtue of the Statute of Uses; some uses remain as uses.

1. The Active Trust

Wherever the person seised to the use of some beneficiary (cestui que use) is given any active duties regarding the land, the use is not executed, and he remains with the legal title, just as the modern trustee does.

2. The Use on a Use

Before the Statute of Uses, a use on a use (e.g., a conveyance "to Bob for the use of Carl for the use of Don,") was void. The use to Don was void as being repugnant to Carl's use. However, shortly after the Statute, the use on a use was declared not void, but was treated rather as an unexecuted use. The first use was executed, so that the first cestui got the legal title, but the second cestui kept the equitable title; there was not a second execution.

Illustration: Feoffment (i.e. livery of seisin) "to Bob for the use of Carl for the use of Don". The Statute executes the use to Carl and gives him the legal title. But it does not go on and execute the use to Don. Don has equitable title, Carl has legal title.

Illustration: Bargain and sale "to Bob for the use of Carl". The bargain and sale gives Bob only a use. But the Statute executes it and gives Bob legal title. No second execution occurs, and Bob has the legal title for the use of Carl.

Illustration: Feoffment "to Bob to his own use to the use of Carl." The first use to Bob is executed, but not the second use to Carl. (This is a "Doe v. Passingham" use).

Illustration: Feoffment "to Bob and his heirs, for the use of Carl for life, and then for the use of Don and his heirs." The uses of both Carl and Don are executed, and both have legal estates. Don has a use after a use, but not a use on a use, since Carl's use is not for the use of Don.

3. Uses and Seisin

Whether or not a use is executed matters wherever it is important to ascertain whether the holder has seisin, as in the case of dower. A widow has dower only in estates of which her husband was seised. On dower, see p. 81.

Illustration: Feoffment "to Bob for the use of Carl and his heirs." Since the statute gives Carl a legal estate, and seisin, Carl's widow will have dower.

Illustration: Feoffment "to Bob for the use of Carl for the use of Don". Since Don's use is not executed, Don does not have seisin, and so Don's widow will not have dower.

VI. THE RULE AGAINST PERPETUITIES (1682)

A. THE RULE

"No interest is good unless it must vest, if at all, not later than 21 years after some life in being at the creation of the interest". This was the common law version of the Rule.

Certain future interests which vest too remotely are invalidated by the Rule. The Rule concerns only the remoteness of vesting, not the duration of the interests once vested or the ability of anyone to alienate an interest, vested or contingent. Interests which vest too remotely are void and are stricken from the conveyance.

B. MEASURING THE TIME PERIOD

An interest had to definitely vest within 21 years, plus actual periods of gestation, after some life in being. If there was any possibility that it might vest at a time thereafter, the interest was void.

Illustration: "To Bob for life, then to Bob's children who reach 25." The gift to the children was void, for it could take effect more than 21 years after the termination of all lives presently in being, i.e., the grantor, Bob, and Bob's children now living. (However, if the doctrine of destructibility of contingent remainders still survives in the jurisdiction where this gift occurs, then the gift is valid, since Bob's children must be 25 by his death in order to take, and the possibility of taking long after his death is no longer possible.)

Illustration: Inter vivos trust "to my grandchildren when they reach 21". The gift is bad. The settlor may have additional children later, who cannot be used as measuring lives since they are not now lives in being. And those unborn children may have children of their own (the grandchildren of the settlor) who will not become 21 until more than 21 years after the settlor and all his presently existing children are dead.

C. INTERESTS WHICH ARE SUBJECT TO THE RULE

1. Contingent Remainders Are Subject to the Rule

Contingent remainders must become vested in interest within the period of perpetuities, or else they fail.

Illustration: "To Bob for life, remainder to his children for their lives, and upon the death of the last of them, remainder to their children who are living at the time of Bob's death and their heirs." The gift to the grandchildren is a contingent remainder. Although it may not vest in possession in time (Bob may have children in the future, whose grandchildren may not be able to take until more than 21 years after the death of all Bob's children presently living), it will vest in interest in time. I.e., the contingent remainder will become a vested remainder upon the death of Bob, since the gift is limited to those living when Bob dies. The gift is valid.

Illustration: "To Bob for life, remainder to his children for their lives, and upon the death of the last of them,

remainder to their children and their heirs." The gift to
Bob's grandchildren is bad, because the contingent remainder will not vest in interest until the last of Bob's children
dies, which may be more than 21 years after the death of
all lives in being now (since Bob may have more children).
It does not matter that Bob may now be 80 years old; the
law conclusively presumed him capable of having more
children (the "fertile octogenarian").

2. Executory Interests Are Subject to the Rule

Executory interests are nonvested until they vest in
possession. There is no such thing as a vested executory interest; if it divests a prior interest before it
takes possession, it then is no longer an executory
interest, but becomes the interest it divested.

Illustration: "To Bob and his heirs, but if liquor is ever
sold on the land then to Carl and his heirs". The gift to
Carl fails. It is possible that this shifting interest will not
take possession until more than 21 years after the lives of
Bob and Carl.

Illustration: "To Bob and his heirs once my will is
probated." This springing executory interest to Bob fails,
for it may take more than 21 years after the measuring
lives to probate the will.

3. Vested Remainders Are Generally Not Sub-
ject to the Rule

Generally the rule does not apply to vested remainders because they are already vested. But in gifts to
classes a different situation obtains and it is held that
the gift must vest in every member of the class in
time.

Illustration: "To Bob for life and then to all his sons
when they reach the age of 25." Bob has a son who is

presently 25. The remainder is vested subject to open since there is one son already able to take. But since it is possible for Bob to sire other sons, not yet born, who could reach 25 more than 21 years after the death of Bob and his living son, the entire gift fails as to all the sons.

4. Reversions Are Not Subject to the Rule

Reversions are always vested estates, and not subject to the Rule. A reversion may not always take, as when it follows a contingent remainder where the contingency does occur in time. But the occurrence of the contingency operates to divest the vested reversion. As far as the reversion is concerned, the occurrence of the contingency is a condition subsequent (terminating the reversion) rather than a condition precedent.

5. Powers of Termination and Possibilities of Reverter Are Not Subject to the Rule

Although considered contingent for many other purposes, powers of termination and possibilities of reverter are here considered vested, and not subject to rule.

6. Other Interests Subject to the Rule

Options to purchase land are subject to the Rule, and powers of appointment are subject to the Rule.

D. CONSEQUENCES OF VIOLATING THE RULE

If a gift is held to be in violation of the Rule, it is stricken and the rest of the limitation stands as written.

Illustration: "To Bob and his heirs, but if liquor is ever sold on the land then to Carl and his heirs." While the gift to Carl fails, the gift to Bob remains valid. It is now a fee simple absolute.

E. MODERN REVISIONS TO THE RULE

Approximately half of the jurisdictions have abandoned the common law version of the Rule and replaced it, either by statute or court decision with a less demanding version.

1. Wait and See

The Restatement and the Uniform Statutory Rule Against Perpetuities test the validity of a future interest against actual rather than hypothetical events. In all of the previous examples, the question is not whether the future interests described there *might* vest outside of the measuring period but whether or not they did under the actual facts of the case. Thus validity of an interest is determined later rather than immediately (unless it has been so well drafted as to survive even under all hypothetical conditions).

Illustration: "To Bob and his heirs, but if liquor is ever sold on the land then to Carl and his heirs." If Bob sells liquor before he dies, Carl's executory interest is valid, but if liquor is not sold until more than 21 years after both Bob and Carl are deceased, that executory interest (now held by Carl's heirs) is defeated.

2. Cy Pres

Another approach is to reform the grant to validate as much as possible in order to thereby carry out the grantor's intent as nearly as possible. This approach may be combined with the wait and see principle previously described (as is the case in the Restatement).

Illustration: Using the same wording as in the prior illustration a court may treat the grant as restricting liquor sales only during Bob's life, thereby saving much of the restriction.

VII. SPECIAL RULES DEALING WITH CONVEYANCES TO HEIRS

A. GIFTS TO HEIRS OF THE GRANTEE—THE RULE IN SHELLEY'S CASE (1581)

"If a freehold is given to a person, and elsewhere within the same document a remainder in fee simple or fee tail is given to the heirs of that person, then that remainder to the heirs becomes a remainder in the ancestor." The rationale is that the reference to "heirs" in the document was intended to be as limitation rather than as purchase. (See p. 31 for the distinction between words of limitation and words of purchase.)

Illustration: "To Bob for life, then to Bob's heirs." As written, this appears to give Bob a life estate, and a remainder in fee simple to his heirs. But the Rule in Shelley's case dictates that both the life estate and the remainder are in Bob. The remainder is transferred from the heirs to the ancestor. So the gift becomes: to Bob for life, remainder to Bob and his heirs.

Illustration: "To Bob for life, then to Carl for life, then to Bob's heirs." The rule converts the remainder in the heirs into a remainder in the ancestor; the gift becomes "to Bob for life, remainder to Carl for life, remainder to Bob and his heirs." The gift to the heirs need not follow directly after the gift to the ancestor (the gift can be "immediate" or "mediate".)

Illustration: "To Bob for life, remainder to Carl's heirs," and Bob then conveys to Carl. Carl will have a life estate, and his heirs will have a remainder in fee simple. The Rule does not apply, since the gifts were not in the same conveyance, which is necessary for the presumption that the grantor intended "heirs" to be words of limitation.

1. Consequences of the Rule

Once the Rule is applied to give the remainder to the ancestor instead of the heir, other consequences usually follow:

a. *The Remainder Generally Becomes Vested Rather Than Contingent*

A remainder to the heirs of a living person is contingent since the taker is unascertained. But once the gift is put into the hands of the ancestor, who is ascertained, the remainder may be vested.

Illustration: "To Bob for life, remainder to Bob's heirs". Before the rule is applied, Bob has a life estate, his heirs have a contingent remainder. Once the Rule gives the remainder to Bob, the remainder becomes a vested remainder since Bob is ascertained. So title now is: life estate in Bob, vested remainder in fee simple in Bob.

Illustration: "To Bob for life, and then if Bob marries Carol before he dies, to Bob's heirs." The Rule gives the remainder to Bob, but it remains a contingent remainder until Bob marries Carol. Before the Rule was applied, the remainder was doubly contingent: given to unascertained persons, and dependent upon a condition precedent.

Switching it over to the ancestor only removed one contingency. Thus title is: life estate in Bob, contingent remainder in fee simple in Bob, (reversion in fee simple in the grantor).

b. The Doctrine of Merger Applies

If the remainder does become a vested remainder in the ancestor, and there are no vested estates between his two estates, then the estates will merge.

Illustration: "To Bob for life, remainder to Bob's heirs." The Rule transfers the remainder from Bob's heirs to Bob. Since Bob is ascertained and there is no condition precedent, it becomes a vested remainder. Since the two next vested estates are in one person, they merge. As a result, Bob has a present fee simple.

Illustration: "To Bob for life, then to Carl for life, then to Carl's heirs." Bob has a present life estate; Carl has a vested remainder in fee simple absolute. The Rule converts the contingent remainder in Carl's heirs into a vested remainder in Carl and the two estates then merge. There is no requirement that the ancestor's estate be possessory.

Illustration: "To Bob for life, then to Carl for life, then to Bob's heirs." Bob has a present life estate, and a vested remainder in fee simple, but the presence of Carl's vested remainder in life estate bars merger.

Illustration: "To Bob for life, then if Carl marries Doris, to Carl for life, then to Bob's heirs." Bob has a life estate; and the Rule gives Bob a remainder in fee simple, which is of course vested here. But since merger would destroy contingent remainders in this case, it does not occur when the two estates are given simultaneously (the exact opposite of the requirement for Shelley to apply.) See p. 55. So title remains as described. But Bob can destroy Carl's contingent remainder by conveying both of his estates to a third person. See p. 56.

2. Characteristics of the Rule

a. *Both Estates Must Be Legal or Both Equitable*

Illustration: "To Bob and his heirs for the use of Carl for life, and then to convey to Carl's heirs upon Carl's death." Carl has an equitable life estate, and his heirs have a legal contingent remainder. The Rule in Shelley's case does not apply since one estate is legal and the other is equitable.

b. *The Rule Is One of Law, Not Construction*

Illustration: "To Bob for life, remainder to his heirs. I intend by this to make a separate gift to the heirs." The Rule applies, giving the remainder to Bob, despite the grantor's intention.

Illustration: "To Bob for life, remainder to his heirs if they have treated Bob, their father, kindly." The Rule does not apply. The grantor obviously meant children here, because a person has only one heir under the doctrine of primogeniture. Therefore, the plural language ("heirs") indicated something else. Furthermore, that he meant children is made certain by the reference to "father".

c. *The Rule Does Not Apply to Executory Interests*

Illustration: Bargain and sale "To Bob for 100 years, if he lives so long, and then to Bob's heirs." The gift to the heirs is that of an executory interest, since a contingent remainder could not be supported by a term of years. The Rule in Shelley's case applies only to remainders. Bob has a determinable term of years; the grantor has the fee simple subject to Bob's term and subject to springing executory interest in Bob's heirs; the heirs have a springing executory interest.

Illustration: Bargain and sale "To Bob for life and one day after to Bob's heirs." The heirs have a springing executory interest, and the Rule in Shelley's case cannot apply. Bob has a life estate; the grantor has a reversion in fee simple subject to a springing executory interest; Bob's heirs have an executory interest.

B. GIFTS TO HEIRS OF THE GRANTOR—THE DOCTRINE OF WORTHIER TITLE

"The inter vivos gift of any remainder to the heirs of the grantor is void". This means that there is left in the grantor a reversionary interest of like size. The heirs of the grantor will then take (if at all) by descent rather than by purchase, which gives them a "worthier title".

Illustration: Al conveys "to Bob for life, remainder to Al's heirs." Bob has a life estate and a literal reading of the gift would be that Al's heirs have a reversion. But under the doctrine Al's heirs have nothing and Al has a reversion in fee simple instead.

1. Characteristics of the Doctrine

a. *"Heirs" Must Be Used in the Correct Sense*

Like the Rule in Shelley's Case, this rule applies only when the reference to heirs is used in the technical sense of an indefinite line of succession, rather than children or merely the first generation of takers.

b. *The Doctrine Does Not Apply to Accidental Heirs*

The rule does not apply to a gift to a named individual who turns out to be the heir of the grantor.

c. *The Doctrine Is Not Limited to Remainders*

Illustration: "To Bob and his heirs so long as the land is used for a farm, and then to my heirs." The possibility of reverter remains in the grantor, and is not given to the heirs (as it might sometimes be after the Statute of Uses).

d. *A Rule of Law, Not Construction*

At common law, this was a rule of law. Today, however, it is generally converted into a rule of construction.

2. A Companion Rule

A devise to a person of an estate of the same quantity as he would have taken by descent if the testator had died intestate is void, and the grantee takes by descent rather than by purchase.

VIII.   RESTRAINTS ON ALIENATION

Special rules deal with the validity of a provision which purports to limit the right of the holder of an estate to transfer it to other persons. The legal effectiveness of such a provision generally depends upon what type of restraint it is.

A.   DISABLING RESTRAINTS

The terms of the grant may expressly deny the grantee the power to transfer the estate to anyone else (or may declare that any attempt to transfer is automatically void). With the exception of spendthrift trusts (not covered in this book), such disabling provisions are always held to be void.

B. FORFEITURE RESTRAINTS

The grant may be made determinable or subject to a condition subsequent bringing about termination of the estate upon any attempt to transfer it. Such a restraint is often upheld if it is restricted as to duration or persons. Provisions compelling the grantee to not convey to any third person without first giving the grantor the right to repurchase or to match the third person's offer (preemptive rights) are usually upheld.

Where an estate smaller than a fee simple is involved, a forfeiture restraint is more likely to be upheld. A provision in a lease prohibiting the tenant from assigning or subletting the property without the consent of the landlord is usually valid. This is also generally true for such restrictions when inserted in life estates, installment land contracts and options. A provision in a mortgage accelerating an installment loan upon transfer of the premises by the mortgagor (a due-on-sale clause), is sometimes treated as a restraint on alienation and held invalid as such, although many jurisdictions uphold such provisions. On transfers of mortgaged property, see Chapter 12, p. 372.

C. PROMISSORY RESTRAINTS

The grant may include a covenant by the grantee not to alienate the property. The validity in such a promissory restraint is generally decided according to the same principles as govern forfeiture restraints.

Coowners of property who covenant not to partition it often do so by way of mutual promises and may be entitled to have the covenants specifically enforced. However, judicial enforcement of racial restrictive covenants in deeds would violate the Equal Protection Clause of the United States Constitution.

IX. WASTE

A. PARTIES

The law of waste prevents the holder of a present possessory estate from acting with regard to the property so as to cause undue harm to the holder of a future interest in the property. It is treated here as a protection of remaindermen against life tenants, but it also protects landlords, nonpossessing coowners and, sometimes, mortgagees.

B. POLICY

The initial assumption of waste law is that the holder of a future interest is entitled to receive the property in the condition it now is in; thus waste is often defined as the commission of any act which alters the appearance of the property, and may include even "ameliorating" waste, i.e., constructing value-adding improvements to raw land.

More commonly today, waste is defined in terms of impairing the value of the future interest, on the assumption that the original grantor intended to limit the present grantee's activities for the benefit of the future grantee, rather than to give the future grantee only what will be left after the present grantee's use.

Illustration: Owen leaves his house to his wife for life and thereafter to his son and his heirs. Unless he explicitly indicated the contrary, Owen's wife will be limited in her use of the property so as to ensure that his son receives the full economic benefit of the house, rather than providing that Owen's son will receive only what is left after his wife makes full economic use of the property. This means that Owen's wife may be prohibited from cutting and selling timber, removing minerals, etc.

C. TYPES

1. Active Waste

This consists of acts done by the possessor which harm the property. It is also known as affirmative or voluntary waste. *Per se* acts of waste at common law were cutting mature trees (except for cultivation, repairs or fuel), changing agricultural use of the land, opening new mines to remove minerals, and demolishing structures not erected by the occupant. These were all acts which destroyed existing features or else exploited limited resources. Today these acts usually constitute waste only when they cause economic harm. Where the acts are done wilfully, it may be called malicious or wanton waste and liability may be trebled.

2. Passive Waste

This consists of the failure to make normal repairs to the property so as to keep it from significant further deterioration, i.e. to keep it windtight and watertight. It is also known as permissive waste. It does not entail a duty to rebuild structures not destroyed by the occupant, although there may be a duty to protect them from further harm (such as boarding up a burned building). The failure to make hazard insurance payments or tax or mortgage payments may be treated as a form of financial waste, since the consequences can be uncompensated damage to the property (if uninsured) or forfeiture of the title (for nonpayment or taxes or the mortgage).

D. REMEDIES

Damages for waste equal the cost of restoration if the action is brought when the future interest holder takes possession, or the reduction in the present market value of the future interest if brought before then. Equity may enjoin the commission of active waste or appoint a receiver to stop passive waste (a step also taken by tenant groups against landlords who will not make repairs).

X. COMMON LAW MARITAL ESTATES

Following a lawful marriage, each spouse may acquire a life estate in the lands of the other if certain further conditions are met. These are "legal" life estates, to be distinguished from the "conventional" life estate which arises due to explicit language in a deed. The legal life estate arises by operation of law.

A. WIFE'S ESTATE—DOWER

Upon the death of her husband, an undivorced wife receives a life estate in one third of certain land owned by her husband during coverture (marriage).

1. Conditions for Dower

a. Seisin

The husband must have been seised of the estate at some time during the marriage.

Illustration: Hubert is seised in fee simple of Blackacre; he conveys it to Xerxes and then marries Wilma. Wilma has no dower in Blackacre when Hubert dies since he was not seised during the marriage.

Illustration: Hubert is seised in fee simple of Blackacre and marries Wilma; then he conveys to Xerxes. Wilma has dower here after Hubert dies since Hubert was seised during coverture; Hubert need not be seised throughout the entire marriage or even at his death so long as he was seised sometime during the marriage.

Illustration: Hubert has a term of years in Blackacre and marries Wilma; he then conveys it to Xerxes. There is no dower here after Hubert dies. Hubert possessed a term of years; but he did not have seisin since a term of years is a nonfreehold estate.

Illustration: Hubert has a use in Blackacre, with title held by Xerxes. Wilma gets no dower on his death, since an equitable owner is not seised, except where the Statute of Uses executes the use and gives the seisin to the cestui que use. See p. 61.

Illustration: Hubert has a remainder in fee simple in Blackacre, but dies before it becomes possessory. His wife has no dower, because seisin was in the holder of the present possessory estate, and not in Hubert as remainderman. It does not matter whether the remainder was vested or contingent.

Illustration: Hubert is trustee of a fee simple for the use of a cestui. The wife of Hubert has no dower, because he has bare legal title only, which is not enough, even though he is seised.

b. Inheritability

The estate must be inheritable by the wife's issue in order for her to claim dower upon her husband's death. There is no need for the wife to have issue in fact, so long as any such issue would qualify as heirs of the husband. Thus an estate held in fee simple by the husband is subject to dower because any issue of the marriage would qualify as heirs of the husband, even if in fact the marriage produces no offspring.

An estate in fee tail is subject to dower even though death without issue would otherwise terminate the estate. In this case the fee tail will not terminate until the widow dies, since her dower estate is viewed merely as an extension of the fee tail. If there are issue of the marriage, they do not take the wife's share until she dies and her dower interest terminates. If the estate is in fee tail special, excluding issue of the present wife, then she cannot claim dower even though her husband may die with other issue capable of inheriting the estate.

There is no dower in a life estate held by the husband, since this estate is not inheritable by her issue; (it is not an inheritable estate at all). The same result applies to a life estate per autre vie;

technically it is not an inheritable estate. (If the husband dies before the measuring life ends, the property is taken by either a general occupant or special occupant; it does not descend to heirs).

2. Extent of Dower

a. Before Death

Before her husband's death, a wife has no estate in his lands. Her right to expect dower is at this point called dower inchoate, and is an interest protected by the courts against fraudulent transfers by her husband.

b. After Death

After her husband's death, the wife takes by dower a life estate in $\frac{1}{3}$ of the lands of which her husband was seised. Usually, the husband's heir sets aside an appropriate share for her, although if the wife is dissatisfied, she may go to court for judicial allocation.

B. HUSBAND'S ESTATE

Somewhat equivalent to the distinction between dower inchoate and dower, the nature of the husband's interest in his wife's estate depends upon their stage of life.

1. Upon Marriage and Before the Birth of Issue—Jure Uxoris

In any estate of which his wife is seised, the husband shares seisin with her by *jure uxoris* (right of marriage). In effect, this is a life estate measured by two lives: hers and his; it terminates upon the death of either unless it has been replaced by curtesy.

2. Upon Birth of Issue Alive—Curtesy Initiate

Once issue are born alive (and if the wife does not die in childbirth), the husband's shared freehold (*jure uxoris*) is converted into a life estate in his own right in his wife's freeholds. This life estate is measured only by his own life, and so his previous smaller life estate (measured by two lives) merges into it. A husband has curtesy initiate in all freeholds of his wife which are inheritable by issue of the marriage. Unlike dower, this includes equitable estates of the wife. Since a husband has a present life estate in his wife's lands, all that she may claim now is a reversion; i.e. a possessory freehold if she survives her husband.

3. Upon the Death of the Wife—Curtesy Consummate

Once his wife dies, the husband's curtesy initiate becomes curtesy consummate. Since he was already entitled to possession, there is no change in that regard. There is no need that the issue born alive still be living. His right is not limited to $\frac{1}{3}$ of her property as is true of dower, but applies to all property of which she was seised.

CHAPTER THREE

CONCURRENT OWNERSHIP

I. FORMS OF CONCURRENT OWNERSHIP

Our legal system recognizes only a limited number of ways in which two or more persons may share ownership of land. The basic forms of ownership now in use are joint tenancy, tenancy in common and tenancy by the entireties. Coparcenary was an earlier form of concurrent ownership, which operated when female heirs took by descent, but it is today generally nonexistent. Tenancy in partnership is a form of concurrent ownership recognized by statute in some states—but it is generally treated in a Business Associations course rather than in Property.

(A life tenant and remainderman may be viewed as sharing the ownership of the entire fee simple. However, their ownership is divided in time, so that at no one time do they share the same rights in the property. Concurrent owners own at the same time and there is no chronological separation in their ownership.)

A. CHARACTERISTICS OF THE VARI-
OUS TYPES OF CONCURRENT
TENANCIES

Joint tenancy and tenancy by the entireties require the existence of certain preconditions, which are not necessary to the existence of a tenancy in common.

1. Unity of Time

In order for two owners to be joint tenants or tenants by the entireties, it is necessary that both receive their interests in the land at the same time. Tenancy in common does not require such unity of time.

Illustration: Owen conveyed to Ann and Bob. Depending on other factors, Ann and Bob may be joint tenants, tenants by the entireties, or tenants in common. There is unity of time: Ann and Bob each became a grantee at the same time. This is not a requirement of tenancy in common, but its presence is not hostile to that estate.

Illustration: Owen conveyed an undivided half interest in Blackacre to Ann in 1971; in 1972, Owen conveyed the other undivided half interest to Bob. Ann and Bob can only be tenants in common. Since they took at different times, there is no unity of time.

Illustration: Ann conveys an undivided half interest in Blackacre to Bob, retaining the other half interest herself. Ann and Bob cannot be joint tenants or tenants by the entireties since there is no unity of time; Bob has taken only now, whereas Ann took her interest long ago.

2. Unity of Title

No joint tenancy or tenancy by the entireties can exist unless both owners receive title from the same source. Tenancy in common does not have such a requirement.

Illustration: Ann conveyed an undivided half interest to Bob, retaining the other half herself. At common law this can only be a tenancy in common. Not only is unity of time lacking (supra), but also unity of title is missing, since Bob's title came from Ann, and Ann's title came from her grantor. The same result occurs if Ann conveyed from herself to herself and Bob as joint tenants. Ann must convey her entire estate to a third person (a "dummy" or "straw man") who then conveys it back to her and Bob as joint tenants or tenants by the entireties, thereby satisfying the requirements of unity of time and title. Today, many jurisdictions permit an owner of property to convey to herself and another person as joint tenants without going through a third person. (Ann can achieve what she wants by conveying the entire estate to Xerxes who then will convey it back to Ann and Bob as joint tenants or as tenants by the entireties. In this way the requirements of unity of time and title would be satisfied.)

Illustration: Owen conveyed undivided half interests to Ann and Bob; Bob conveyed his undivided half interest to Carl. As between Ann and Carl, only a tenancy in common is possible. Carl's title came from Bob, while Ann's title came from Owen.

3. Unity of Interest

Joint tenancy and tenancy by the entireties require that all owners have equal interests in the land. If one has a greater interest than another, only a tenancy in common exists.

Illustration: Owen conveyed an undivided ⅓ interest to Ann and an undivided ⅔ interest to Bob. Ann and Bob can only be tenants in common because there is no unity of interest.

4. Unity of Possession

Joint tenancy, tenancy by the entireties and tenancy in common require that each tenant have an equal right to possess the whole. This is the significance of "undivided", i.e. if separate (divided) rights to geographic segments are given, there is separate ownership of different parts. (The parties are neighbors, not co-owners). If possession is given to one but postponed to others, there is a division of estates into possessory and future interests, rather than concurrent ownership, and again the rights are "divided".

Illustration: Owen conveyed to Xerxes for life, and then in equal undivided shares to Ann and Bob. Ann and Bob may be tenants by the entireties, joint tenants, or tenants in common here. Although neither has a present right to possession, their rights to possession in the future are equal as between themselves. Xerxes is not a cotenant of any sort with Ann and Bob; Xerxes has an exclusive right of possession for the present which is not at all shared with Ann and Bob.

5. Unity of Person

The estate of tenancy by the entireties requires that the takers be validly married. (There is unity of person between husband and wife at common law). Neither joint tenancy nor tenancy in common has this requirement.

B. PREFERENCES FOR ONE ESTATE OVER THE OTHER

At common law, the joint tenancy was preferred over the tenancy in common. This meant that if it were possible to construe a gift to two or more persons as a joint tenancy, rather than a tenancy in common, then it would be so construed. Today, the constructional preference is for tenancy in common over a joint tenancy. In order to create a joint tenancy it may be necessary for the deed to state "to * * * as joint tenants, and not as tenants in common, together with the right of survivorship" (See below on survivorship). It was also the case at common law that an ambiguous gift to spouses was construed to create a tenancy by the entireties. Today about half of the states have abolished this form of ownership, but where it does survive, there is still a constructional preference for this estate.

II. CONSEQUENCES OF DIFFERENT TYPES OF OWNERSHIP

A. SURVIVORSHIP

The chief and special aspect of joint tenancy and tenancy by the entireties is that of survivorship: upon the death of one of the cotenants the surviving tenant becomes the sole owner of the entire estate. It is not a question of inheritance or descent because the survivor will take all even if he or she is not an heir of the other and even though true heirs of the deceased would otherwise take all of the deceased's property. During the lives of both tenants each is viewed as owning the entire estate, subject only to the equal claims of the other; upon the death of one of them the other's already full ownership is merely freed from the one disability previously existing (the equal claim of the other). Thus the survivor does not "inherit" the other's share, but merely continues his or her full ownership, now alone rather than jointly.

Tenants in common have separate (although still undivided) interests in property, i.e. the interests of each are inheritable by heirs on death and are subject to separate testamentary disposition. A surviving tenant in common takes the entire estate only when he or she qualifies as the heir of the deceased or is so named in the will.

Illustration: Ann and Bob were joint tenants. Bob died, leaving Wilma, his widow, as his only heir. However, Wilma takes nothing by descent, and Ann takes all by survivorship. (Any claim to dower by Wilma is also defeated, since this is not an estate inheritable by issue. See Chapter 2, p. 82). Ann is now the sole owner.

Illustration: Ann and Bob were joint tenants. Bob died, leaving Wilma, his widow, as his only heir. Then Ann died, leaving a son, Harry, as her only heir. Harry now owns the entire estate. Ann took all by survivorship, defeating any claims of Wilma. And upon Ann's death her son Harry inherits her entire interest.

Illustration: Ann and Bob were joint tenants. Bob died, leaving a will giving all of his property to his wife Wilma. Wilma does not take any interest in the estate because Ann's rights of survivorship prevail over Bob's will. (Had Bob outlived Ann, then under the terms of his will Wilma would take the entire estate because Bob would have become its sole owner when he survived Ann).

Illustration: Ann and Bob were tenants in common. Bob died, leaving Wilma, his widow, as his only heir. On Bob's death Wilma inherits his tenancy in common interest in the property and becomes a tenant in common with Ann.

Ann's interest is unaffected by Bob's death, and since this is not joint tenancy she does not take any part of Bob's interest by survivorship.

Illustration: Ann and Bob were tenants in common. Bob died, leaving a will giving all of his property to his wife Wilma. By virtue of the will Bob's entire interest in the property passes to Wilma, making her a tenant in common with Ann.

Illustration: Ann, Bob and Carl were joint tenants. Carl died, leaving a son, Jay, as his only heir. Jay takes nothing, because this is joint tenancy and the principle of survivorship prevails over the rules of descent. Ann and Bob survive to Carl's interest. Thus the property becomes the joint tenancy property of Ann and Bob alone; they now hold half interests rather than third interests in it.

B. SEVERANCE

A joint tenancy may be severed, converting it into a tenancy in common. Severance occurs when one of the joint tenants conveys his or her interest to a third party, thereby eliminating the unity of time and title which previously existed. The transferee holds an undivided interest in the property and concurrent ownership remains, but the parties become, of necessity, tenants in common.

Illustration: Ann and Bob were joint tenants. Bob conveys his interest in the property to Carl. Ann and Carl are now tenants in common. There is no unity of time or title between Ann and Carl, since Carl took at a different time and under a different instrument than did Ann. The joint tenancy has been severed and a tenancy in common relationship now exists.

Illustration: Ann, Bob and Carl were joint tenants. Carl conveys his interest to Dora. The effect of the conveyance is to give Dora a ⅓ interest in the property as a tenant in common with Ann and Bob. But Ann and Bob continue as joint tenants with regard to the ⅔ interest they still hold, although they stand as tenants in common to Dora. This means that if Ann dies first Bob will take her ⅓ interest by survivorship and Dora will be unaffected; Bob and Dora will then be tenants in common, with Bob owning ⅔ and Dora owning ⅓. The same result will occur if Bob dies first, making Ann and Dora tenants in common with a ⅔–⅓ division. If Dora dies first, her heir will inherit her ⅓, and Ann and Bob will be unaffected. When Ann or Bob dies, the survivor will then hold the ⅔ interest in common with the ⅓ interest held by Dora's heir.

1. Severance of Tenancy by the Entireties

A tenancy by the entireties is not severed by a conveyance of one of the tenants, since no conveyance of such an estate is valid unless both spouses join in. Tenancy by the entireties is ended when there is a divorce. In some states the estate is converted into a joint tenancy, in others it is converted into a tenancy in common.

2. Severance of Joint Tenancy

Any conveyance, voluntary or involuntary, by one joint tenant severs the joint tenancy. Generally, a contract to convey the property also works a severance (by virtue of the doctrine of equitable conversion. See Chapter 8, p. 268). In some states a lease works a severance, but in other states the lease is not treated as severing the reversion. In states where a mortgage is viewed as conveying a title to the mortgagee, the mortgage causes a severance. The same result is sometimes reached even in states where the mortgage gives the mortgagee only a lien on the property.

C. PARTITION

A partition is a physical division of the property, converting the former co-owners into neighbors. Instead of undivided ownership in the entire property, there is now divided ownership, each owning a separate parcel. Thus it differs from severance in that severance does not alter undivided ownership, but merely eliminates the element of survivorship. The parties remain co-owners after a severance; they become tenants in common rather than joint tenants, whereas there is no co-ownership after a partition.

Partition may be physical, whereby each cotenant receives a separate geographic portion of the property. This can occur by court action (resulting from a suit for partition), or by voluntary action (resulting from cross deeds between the parties). Where physical partition does not make sense, a court will order a sale of the entire parcel with a division of the sale proceeds between the parties.

III. POSSESSION, PROFITS AND EXPENDITURES

The one unity shared by all forms of cotenancy is unity of possession. Each tenant has an equal right to possess the whole of the property, and none is entitled to exclude the others or to claim sole possession of any part. When one cotenant does "oust" the other, the excluded tenant may bring an action in ejectment to be let back in (or else face losing title by adverse possession by failing to act in time).

A. RENTS

1. Rents From the Possessing Cotenant

Since each tenant is entitled to possess the whole of the property, the majority rule is that a tenant in sole possession is not liable to the other (nonpossessing) tenant for rent. The other tenant cannot—by staying out of possession—compel the possessor to pay for what he or she has a right to do. The right of the nonpossessing cotenants is to share the possession, not to charge the other for his or her possession. However, if the possessor makes expenditures and seeks contribution from the nonpossessor for them, then the value of his possession may be allowed as an offset against the duty to contribute. Also a cotenant who ousts the other is liable for one half the rental value in any ejectment action brought by the excluded cotenant to recover possession.

2. Rents and Profits From Third Parties

A cotenant is free to lease his or her possessory interest out to strangers. A lease signed by one cotenant is as effective as a deed so executed and conveys to the third person whatever possessory rights that co-tenant has. There is no requirement that the other cotenant join in the execution of the lease. Such a lease will therefore entitle the tenant to take possession of the property, subject to the restriction that the other co-owner be not excluded from possession. For this reason, the common law originally held that the leasing cotenant was entitled to retain all of the rent paid by the tenant. However, the Statute of Anne (1705) compels the possessing cotenant to share rents and profits received from a third person with the other cotenants. Not all states have followed this statute.

Illustration: Ann and Bob are tenants in common (or joint tenants). Ann was in exclusive possession, farming the land herself, but recently she has rented the farm to Carl, for a rent of $1000 per year. Bob here is entitled to $500 per year if the statute of Anne is law in the state. Otherwise Ann is entitled to keep all of the rent. In neither case may Bob recover from Ann for rental value while Ann herself was in possession (under the majority rule).

B. EXPENDITURES

1. Payment of the Purchase Price

Where the parties make unequal contributions towards the purchase price, a court may, on partition, award them correspondingly unequal shares of the property.

Illustration: Ann and Bob purchased property as tenants in common, with Ann paying $20,000 of the price and Bob paying $10,000. A court may determine that they intended that the property would be owned ⅔ by Ann and ⅓ by Bob.

Illustration: The same facts as above except that Ann and Bob took title as joint tenants. A court may now conclude that the taking of title in joint tenancy, with its attendant unity of interest, requires that the parties be treated as equal one-half owners. The excess contribution made by Ann would then be treated as a gift or loan to Bob.

2. Necessary Payments

Payments necessary for the preservation of the title, e.g. taxes, and mortgage payments are generally recoverable by the paying cotenant in an action for contribution or for an accounting or in a partition suit.

Illustration: Ann and Bob are both in possession of the property, but Ann makes the entire payment of $500 for the annual property taxes. Ann is entitled to sue Bob to recover $250. The usual remedy is to give Ann a lien on Bob's interest in the property rather than a personal judgment against Bob.

Illustration: Ann is in sole possession and makes the same tax payment. Ann is entitled to contribution from Bob, but Bob may be permitted some offset for the value of Ann's possession during that time.

3. Improvements

There is no right of contribution for improvements, because the improver cannot force the cost of them onto an unwilling co-owner. For the same reason, the improver can claim them in any accounting of rents and profits collected from a third party, only to the degree that they contributed to an increase in the rents. However, in a partition action, the improved part may be set aside or an increased share of the proceeds may be awarded to the improver.

Illustration: On a two-acre tract Ann has built a house at her sole expense. On partition Ann should be awarded the acre containing the house and Bob should get the unimproved acre.

Illustration: Ann has built a house on a one acre tract adding $20,000 to the value of the property. If the value of the land alone is $10,000, and there is a partition sale for $30,000, Ann should receive $25,000 of the proceeds and Bob should receive $5,000.

4. Repairs

There is generally no right of contribution for repairs because it is considered too difficult to distinguish these from improvements. Adjustments may be made in a partition or in an accounting action.

IV. COMMUNITY PROPERTY

Some jurisdictions add another form of co-ownership, derived from the civil law system, that of community property ownership. In general, property may be held as community property only between parties who are validly married (although certain similar property rights may be held to exist between persons who believe themselves to be married or hold themselves out as married or, sometimes, merely live together). "Marital" property is treated similarly under the Uniform Marital Property Act (1983). The Act treats all other property as "individual" property (the equivalent of "separate" property in community property jurisdictions).

Community property generally includes everything spouses acquire during their marriage. Wages earned by either spouse during the marriage are usually the most significant form of community income, together with income closely related to wages, e.g. pensions (saved wages) and personal injury awards (wage substitutes). Any asset acquired with such income thereby becomes a community asset.

Separate property includes property either spouse had prior to the marriage (i.e. an individual's premarital property is not converted into community property by marriage). The income earned from separate assets, e.g., dividends from separately owned stock, is commonly treated as separate property, though not always. Generally gifts received by one or the other spouse are treated as his or her separate property rather than as owned by the community. Property which the spouses acquire during the marriage but to which they take title as tenants in common or joint tenants is also separate property. (However, some states have a presumption that family residences are presumed to be community property notwithstanding that title appears otherwise).

Separate property may be transmuted into community property, and vice versa, by agreement or gift between the spouses. Where parties have "commingled" separate and community funds, a court will either trace currently held assets to their separate original sources or, if untraceable, treat such assets as entirely community property.

Illustration: Bob married Ann and moved into the house she owned. Both of them thereafter paid the mortgage from their salaries. The house was originally Ann's separate property and did not become community property because she married or because Bob moved in (unless it can be shown that she elected to make it a gift to Bob or to the community). But after the marriage, community income (salary) was used to acquire the balance of the house. It does not matter whose salary was used, both salaries were community property. Therefore the house is now either partly Ann's separate property (what she owned before the marriage) and partly community property, or else entirely community property if tracing cannot allocate respective interests. Ann would have to show that Bob made a gift of all his interest in the community earnings to her in order to make the entire house her separate property. Bob would have to show that Ann made a gift of her separate interest in the building to him or to the community in order to claim a larger share of it.

Illustration: Ann continued to manage the apartment building she owned prior to her marriage to Bob and used the rents from it to acquire a car after the marriage. The apartment building was and is Ann's separate property and much of the rent it produced is therefore also her separate property. But to the degree some of the rental income is attributable to her management efforts, it is community income (earnings from services) and makes some part of the car community property rather than her separate property.

Illustration: As a wedding present, Ann's parents purchased a house for them to live in. If her parents had title placed in her name, it is probably her separate property notwithstanding the marriage because it was a gift. This would also be true if Bob paid for the house from his previous inheritance but put title in Ann's name. If her parents put the title in both names, it would be community property unless the deed said "Ann and Bob as joint tenants", in that case both spouses would have separate property interests as joint tenants, (unless residential joint tenancies are presumed by state law to be community property or if the spouses had agreed it was community property notwithstanding the form of the title).

A. CHARACTERISTICS OF COMMUNITY OWNERSHIP

1. Management and Control

Until recently, the husband, as head of the household, had the sole power to manage and control the community property, and thus could convey it without his wife's signature or consent. However, now the spouses are generally given equal rights to management and control, and both may be required to join in the execution of any document affecting title.

Illustration: Ann and Bob, spouses, hold title to their house in joint tenancy. If this is truly a joint tenancy, either may convey his or her half interest without the knowledge or consent of the other, thereby making the grantee a tenant in common with the other spouse (the joint tenancy being severed by the conveyance). But if the house is deemed to be community property, then a deed executed by just one of them is entirely ineffective to transfer any part of the title. The same may be true for mortgages executed by either spouse.

2. Severance

In light of the inability of either spouse to convey away any fractional interest in the property, community property is not subject to severance as joint tenancy property is. Nor can it be partitioned by a court in an ordinary judicial proceeding like joint tenancy or tenancy in common can. Instead, it is divided or awarded to one or the other of the spouses as part of a marital dissolution proceeding. Distribution will either be based on fault (the old rule), or "equitably" or equally, depending upon the jurisdiction's policy.

3. Death Transfers

Each spouse has testamentary control over one-half of the community property. If this power is not exercised, however, that half will pass to the surviving spouse. In this respect community property resembles joint tenancy in that if one spouse dies intestate, their share goes to the surviving spouse rather than the heirs of the decedent. But it resembles tenancy in common if he or she dies testate, since the legatees under the will take in preference to the surviving spouse.

4. Liabilities

Community property is not liable to seizure for the separate debts of either spouse (notably those they brought to the marriage). For those claims a creditor must look solely to the separate property of the debtor spouse. Debts incurred by either spouse during the marriage may or may not entitle the creditor to reach community assets for satisfaction, depending upon whether it was a community debt, was acknowledged by both spouses, was for common necessaries, was contract or tort, or based on other relevant factors under local law.

V. CONDOMINIUMS

A condominium is not a form of ownership different from those previously discussed, but is rather a special combination of other forms. In a typical condominium project, for instance, each owner holds a title in fee simple absolute to his or her individual "unit" and also holds title to the "common areas" of the project as a tenant in common with the other condominium owners. In a typical residential condominium, a unit is the equivalent of the apartment that its owner would occupy under a lease. The unit owned is generally the area encompassed by the interior walls. The walls themselves (as well as the halls, plumbing, etc.) are common areas or elements owned by all unit owners as tenants in common.

If title to the common areas is held by a homeowners' or community association (to which the individual owners belong), rather than in common by all of the individual owners, then the project is generally referred to as a "planned unit development" (PUD).

A. CONDOMINIUM OWNERSHIP

Condominium ownership gives exclusive right of possession over the unit owned and shared possessory rights to the common areas.

Illustration: Ann and Bob own different units in a condominium project. As the sole owner of Apartment # 101, Ann is entitled to exclusive possession of it, and she may exclude Bob from it, or rent it out to Tina. As co-owner of the hallway and the project swimming pool, Ann is entitled to use these facilities along with the other unit owners and she cannot exclude Bob from these areas. If the project includes a garage, both Ann and Bob may have exclusive easements for designated parking spaces.

B. CREATION OF A CONDOMINIUM PROJECT

No title starts out as condominium. It is made into one by virtue of its owner bringing it within the condominium enabling statute of the jurisdiction. This is generally done by recording: 1) a condominium declaration which describes the units and the intended condominium arrangement; 2) a map of the entire project (which will include vertical as well as horizontal dimensions); and 3) various supplementary documents regulating the operation of the condominium, such as the articles of incorporation and by-laws of the owners' association, and the covenants, conditions and restrictions applicable to the project. Thereafter, deeds are executed and delivered to purchasers who become owners of individual units, co-owners of the common areas, and members of the owners' association, being subject to the rules of the association and the covenants and restrictions running with the land.

In most condominiums, management of the common areas is vested in a community or homeowners' association, composed of all unit owners in the project. The condominium documents generally will have covered the questions of membership and voting rights in the association, its rights and duties with respect to the common elements, and its power to levy assessments on individual units in order to maintain the common elements. Also generally covered in these documents are restrictions on partition, and provisions dealing with partial and total destruction of the buildings.

C. TIME SHARING ARRANGEMENTS

Condominiums and other forms of coownership may be divided up on a time-sharing basis, so that different parties have exclusive rights of possession at different times of the year. One way this can be accomplished is by conveying to each purchaser ownership during an annual recurring period for a term of years, together with an undivided fee in the remainder ("interval ownership"); another way is to convey a tenancy in common interest to each purchaser together with an exclusive right to possess the unit during a certain period of time each year ("timespan ownership").

Illustration: An interval ownership time-sharing deed would provide that the grantor conveys a designated unit and an interest in the common elements from January 1 to January 31, each year, until 2001 A.D., together with a remainder over in fee absolute to the unit as a tenant in common with the other owners of the unit. A time-span deed would provide that the grantee takes an undivided interest in the entire project together with the exclusive right to occupy a designated unit and the common areas during the specified use periods, and excepting from the grant the right to make such uses at any other time of the year.

D. COOPERATIVES

In a cooperative, title to all the property is usually held by a corporation; an individual then purchases stock in the corporation and receives, along with the stock, a lease to an individual unit within the project rather than a title to real property. In both a condominium and a cooperative, the common expenses are shared by all members. However, because condominium owners hold fees to their individual units, those units may be separately mortgaged and taxed, which is often not the case for cooperatively held units.

Failure to make such payments may be treated as a form of financial waste, since the consequences can be uncompensated damage to the property (if uninsured) or forfeiture of the title (for nonpayment or taxes or the mortgage).

E. REMEDIES

Damages for waste equal the cost of restoration if the action is brought when the future interest holder takes possession, or the reduction in the present market value of the future interest if brought before then. Equity may enjoin the commission of active waste or appoint a receiver to stop passive waste (a step also taken by tenant groups against landlords who will not make repairs).

CHAPTER FOUR

LANDLORD AND TENANT

I. TYPES AND CREATION OF TENANCIES

The owner of a fee simple absolute, holding a potentially infinite estate in land, may transfer only a fraction of it, i.e. an estate for a shorter time period, to another person and retain the balance of the time for herself. In most commercial transactions, such a limited conveyance is done by execution of a lease rather than a deed and the parties are then referred to as landlord and tenant or lessor and lessee. The tenant usually pays the price for his temporary usage of the property in the form of "rent". It is often appropriate to think of the tenant as the owner of the property for the time being. In this section "Lil" will indicate the landlord in the illustrations, and will be referred to by feminine pronouns in the text. "Tom" will indicate the tenant and will be referred to with masculine pronouns in the text.

Illustration: Lil, who owns a building in fee simple leases it to Tom for a period of five years. During that time period Tom has possession of the building and many of the normal incidents of ownership of it. He may decide what to do on the premises, e.g. whether to permit others to enter, and whether to repair or improve it, unless the lease denies him these powers. At the end of the lease, posses-

106

sion and control of the building revert from Tom back to Lil. During the five year period, Lil may be regarded as having a reversion or else as having the fee, subject to a five year leasehold. In this case, Tom and Lil are not neighbors, as would result from a physical division of the building, nor cotenants, as would result from a division of present interests, nor dominant and servient tenants relating to an easement as would result from a division of permitted uses on the property. The landlord-tenant relationship divides ownership in a different way from those other relationships. (Revise first illustration on p. 104 to delete titles landlord & tenant in first line).

There are four kinds of interests in land which are generally referred to as tenancies. They are the tenancy for a term, the periodic tenancy, the tenancy at will, and the tenancy at sufferance. However, tenancy at will, as it existed at common law, has generally disappeared, or exists now only on paper. The tenancy at sufferance is hardly a tenancy at all, and does not function at all like the other tenancies do. The distinction between the various tenancies is relevant primarily in terms of how they are created and how they are terminated.

A.　TENANCY FOR A TERM

A tenancy for a term, or a tenancy for years as it is sometimes called, arises whenever the two parties agree that the tenant will hold the property for a certain length of time, and no longer. A lease is the classic example; it gives the tenant the right to possess the property for 6 months or one year or 5 years or 99 years. Both parties understand that at the expiration of the lease the tenancy will end, unless a new lease is executed. Generally, the statute of frauds requires that any lease for over one year be in writing.

B.   PERIODIC TENANCY

The tenancy from period to period or periodic tenancy, arises whenever the parties agree that a periodic rent will be paid by the tenant (e.g., every week or every month or every year) but do not make any agreement as to when the tenancy will end. The estate is automatically renewed each successive period unless either party gives timely notice of an intent to terminate it. The period is almost never over a year and there is no requirement of a writing as a result.

1.   Inadvertent Periodic Tenancies

Since a periodic tenancy requires only the payment of a regular rent without an agreement as to a termination date, this estate may arise by virtue of acts of the parties without their ever having expressly agreed to create it.

Illustration: Lil and Tom wrote a five year lease calling for a yearly rent, but failed to sign it. Since the statute of frauds requires that such a lease be signed, it is invalid, and Tom does not have a five year term. But if Tom takes possession and does pay Lil the yearly rent, Tom then has a periodic tenancy (from year to year).

Illustration: Lil and Tom executed a one year lease, calling for an annual rent. Tom entered and paid the rent, but then held over after the year ended, and made another rental payment to Lil, which she accepted. Tom is now, probably, a periodic tenant (from year to year) since there is a regular rent and no agreement as to termination. (On the nature of "holdover" tenancies, see p. 118).

2. The Length of the Period

In most jurisdictions the period is measured according to the interval over which the rent is paid. Thus a weekly rent creates a tenancy from week to week, a monthly rent makes a tenancy from month to month, and a yearly rent makes a tenancy from year to year. Occasionally the period is based upon how the rent is calculated (or estimated) rather than how it is paid. Thus a rent of $1200 per year, payable $100 per month could be regarded as creating either a tenancy from year to year or a tenancy from month to month.

C. TENANCY AT WILL

This estate arises whenever a landowner permits another person to possess the property without any agreement between them as to a termination date or as to the payment of rent. In most states, as soon as the possessor begins to pay rent to the owner this estate is converted into a periodic tenancy.

1. Inadvertent Tenancies at Will

Since the essence of this estate is that the landlord had not objected to the tenant's possession, this estate may arise in a number of "unconventional" ways.

Illustration: Lil and Tom prepared a five year lease but did not sign it, as the statute of frauds requires. If Tom takes possession under it, he is a tenant at will. As soon as he begins paying rent, however, he usually is treated as a periodic tenant.

Illustration: Owen conveyed property to Ann by a void deed and Ann took possession. Since the deed failed to transfer title, Owen is still the owner of the property and Ann's possession under the void deed makes her a tenant at will.

D. TENANCY AT SUFFERANCE

A person becomes a tenant at sufferance by holding over after the expiration of the term without the prior consent of the landlord. If the landlord permits this and accepts rent from the tenant, the tenant becomes a periodic tenant (See p. 108); if the landlord orders the tenant to leave and sues to recover possession, the tenant who still stays becomes a trespasser. But in the interval between the point when the old tenancy ended and the point that the landlord elected what to do, the tenant is labelled a tenant at sufferance, i.e. a former rightful possessor whose continued presence there is justified only by the landlord's inaction. The tenancy at sufferance can arise after the termination of any of the three previous estates.

Illustration: Tom's lease expired on January 1, but on January 2 Tom is still there. He is a tenant at sufferance until Lil elects to make him stay (as a periodic tenant) or to make him leave.

Illustration: Tom was a month to month tenant, and Tom or Lil gave proper notice of termination as of the following month. However, Tom is still there when the next month begins. He is a tenant at sufferance until Lil makes an election.

Illustration: Tom was a tenant at will and Lil terminated the tenancy, but Tom does not leave. He is a tenant at sufferance.

II. TERMINATION OF TENANCIES
A. TERMINATION ACCORDING TO TYPE OF TENANCY

1. Tenancy for a Term

Since the original lease agreement specifies a termination date, the tenancy for a term automatically ends on that date. No notice is required. The tenancy ends when the term ends.

2. Periodic Tenancy

This tenancy will automatically renew unless a timely notice of termination is given by one of the parties. Usually such notice must be given at least one period in advance. Thus a tenancy from week to week usually requires 7 days notice of termination, and a tenancy from month to month usually requires 30 days notice. The tenancy from year to year required only 6 months notice of termination at common law, or even less today. The notice usually must coincide with the rental period, i.e. a tenancy from month to month commencing on the first day of each month can only be terminated by a notice effective on the first day of a month. Some states permit the parties to agree to a shorter notice period, e.g., 7 days notice for a month to month tenancy. Some require that even weekly tenancies be given 30 days notice of termination, or require 60 days notice of termination of monthly tenancies.

3. Tenancy at Will

This estate terminates upon either party giving notice to that effect to the other. At common law, the notice could take effect immediately and was not required to be given in advance. Today many states do impose a waiting period, thereby making the tenancy at will very much like a periodic tenancy. Where the agreement gives one party the option to terminate early, the estate may be treated as a defeasible term rather than as a tenancy at will (e.g. a term of five years subject to defeasance by landlord or tenant at an earlier time).

4. Tenancy at Sufferance

No notice should be required by the landlord to end this tenancy, since the tenant is already there past the original termination date. However, if the holdover becomes a periodic tenant by virtue of the landlord's election, then this estate must now be terminated the same as all other periodic tenancies.

B. OTHER WAYS OF TERMINATING A TENANCY

1. Destruction of the Premises

At common law, the destruction of the premises did not bring about an end of the tenancy. The tenant still had a nonfreehold estate in land (even though it could hardly be used). Today many states provide by statute that a destruction of all or a material part of the premises automatically terminates the tenancy or else gives each of the parties an option to terminate. Most leases also provide for this contingency.

2. For Breach by the Tenant—The Doctrine of Independent Covenants

At common law, a failure of the tenant to perform covenants under the lease did not entitle the landlord to terminate the estate. Covenants in leases were independent, so that nonperformance by one did not excuse performance by the other. Thus even though the tenant was not paying rent, the common law landlord remained obliged to let the tenant retain possession. The landlord's remedy was to enforce the particular covenant involved; e.g. if the tenant did not pay rent, the landlord could sue to recover the rent (or bring the old remedy of distress and levy on the tenant's chattels).

Today, either by statute or by provisions in the lease a landlord is inevitably allowed to terminate the tenancy if the tenant defaults in the performance of any major covenant, particularly rent. Most leases make the performance of all covenants by the tenant conditions for the continuance of the estate. This has the effect of giving the landlord a power of termination (usually called a right of entry) incident to the reversion. After default by the tenant the landlord is usually required to give a short notice requiring the tenant to correct the breach or quit the premises, and if the tenant fails to do either the landlord may then commence summary proceedings to terminate the tenancy and recover possession.

3. For Breach by the Landlord—The Covenant of Quiet Enjoyment

There is implied in every lease a covenant of quiet enjoyment, i.e. a promise by the landlord that he or she will do nothing personally to disturb the tenant's possession of the premises. If the landlord breaches this covenant, the tenant is entitled to terminate the tenancy.

Eviction by the landlord: Illustration: Tom has a tenancy for a term with 6 months to go. However, Lil changes the locks on the door, thereby locking Tom out. Tom may now regard the tenancy as terminated and cease paying rent. (Tom may also treat the lock out as a tort—either a trespass or a forcible entry—and may sue for damages. In addition, Tom need not regard the tenancy as terminated if he does not so elect, and may sue to be restored to possession).

Eviction by a third party: Illustration: Tom has a tenancy for a term with 6 months to go, and third parties intrude, making it impossible for Tom to possess the premises any longer. Tom may not terminate here, since there is no breach of any covenant by Lil. The landlord's covenant of quiet enjoyment applies only to acts of Lil or her agents. She does not insure Tom's possession against third parties. (It was this same reasoning that led the common law to deny termination as a remedy upon destruction of the premises, unless the landlord caused the loss.)

Eviction by other tenants: Illustration: Tom's possession is disturbed by the acts of other tenants in the building. In some jurisdictions Tom may terminate under these circumstances, but many states do not make the landlord responsible for the acts of other tenants and Tom is not free to leave. Sometimes the outcome will depend on whether the disturbing acts of the other tenants violated provisions in their leases. If so, Lil's power to prevent Tom's neighbors from so behaving may entitle Tom to treat her as responsible for them.

Eviction by paramount title: Illustration: Lil failed to pay her mortgage and as a result the mortgagee foreclosed and evicted Tom. This is eviction by paramount title, and Lil's covenant of quiet enjoyment does warrant protection against that contingency. Tom may treat the lease as terminated.

a. Mortgages and Leases

If the landlord mortgages the property and then leases it, the mortgage is superior to the lease, and the tenant takes a lease on mortgaged property. The mere existence or assertion of a mortgage or any other adverse claim does not of itself constitute a breach of the covenant of quiet enjoyment. There must first be an "eviction". If the mortgagee forecloses, the tenancy is destroyed because the leasehold as well as the reversion was subject to the mortgage. An eviction has now occurred and the tenant may stop paying rent and quit the premises even if the mortgagee desires to keep him. On foreclosure of mortgages see Chapter 12, p. 365. If, instead, the landlord leases the property first and then mortgages it, the lease is paramount to the mortgage and the mortgagee takes a mortgage only on the reversion. In this case a foreclosure of the mortgage only gives the mortgagee the reversion and makes the mortgagee the new landlord of the tenant without destroying the tenant's estate. (Since most mortgagees will not accept a mortgage which is subject to outstanding leases, it is common for leases to provide that they will be subject to all mortgages even though executed after the lease.)

b. *Constructive Eviction*

The failure of the landlord to perform covenants she has made does not by itself entitle the tenant to terminate. Covenants in leases are independent and the tenant's remedy is to sue for breach of the covenant but not to terminate. However, if the landlord's failure to perform some covenant materially impairs the tenant's ability to enjoy the premises, this will be treated as a breach of the covenant of quiet enjoyment. When that covenant is breached by an actual eviction the tenant is always able to terminate. And, by analogy, when it is breached indirectly (by a material failure of the landlord to perform covenants), there is a constructive eviction, and the tenant may terminate. Constructive eviction is examined in more detail at p. 147.

4. By Agreement—Surrender

The parties may always agree to terminate a tenancy before it would naturally end. Unlike a contract, however, this is not accomplished by tearing up the lease (rescission). Since the lease conveyed an estate in property to the tenant, it is technically necessary for the tenant to reconvey that estate back to the landlord, by a surrender deed if the estate is large enough to come under the Statute of Frauds. (A conveyance of the landlord's reversion to the tenant would be by release deed). However, a surrender by operation of law is sometimes held to occur when the tenant abandons the property and the landlord reenters. Surrender by operation of law eliminates the need for a writing. See p. 123.

5. Eminent Domain

The government has the power to acquire private property for public use. When leased property is taken, the government acquires the tenant's as well as the landlord's interest, and thereby terminates the lease.

The government is required to pay just compensation (i.e., the fair market value of the property), and both landlord and tenant may share in the condemnation award. If the value of the tenant's leasehold was equal to his rent burden, then he has no claim to any part of the award since his loss (future use of the premises) was offset by an equivalent gain (future rent liability). But if his leasehold had a value in excess of his rent, some of the award belongs to him.

Illustration: Tom leased the premises for five years at $1000 per month. Because of general improvement of neighborhood conditions, the fair rental value of the premises was $1200 per month (i.e. he could have sublet the premises for that much). If the government takes the property while Tom's lease has one year to go, he should receive the lost bonus value of his lease: $200 × 12 months, reduced to present value. (Assume this equals $2000, for simplicity purposes).

Since $2000 of the award will go to Tom, Lil will necessarily receive that much less, since the government is liable only for the market value of the land and cannot be made to pay more than that because the premises are leased. But the value of Lil's interest is in fact worth $2000 less than otherwise because of the depressing effect of Tom's lease. If her property would be worth $100,000 if there were no lease on it or if the lease produced a market value rent, $1200 per month, the fact that it produces a below market rent means that any buyer would require the price be reduced to cover the shortfall in rent, i.e. the property is worth only $98,000 rather than $100,000 because of Tom's lease.

Where the government takes the property only temporarily and for a shorter duration than the remainder of the tenancy, the lease is not terminated and the award goes entirely to the tenant, who continues to owe the rent to the landlord. Where a physical part of the property is taken, most courts hold that rent liability is unaffected and the tenant is therefore entitled to receive both the future rent owed for the part taken as well as its bonus value. The balance goes to the landlord.

C. LANDLORD'S REMEDIES AGAINST CONTINUED POSSESSION AFTER THE TERMINATION OF THE ESTATE—HOLDOVER TENANTS

It is expected that the tenant's possession will end when the leasehold ends. However, when a tenant holds over after the term, the landlord has a choice of remedies.

1. Double Damages

Statutes in many states permit the landlord to recover twice or three times the regular rent for the time that the tenant actually holds over. Sometimes this remedy is limited to willful or malicious hold-overs.

2. Increased Rent

The lease may provide that any holding over past the term will be at some higher specified rent. Or the landlord may notify the tenant before the end of the term of this same consequence. Generally, such a provision in a lease or in a notice sent later is upheld if not unreasonable. If the tenant has already begun holding over, the landlord may have special problems with regard to giving any subsequent rent raise notice. See p. 121.

3. Eviction and Damages

In every state a landlord may proceed to evict a holdover tenant and recover damages for the fair rental value of the premises during the time of holding over.

4. Self–Help

While a landlord may be entitled to evict a hold-over tenant, this does not mean that the landlord may enter without a court order and use self-help to oust the tenant (e.g. by changing the locks). In many states such acts make the landlord guilty of forcible entry or forcible detainer; the tenant is a peaceable, albeit wrongful, possessor. A landlord's right to evict is mainly a right to go to court to bring summary dispossession proceedings against the tenant.

5. Compelling the Tenant to Stay

The landlord may elect to make a tenant who holds over remain for another entire period, usually equal to the length of the original term, regardless of how long the tenant actually held over. In most states the tenant then becomes a periodic tenant but in some others the tenant becomes a tenant for a term.

Illustration: Tom had a one year lease, and held over 5 days after its expiration. Lil may elect to make Tom stay another period, either as a periodic tenant (majority rule) or as a tenant for a term (minority rule). Among those states where the holdover tenant becomes a periodic tenant some treat him as a tenant from year to year (because the original term was a year), while others make him a tenant from month to month (if the rent was paid on a monthly basis).

Illustration: Tom was a tenant from month to month. Either Lil or Tom gave 30 days notice of intent to terminate the tenancy effective the following month. Tom, however, held over for 3 days into the month after that. As a result, Lil can hold Tom for the entire month, either as a tenant from month to month all over again, or as a tenant for a term (a month).

a. The Consequence of a Tenant for a Term Becoming a Periodic Tenant

As stated, a tenant for a term who holds over may, at the election of the landlord, be converted into a periodic tenant. Since periodic tenancies are terminated only by the giving of notice, that tenant may then be required to stay for a third period, even though there was no holding over after the second period, if the tenant failed to give timely notice of intent to terminate during the second period.

Illustration: Tom held under a one year lease commencing January 1, 1980, and expiring December 31, 1980. Tom held over until January 5, 1981 and Lil then elected to make Tom stay. Under the law of that state this converted Tom into a tenant from year to year. On December 31, 1981 Tom vacated. However, Lil can now hold Tom for the next year (1982) since the tenancy from year to year which was created in 1981 was automatically renewed in 1982 when neither party gave timely notice of termination.

b. *Increasing the Rent*

Since most states require notice of rent increases to be given as far ahead of time as notices of termination, a landlord may not be able to insist on an increased rent owed by the holdover unless notice of such rent raise was also given sufficiently in advance.

Illustration: Tom held over and Lil then announced that if Tom continued to stay he would owe a higher rent. Unless this notice was given 7 or 30 days in advance of the date of increase, it is not valid.

D. THE CONSEQUENCES OF A TENANT ATTEMPTING TO SURRENDER THE ESTATE BEFORE THE END OF THE TERM—ABANDONMENT AND SURRENDER

A tenant has an estate in land which, in the case of tenancies for terms and periodic tenancies, endures for a certain length of time, and the duration of that estate is not dependent upon the tenant remaining in possession of the land. The tenant has a possessory estate even though he or she may not be there to possess it. Consequently, even the nonpossessing tenant owes rent.

1. Failure to Pay Rent

A tenant does not terminate his or her estate simply by failing to pay rent. At common law, where covenants were independent, the landlord could not terminate the estate merely because the tenant failed to honor the rent covenant. Today, however, a landlord generally may terminate the tenant's estate for nonpayment of rent, but such a result requires affirmative action by the landlord, and nonpayment of the rent does of itself not terminate the estate.

2. Failure to Retain Possession and to Pay Rent

If a tenant abandons and also stops paying rent, the common law did not treat the tenancy as automatically terminated. The landlord could still treat the lease as subsisting, and bring action each period for the rent then due.

Illustration: Tom is a tenant for a term of 5 years, paying a rent of $100 per month. After one year of possession, Tom abandoned and paid no more rent. Lil may, among other things, elect to sue for $100 each month thereafter, entirely ignoring Tom's abandonment. Lil may also wait three months and then sue for $300 back rent, or wait 6 months and then sue for $600, etc. Only the statute of limitations regulates how long Lil may wait. (But Lil may sue for rent only when it becomes due and cannot sue for the rent for the balance of the term immediately upon Tom's abandonment. Even if the lease has a rent acceleration clause making all of the rent fall due when Tom breaches, it is most unlikely that Lil will be permitted to have this extreme form of relief).

Illustration: Tom is a tenant from month to month. Tom paid January's rent, but then abandoned the premises on January 20 and paid no rent thereafter. Lil filed suit on May 15. Lil may recover four months rent, from February through May. A periodic tenancy is terminated only by notice, and Tom has given no notice. Therefore the tenancy is still alive and rent for each month of its existence is owed. Tom's abandonment and default in the rent gave Lil the option of terminating the estate but do not require her to do so. She may elect not to terminate the tenancy and may continue to hold Tom for rent until Tom properly terminates the tenancy.

a. *No Duty to Mitigate*

The two previous illustrations both assumed that a landlord is entitled to permit the premises to stay vacant and hold the tenant for the rent. This has been the majority rule in the United States, and only a minority of jurisdictions compel the landlord (either through statute or court decision) to mitigate damages by looking for a new tenant. Even under the rule that a landlord must mitigate, the above measure of recovery applies whenever the landlord is unable to find a new tenant.

b. *Surrender by Operation of Law*

If a tenant abandons the property and ceases paying rent the landlord may treat these acts as an offer by the tenant to surrender the leasehold estate, and may accept this offer by reentering the premises and retaking possession. This will terminate the tenancy and end the tenant's rent liability.

Illustration: Tom was a tenant for a term with 8 months to go on his lease. But Tom quit paying rent and left. Lil immediately reentered, remodeled, and began to use the premises herself. These acts terminate the tenancy and Tom is therefore not liable for the remaining 8 months' rent.

Since the original lease conveyed an estate in land to the tenant, common law formalities required that such an estate be terminated only by its reconveyance back to the landlord (by a surrender deed). However, to solve the practical problems confronting both parties upon a tenant's abandonment, the courts created the fiction that an abandonment by the tenant constituted an offer to surrender the leasehold estate and a reentry by the landlord was an acceptance of that offer, working a surrender "by operation of law" (in lieu of a conventional surrender deed). Thus the estate revested in the landlord without a writing.

3. Failure of the Tenant to Pay Rent or Honor Other Provisions of the Lease

Today, either by statute or by provisions in the lease, the landlord is usually entitled to bring proceedings to evict the tenant after a default. These proceedings usually operate not only to dispossess the tenant but also to terminate the tenant's estate. Consequently, further rent liability is also terminated.

Illustration: With 6 months to go on his lease, Tom fails to pay rent and Lil brings a summary dispossession action against him, also praying to have Tom's tenancy forfeited. The suit will lead to a restoration of possession in Lil, but Tom will no longer owe rent for the remaining 6 months.

a. Dispossession Without Termination

Some states permit a landlord to dispossess a defaulting tenant without terminating the leasehold estate. When this is permitted the tenant is denied possession but remains liable for the rent for the balance of the term. This fairly inequitable combination is rare.

4. Reletting for the Tenant's Account

When the tenant abandons the premises the landlord may have a third remedy, midway between the choices of permitting the premises to stay vacant (and suing for the rent) and terminating the estate. The landlord may reenter and relet the premises as the tenant's agent, or for the tenant's account, so that the tenant's liability is then limited to the rent due before a new tenant was found, plus any rent differential if the new tenant pays a lower rent.

Illustration: Tom abandoned at a time when his lease had one year to run, at a monthly rent of $1000. Lil reentered and after one month was able to relet the premises to another for a monthly rental of $900. At the end of that year Lil may sue Tom for $1000 (the one month that the premises were vacant) plus $1100 ($100 per month loss for the remaining 11 months).

In some states this remedy is not available to the landlord unless the lease so provides, or unless notice is sent to the tenant of an intent to pursue this remedy. The tenant's consent however, is not generally required as a precondition for this remedy.

Since reentry and reletting are highly possessory acts, there is a danger that a court will treat them as a retaking of possession for the landlord's own account, thereby causing a surrender of the lease and a termination of the tenancy. It is generally required that the landlord make it plain throughout that these acts are solely for the tenant's account. But sometimes the acts themselves may defeat statements of contrary intent, as where the premises are entirely reconstructed by the landlord to suit a new tenant who agrees to rent the premises for a much longer period than the balance of the original term. In such a case it may be held that a surrender has occurred, despite the landlord's assertion of acting only as the tenant's agent.

5. Difference Value Damages

There is a growing tendency to award the landlord damages, measured by the difference between the fair rental value and the rent reserved for the balance of the term when the tenant abandons. This allows the tenant to avoid liability for the full rent, and also benefits the landlord by allowing suit to be brought immediately after the abandonment, rather than at the end of the term. Where this standard applies, it often excludes all alternative measures of recovery.

Illustration: Tom had one year remaining on his lease when he abandoned. The rent reserved under the lease is $1000 per month, but the fair rental value of the premises is only $900. Under this remedy Lil may sue immediately for $1200, the difference between $900 and $1000 for the remaining 12 months (12 × 100) and this may be the only remedy allowed to Lil.

Illustration: Tom had one year remaining on his leasehold when he abandoned. The rent reserved under the lease is $1000 per month, but the fair rental value of the premises is $1100 per month. Here Lil can recover no damages, since Tom's abandonment in fact benefited her. (Before Tom's departure Lil was renting premises worth $1100 per month for only $1000, and thereby "losing" $100 a month for every month that Tom stayed).

Illustration: Tom defaulted in his rent, and Lil sued to terminate his estate, which had one year to go at $1000 per month. The fair rental value is $900. Along with terminating Tom's interest in the land, Lil may recover $120 (the differences between $900 and $1000 over 12 months plus any unpaid back rent. It does not matter that the tenancy was terminated by Lil rather than Tom in this case. Her damages are the same.

III. THE TENANT'S POSSESSORY INTEREST

The essence of a lease is its transfer of a temporary right of possession from landlord to tenant. By obtaining possession (instead of just a right to make some limited uses of the property) the tenant is regarded as having a leasehold estate in the property rather than an easement. The tenant has a nonfreehold possessory estate.

During the duration of any leasehold estate, the tenant has the exclusive possessory right. As a possessor, the tenant is entitled to exclude all others from the property. Even the landlord may be excluded unless the lease permits entry without the tenant's consent. (The common law, however, recognized a limited right in the landlord to enter to "view waste").

A. TENANT'S REMEDIES FOR DISTURBANCE OF POSSESSION

1. Remedies Against Strangers

By virtue of having the possessory right the tenant is entitled to protect that possession against all others. If trespassers intrude it is the tenant rather than the landlord who may sue. The tenant may recover damages for trespass or may recover possession from intruders in an ejectment action. (This is one reason for holding that the tenant is not excused from rent when he is dispossessed by strangers since it is he, not the landlord, who can have the strangers ejected).

2. Remedies for Interference by the Landlord

The tenant may exclude the landlord from the premises the same as he may exclude everyone else. However, if the landlord is the person who dispossesses the tenant, the tenant may be allowed the additional remedy of terminating the tenancy.

Illustration: Lil entered and dispossessed Tom at a time when he had one year remaining on his lease. Tom may, if he desires, sue to recover possession. Or alternatively, Tom may treat the eviction by Lil as a breach of the implied covenant of quiet enjoyment and declare the leasehold terminated.

Illustration: For failure to pay rent, Lil brought a summary dispossession proceeding against Tom and recovered possession. Tom is probably excused from further rent as a result. Lil may have been entitled to enter, and thus is not liable in ejectment or tort or for breach of covenant. But the fact that Lil has dispossessed Tom means that the condition on which Tom owed rent—possession—has been eliminated by Lil, and Tom's rent liability should cease.

3. Eviction by Paramount Title

If a tenant is dispossessed by an entry made by one under paramount title, he or she has no remedy to recover possession, but may terminate the lease and may recover damages for breach of covenant (of quiet enjoyment) from the landlord.

Illustration: Lil failed to pay the mortgage and the mortgagee foreclosed and took possession of the property. If the mortgage is superior to the lease (as it will be if it is executed before the lease), then Tom cannot resist the mortgagee's power to enter. But Tom is excused from further rent liability to Lil.

B. REMEDIES WHEN A NEW TENANT IS PREVENTED FROM TAKING POSSESSION BY VIRTUE OF A HOLDOVER TENANT

1. When the Landlord Is at Fault

If the landlord is personally in possession when the tenancy is about to commence and fails to leave, the tenant has the same remedies as if the landlord subsequently interfered with his or her possession, i.e. to sue to recover possession or to terminate the lease and/or recover damages. When a third person is in possession with the landlord's consent the tenant may also terminate the lease and recover damages from the landlord for breach of covenant. Whether the tenant can sue to recover possession from the third person depends on which of them has the superior right to possession: if the tenant took his lease first, then his right of possession should be superior, but if the third person is in possession under a lease executed before the tenant's lease then the tenant will probably not be able to eject the third person.

Illustration: Tom signed a lease on January 1, to take effect on February 1. But on January 15, Lil signed another lease with Ann putting Ann into possession immediately. On February 1, when Tom is unable to enter because of Ann, he may terminate his lease with Lil and sue Lil for damages, or he may bring ejectment against Ann.

Illustration: Tom signed a lease on January 15 to take effect on February 15. But on January 1, Lil had executed a lease with Ann and Ann took possession under it on February 1. On February 15, when Tom is unable to enter, he may terminate his lease and sue Lil for damages but he probably cannot eject Ann.

Illustration: Tom's tenancy is to commence on February 1 and the tenancy of Lil's former tenant, Ann, was to end on January 15. However, Ann held over and on January 20, Lil elected to make her stay (as a periodic tenant, from month to month). Thus Tom cannot enter on February 1. Tom may terminate the lease or may be able to recover possession from Ann.

2. When No One Is at Fault

The states are divided as to whether a tenant may terminate his tenancy if he is unable to take possession at the start because of the hostile possession of some third party whose presence there is not the result of the landlord's consent.

a. The English Rule

The rule of several states (referred to as the English rule) is that under such circumstances the tenant may terminate the tenancy. This rule thus imposes an obligation on the landlord to put the tenant into actual possession at the commencement of the tenancy.

b. The American Rule

Under this rule the landlord is obliged to deliver only "legal" possession (i.e. the right of possession) not actual possession. This rule does not permit the tenant to terminate the lease, but limits him to relief against the wrongful possessor.

Illustration: Tom is unable to take possession when his lease begins because Ann, the former tenant, has failed to leave, although Lil has requested her to do so. Under the American rule, Tom still owes rent and must be the one to bring an action to eject Ann. Under the English rule, Tom may elect to terminate his lease.

C. RIGHTS INCIDENTAL TO POSSESSION

In a multi-unit building, the tenant has possession only of that part of the building actually leased to him or her. However, the tenant also shares with all of the other tenants the right to pass through the hallways, ride the elevators, use the laundry room, etc. In these "common areas" the tenant's right is one of shared use rather than exclusive possession. These rights may be regarded as easements in the common areas which are incidental to the possessory right to the space actually leased.

D.   LIABILITIES AS A POSSESSOR

Since the tenant is the one in possession of the premises actually demised to him, it is generally the case that he, rather than the landlord, will be subject to the normal tort duties owed by occupiers of land towards invitees, licensees, trespassers, etc.

IV.   RENT

Rent refers to the periodic charge imposed on the tenant for his use of the landlord's property. Usually the lease sets forth the amount, the "rent reserved". However, if the lease is silent as to the amount, a rent equal to the fair rental value of the property is implied whenever one party uses the property of another with her consent and where a gift was not intended.

A.   PAYMENT

Cash rent is usually paid at the beginning rather than the end of the rental period. For common law agricultural tenancies, rent was a share of the crops harvested by the tenant (which led to its being called "rent", i.e. something torn or "reserved" from the land of the landlord). Currently rent may include a share of the tenant's profits from the business he conducts on the premises ("percentage rent").

The amount owed as rent is frequently held constant over the lease term, but it may be increased periodically either by a fixed amount as provided for in the lease or by the inclusion of a cost of living ("escalator") clause in the lease. For periodic tenancies, a unilateral demand by the landlord for an increase often must be given at least one period in advance (perhaps in the form of an alternative notice of termination or increase if the tenant stays thereafter).

B. RENT CONTROL

By ordinance, many cities now limit the amount by which residential landlords may increase the rents paid by their tenants. Such local exercises of the police power have generally been upheld against attacks charging that they are preempted by state law, constitute a "taking" of the landlord's property, deny landlords due process or equal protection, or violate the antitrust laws. Common features of such ordinances are described below.

1. Premises and Persons Covered

Rent control rarely extends to commercial premises. By virtue of existing under local ordinance, the city limits confine its geographical coverage to residential premises. Certain forms of housing may also be excluded, e.g. boarders in single family houses, single family or two family dwellings, luxury housing. The tenant may also be required to show that the premises constitute his "primary residence" or that he is a member of the family of the originally protected tenant in order to continue his own protection under the ordinance. He may also be limited in the amount he can charge if he sublets the premises.

When the premises become vacant, some ordinances permit the landlord to increase rents without restrictions ("vacancy decontrol"), while others continue the rent control in effect notwithstanding. Ordinances which permit vacancy decontrol generally prohibit landlords from evicting tenants merely in order to increase rentals. Such "good cause eviction" restrictions confine tenant removal to cases of tenant default or misbehavior or the landlord's need to occupy the premises personally.

2. Rates

In order that all landlords not raise rents in anticipation of the enactment of rent control most ordinances use as a base rent the rent charged at some earlier date (e.g. one year before the ordinance was enacted or first considered) and "roll back" the allowable rent to that amount. Increases may then be made only pursuant to a formula applicable to all such units, e.g., an annual raise equal to 50% of the consumer price index increase for that period or consent of the rent control board in an individual case pursuant to a proper showing by the landlord (e.g., that the cost of necessary services has increased or that she cannot make a fair return on investment otherwise).

3. Ancillary Restrictions

Landlords confronted with limitations on the amount they may charge for residential rental properties may seek to convert their buildings to more profitable unrestricted uses. In order to prevent such depletions in the rental housing stock, rent control ordinances are often accompanied by restrictions on condominium conversions or conversions to nonresidential use or demolition of the premises. Such restrictions may be in the form of a complete prohibition or may be granted under a rationing system (e.g., 1000 conversions a year) or may be subject to payment of compensation by the landlord to the existing tenants (e.g., by way of mandatory relocation services or entitling them to reduced "insider" prices or lifetime rental tenancies in newly converted condominiums.

V. PROBLEMS ARISING FROM CONDITIONS OF DISREPAIR

A. THE BASIC DUTIES OF THE PARTIES

Because the common law viewed a lease as transferring an estate in land, rather than land itself, the landlord was held to have no responsibilities concerning the condition of the premises. With regard to disrepairs which existed at the time of the execution of the lease the doctrine of caveat emptor applied, and there were no implied warranties in a lease. The same was true with regard to subsequently arising dilapidations: the landlord had no duty to repair or correct these conditions. The only obligation imposed on a landlord was the same one imposed on everyone else in the world as well—not to do any harm personally to the premises after the tenant had taken possession.

The only obligation which the tenant owed to the landlord with regard to the condition of the premises was the duty not to commit waste. The tenant had the duty not to commit active waste, i.e. not to cause harm to the premises by his or her own acts. And there was also the duty not to commit passive waste, i.e. not to fail to make minor repairs which kept the premises windtight and watertight and which, if not made, would have led to subsequent material injury. The landlord was entitled to receive back the premises at the end of the term in the same condition as they were at the start, reasonable wear and tear excepted. Apart from these duties as to waste the tenant had no general duty to repair.

Illustration: Lil broke a fence on the premises before she rented them to Tom. Lil has no duty to repair the fence since she made no warranties to Tom as to the condition. But neither does Tom have any duty to repair the fence since he did not break it nor will its continued disrepair cause any material harm to the reversion.

Illustration: Lil broke a fence on the premises during Tom's term. Tom may charge Lil for the damage the same as he could recover from anyone else who broke the fence.

Illustration: Tom broke a fence on the premises during his term. Tom owes Lil a duty to repair the fence since this is active waste.

Illustration: A third party broke a fence on the premises during Tom's term. Neither Lil nor Tom has any duty to the other to repair the fence. The third party is liable for the damage, and any damage award should either be used to repair the fence or else apportioned between Lil and Tom according to their respective losses (Tom loses the use of the fence for his term; Lil loses the use of the fence thereafter).

Illustration: An unknown third party broke a window during Tom's term. If the window is not repaired, rain may get inside and cause the floors to warp. Here Tom does have a duty to repair the window in order to avoid waste. This minor repair now will avoid major costs later and therefore is imposed upon Tom as possessor of the property.

(*Duties Owed to Third Persons*) Even though neither party may owe a duty to the other to make a certain repair, either or both of them may owe duties towards the public generally insofar as they may be held liable in tort for injuries to others due to the disrepair. See p. 152.

1. Modern Changes in the Basic Duties

The possibility of neither party having any obligation to correct a disrepair frequently no longer exists due to modern building and housing codes. Thus there may be a duty to repair owed at least to the municipality under its housing code. And such a duty owed to the municipality may affect the duties owed to the other party to the lease. More directly, in some states statutes impose duties of repair upon either landlord or tenant with a direct right of enforcement vested in the other party.

2. Duties Regarding Common Areas

The tenant's duties in regard to waste apply only to those premises actually demised to him, i.e., where he is the true possessor. As for common areas, the landlord is regarded as still the possessor. Consequently instead of a landlord-tenant relationship in the hall, there is rather a relationship of possessor-invitee. The tenant therefore has no duty regarding waste, but both landlord and tenant may have duties arising out of their possessor-invitees relationship.

Illustration: Tom damaged a step in the common stairway. Tom is as liable as any third person would be.

Illustration: Lil cared for the common steps so negligently that Tom was injured. Tom may recover for his injuries from Lil the same as any outsider could recover from a possessor of land for negligent care of the land.

B. ALTERING THE BASIC DUTIES BY COVENANT

Unless prohibited by statute, landlord or tenant can agree to undertake duties of repair not otherwise existing. Either can agree to make general or special repairs.

1. Enlarging the Scope of the Tenant's Duties by a Tenant's Covenant to Repair

If there is no covenant, the tenant's duty to avoid waste does not extend to extensive structural work or rebuilding except where the tenant is the cause of the injury. However, many states interpret a general covenant to repair made by the tenant as including the obligation to rebuild regardless of the source of the destruction.

2. Diminishing the Scope of the Tenant's Duties by a Landlord's Covenant to Repair

Where there is a covenant to repair executed by the landlord the tenant may thereby be relieved of obligations to repair which would ordinarily be imposed upon him or her under the doctrine of waste. A landlord's covenant to repair however generally does not include a duty to repair damage caused by the tenant or a duty to rebuild the premises if they are substantially destroyed.

C. ONE PARTY'S RIGHT TO RECOVER THE COST OF REPAIRS WHEN THE OTHER FAILS TO REPAIR

Different consequences may result when both parties fail to correct a condition of disrepair. Whether a particular kind of relief is available to one of the parties is not always resolved by the mere demonstration that the other party had a duty to repair which was not performed. This section deals with the specific question of when one of the parties to a lease may sue the other for the cost of making a repair after the other party has refused to make the repair.

1. No Right to Recover When No Duty to Repair

If the nonrepairing party were not obliged to make the repair, then obviously the other party cannot recover the cost of making the repair.

Illustration: Lil refuses to repair a fence which was broken by an unknown third party. Since a landlord has no general duty to make repairs, Tom cannot repair the fence himself and sue Lil for the cost.

Illustration: Tom refuses to repair a fence which was already broken when he took possession. Since it is not waste to fail to repair a preexisting defect which will not lead to greater loss later, Lil cannot repair the fence herself and then sue Tom for the cost.

2. Tenant's Right to Recover When the Landlord Has a Duty to Repair

a. Duty Arising From a Building Code

Building codes generally impose duties upon owners (i.e., landlords). But it is generally held that unless the building code specifically declares that a tenant may enforce its obligations, the tenant has no right under it to recover the cost of repairs from the landlord.

Illustration: The fence is in disrepair and the local building code requires an owner of property to keep fences in good repair. Tom cannot repair the fence himself and then sue Lil for the cost. Lil's obligation is to the county, not to Tom. The county can compel her to fix the fence, but Tom can not.

b. Duty Arising From a Special Habitability Statute

More and more states today are requiring that a landlord of residential premises keep the premises in a habitable condition throughout the term. These statutes usually permit the tenant to make the repair and deduct up to one month's rent to cover its cost. There are frequently additional statutory provisions stating how often this right can be exercised and whether the tenant can make the repair personally or must hire outside contractors. It is unsettled whether several tenants can cumulate their rights to make a single large repair, or whether one tenant can make an expensive repair and then deduct one month's rent as a part of the cost.

c. Duty Arising From a Covenant

If the landlord covenants to make repairs and then fails to do so, the tenant is generally entitled to then make the repair and recover the cost from the landlord. In fact, as a way of mitigating damages, the tenant may be required to make the repair promptly before the disrepair becomes aggravated. Obviously the resolution of most questions concerning rights and duties under a covenant to repair depends upon the precise wording of the covenant.

d. Duty Arising in Common Areas

If the landlord fails to keep common areas in good repair it is doubtful that the tenant can make the repair and then recover the cost. The landlord may be liable in tort to the tenant for some of the consequences of a dilapidated common area, but one remedy which is generally not available to the tenant is recovering the cost of repairs.

3. Landlord's Right to Recover When the Tenant Has a Duty to Repair

If the tenant owes a duty to repair, either by virtue of the doctrine of waste or under a tenant's covenant to repair, then the landlord is generally entitled to recover the cost of repairs from the tenant. The cost of repairs is the usual measure of damages when the landlord waits until the end of the term before suing. If the landlord sues before that time the measure of damages may be the diminution of value of the reversion instead.

Illustration: Tom breaks the fence with one year to go on his lease and Lil sues immediately. Testimony is introduced showing that it will cost $500 to repair the fence, but that the value of Lil's reversion (i.e. how much she could sell her interest for) is only reduced by $400 due to the broken fence. Either Lil will be compelled to wait until the term is over before she may sue or else her recovery will be limited to $400 if she is allowed to sue now.

a. Recovery When a Building Code Is Applicable to the Tenant

Generally building and housing codes impose duties on the landlord (as owner) rather than on the tenant. However, when a tenant's special use of the property subjects the land to special code requirements this new burden may be imposed upon the tenant. But just as a tenant is generally not entitled to enforce the code against the landlord so also the landlord probably cannot sue the tenant for the cost of code compliance.

b. Recovery Under Modern Statutes

Some recent residential statutes, modeled after the proposed Uniform Residential Landlord and Tenant Act, impose certain duties of repair upon the tenant. These statutes also provide that when the tenant fails to perform such duties the landlord may make the repair and add the cost to the rent.

c. The Effect of Insurance

Both landlord and tenant have insurable interests in the property. If either party separately insures himself against the disrepair or destruction he alone should be entitled to those funds. This right to recover under the policy may be independent of any rights given to either party under the lease.

Illustration: A fire destroyed the premises. Tom has covenanted to repair, but Lil has also taken out her own casualty insurance policy. Tom's duty to repair is not eliminated because Lil receives an insurance award. (However, Lil's insurance company may be subrogated to her rights against Tom).

Illustration: A fire destroyed the premises. Tom has his own insurance policy and has not covenanted to rebuild. The majority rule is that Lil is not entitled to share in Tom's insurance award, and Tom may keep the award even though he is not obliged to rebuild. (A minority rule lets the landlord compel the tenant to use the proceeds to restore the premises).

D. THE RIGHT TO TERMINATE
THE TENANCY

The question discussed in this section is that of either party's right to terminate the tenancy by virtue of the other's failure to correct a disrepair.

1. Landlord's Right to Terminate

The common law did not initially permit a landlord to terminate the tenant's estate for disrepairs even if the tenant were guilty of waste or breach of covenant to repair. The landlord might sue to recover damages or for an injunction, but could not forfeit the tenant's estate since the obligations of the parties were treated as independent. This doctrine is generally modified now either by statute or lease provision so that a landlord may terminate the tenancy if the tenant either commits waste or fails to honor a covenant to repair.

a. No Right to Terminate When There Is No Duty on the Tenant

If the disrepair is not caused by the tenant and is one which the tenant is not otherwise obliged to repair, then the landlord cannot terminate the estate for failure of the tenant to repair.

b. Right to Terminate After Destruction

Many statutes today permit either party to a lease to terminate it if all or a substantial part of the premises are destroyed. Even when there is not a statute to this effect it is likely that the lease will so provide. Under these circumstances, a landlord (or a tenant) may terminate the tenant's estate after any destruction.

2. Tenant's Right to Terminate

Statutes or lease provisions often permit a tenant to terminate the tenancy if the premises are destroyed. If, however, there is no such statute or provision in the lease, then the common law rule that destruction of the premises does not terminate the tenancy still applies. See p. 112.

Illustration: The premises are destroyed by a fire of unknown origin, and there is neither a statute nor a lease provision covering this. Neither party can terminate the tenancy. (At the same time, neither party can compel the other to rebuild. Tom is obliged to pay the rent, but is not obliged to pay the cost of a new building. Nor is Lil obliged to rebuild.)

Illustration: The premises are destroyed by fire and there is a statute or a lease provision permitting termination after such a casualty. Tom or Lil may now terminate. (But even so, neither party is obliged to rebuild. Tom has the right to terminate, but not the right to compel Lil to rebuild; and the same is true for Lil).

Illustration: The premises are destroyed by fire; there is no statute or lease provision dealing with termination, but there is a covenant to repair by Tom. Here Tom cannot terminate and Lil can compel Tom to rebuild. If Tom fails to rebuild, Lil can probably terminate for breach of covenant and/or recover the cost of rebuilding.

Illustration: Tom caused the premises to be destroyed by fire. There is a statute permitting termination after destruction. However, such a statute probably is inapplicable to destructions caused by the party desiring to terminate. Thus Tom cannot terminate. Lil may terminate (under the statute) and may also sue Tom for the cost of repairs (for active waste). This should be true even if the lease contained a covenant by Lil to repair and rebuild.

Illustration: Lil caused the premises to be destroyed by fire. Tom has covenanted to rebuild and there is a statute permitting termination after destruction. Lil cannot elect to terminate, since she caused the fire. But Tom can terminate, even without the statute, since Lil has breached the covenant of quiet enjoyment. Alternatively, Tom may perhaps stay and compel Lil to rebuild, or Tom may receive monetary compensation for the loss of the building. However, Tom cannot compel Lil to rebuild if Tom elects to terminate the tenancy.

Where there is a disrepair (rather than a destruction), the tenant may terminate only if the landlord is under an obligation to repair and fails to do so. See p. 140.

a. Where a Building Code Applies to the Landlord

Generally the mere failure of the landlord to comply with the building code is not regarded as entitling the tenant to terminate the lease. The duty of code compliance is owed to the government, not to the tenant.

b. Where a Special Statutory Duty Applies to the Landlord

In jurisdictions where a landlord is required to put or keep residential premises in habitable condition a tenant is often, by the same statute, allowed to terminate the tenancy if the landlord fails to do so. This remedy of termination is often provided by the statute as an alternative to the tenant's remedy of making the repair and deducting its cost from the rent.

c.　Failure to Repair the Common Area

The landlord's failure to maintain the common area in good repair does not entitle the tenant to move out unless it can be shown that this condition also seriously impairs the tenant's enjoyment of the demised premises.

d.　Failure to Honor a Covenant to Repair—Constructive Eviction

If the landlord has covenanted to make repairs and fails to do so, the tenant may be entitled to terminate the tenancy. Although covenants in leases are generally independent, the tenant's covenant to pay rent is regarded as dependent upon the landlord's covenant of quiet enjoyment. The covenant of quiet enjoyment is breached by a landlord evicting the tenant, but it is also considered breached when the landlord's failure to perform contractual obligations materially impairs the tenant's enjoyment of the premises.

Illustration: Lil has covenanted to make repairs. The fence is broken from external causes and Lil refuses to repair it. Tom cannot leave merely because Lil has breached her covenant to repair. But if the nonrepair of the fence is regarded as materially impairing Tom's enjoyment of his premises then he is entitled to leave and terminate the tenancy.

For a plea of constructive eviction to succeed the tenant must show that there was an obligation imposed upon the landlord (having its source either in the lease or imposed by law), that the landlord failed to perform the obligation, that the failure materially impaired the tenant's enjoyment of the premises, and that the tenant promptly quit the premises thereafter.

Illustration: Tom's lease is silent on the question of heat, and Lil fails to provide any to him in winter. At common law he may not quit the premises claiming a constructive eviction, since she had no duty to furnish heat. She has breached no covenant in her lease to him and she has not impaired his quiet enjoyment of the premises. However, if these are residential premises, there may be a statutory or judicial requirement that a landlord furnish heat in winter; in that event Lil's failure would constitute a breach of an implied obligation to Tom and—if the failure were sufficiently serious—entitle him to quit.

Illustration: Tom desires to convert the warehouse he has leased from Lil into a movie theatre. The local authorities inform him that he must install an additional washroom on the premises if he wants to open the theatre to the public. This requirement arises solely because of Tom's special use of the premises, and therefor is not imposed on Lil. Tom cannot compel Lil to add a washroom nor can he quit the premises if she fails to add one for him. (Nor, under these circumstances, can Lil compel Tom to add the washroom).

When a landlord is guilty of actual eviction the tenant's obligation to pay rent is entirely suspended even though the tenant is not totally gone from the premises. Based upon this doctrine of partial actual eviction, some tenants have argued for a doctrine of partial constructive eviction, claiming that they are entitled to stop rent entirely even though they have not entirely quit the premises. As yet, however, this doctrine has not persuaded any court. The general rule, therefore, is that a claim of constructive eviction requires the tenant to quit if it is to succeed.

Illustration: Lil shuts off the air conditioning after 5:00 p.m. each day, making the premises unusable until the next morning. Tom does not move out, but refuses to pay rent, claiming a partial constructive eviction after 5:00 p.m. each day. Under traditional rules, the claim will fail: Tom may move out and terminate his lease but he cannot stay and refuse to pay rent.

Illustration: Lil fails to repair a leak and as a result, the basement remains flooded and unusable. Tom continues using the rest of the house but refuses to pay rent claiming a partial constructive eviction from the basement. Traditional concepts of constructive eviction, however, hold that Tom's only right is to quit the premises entirely if he wishes to terminate his rent liability.

A tenant who is constructively evicted, not only ends his rent liability, but may also have a cause of action against the landlord for breach of covenant (either the covenant to repair or the covenant of quiet enjoyment). (See p. 114.)

If a tenant leaves claiming constructive eviction but it is subsequently held that the claim was unfounded, then the tenant has instead merely abandoned the premises, and is subject to all of the liability that an abandoning tenant incurs. (See p. 121.)

E. THE RIGHT TO A RENT REDUCTION

This section deals with the tenant's right to reduce or withhold rent by virtue of conditions of disrepair which exist on the premises.

1. Where There Is a Covenant to Repair by the Landlord

Generally the doctrine of independent covenants does not permit the tenant to withhold or reduce rent when the landlord has failed to comply with a covenant to repair. If the tenant seeks a dollar remedy, it is usually limited to the cost of repairs (which the tenant may be allowed to offset against the rent) rather than the reduction of rental value.

2. Where There Is a Repair and Deduct Statute

Most of the statutes which require a landlord of residential premises to keep the premises in tenantable condition limit the tenant's monetary relief to repairing and deducting up to one month's rent and do not permit the tenant to pay a reduced rent based upon reduced rental value.

3. Where There Is an Implied Warranty of Habitability

Since 1970, an increasing number of courts have held that there is to be implied in every residential lease a warranty of habitability, i.e. a warranty that the premises do and will continue to comply with local codes. Where such a warranty is found, the tenant's rent is reduced by so much as the rental value of the premises is decreased by code violations.

Where an implied warranty of habitability does exist, litigation between the parties usually is initiated by the tenant's withholding of rent. Thereupon the landlord brings an action to dispossess the tenant for nonpayment of rent and the tenant raises as a defense the contention that rent is not due because of the code violations. As a condition to permitting this defense to be asserted (since summary dispossess actions generally do not permit affirmative defenses), the tenant may be required to pay all or part of the rent into court each month while the case is pending, and the rent so escrowed is then allocated between landlord and tenant at the conclusion of the trial.

4. Retaliatory Eviction

States are now beginning to prohibit, either by statute or by judicial decisions, evictions by the landlord in retaliation for the tenant's assertion of rights created by a habitability statute or an implied warranty.

Illustration: Tom, a tenant from month to month, withheld one month's rent to make a repair under a repair and deduct statute. Thereupon Lil gave notice of intent to terminate the tenancy, complying with the requirements for the correct termination of periodic tenancy. If the dominant purpose of Lil's termination is retaliation for Tom's assertion of his statutory right, the trend is to deny Lil the right to terminate (for 6 months or a year following the repair).

Illustration: Tom, a periodic tenant, made the same repair and deduction as above. Thereupon, Lil served notice that the rent would be trebled as of the following period, and then sought to dispossess Tom when he refused to pay the increase. This too is a retaliatory eviction, impermissible in the modern view.

Illustration: Tom notified municipal health inspectors about code violations occurring on the premises and as a result Lil either terminated the tenancy or raised the rent.

Either way, if the state prohibits retaliatory evictions Lil will not succeed.

F. TORT CONSEQUENCES OF DISREPAIRS

1. The Relation of the Tenant to Visitors

The tenant is the possessor of the demised premises and a large body of tort law deals with the liability of an occupier or possessor of land to other persons on the land who are injured due to conditions of the premises. The older view made much depend on the status of the person injured: different duties of care were owed to licensees, invitees and trespassers respectively. A more modern view sets the standard as one of due care under all the circumstances, treating the status of the injured party as only one of many considerations. These issues are for more detailed analysis in a torts text. In this section all nonpossessing persons entering onto the premises will be called "visitors" without regard to common law status, and the phrase "negligent care of the premises" will be used to mean that the possessor has failed to exercise the duties deemed owed to the visitor under the law of the state.

2. The Relation of the Landlord to Visitors

Since a lease turns possession of the premises over to the tenant the landlord is no longer a possessor once the tenant enters. Thus the basic doctrines of tort liability which are applicable to occupiers of land do not apply to the landlord. There is not, therefore, any general duty of care owed by a landlord to visitors.

3. The Relation of the Landlord and Tenant to Each Other

a. Tenant's Liability

A landlord visiting the tenant's premises is as much a visitor as anyone else. As a general proposition, therefore, the tenant is liable for injuries suffered by the landlord resulting from the tenant's negligent care of the premises.

b. Landlord's Liability

Since a landlord is not a possessor and since there are no implied warranties in a lease, the common law landlord owed no general duty of care to the tenant. However, the landlord is a "seller" of the premises to the tenant (and perhaps also a former possessor) and doctrines somewhat analogous to products liability may add a different dimension of liability to the landlord. With regard to common areas, where the landlord is a possessor and the tenant a visitor, a general duty of care is owed to the tenant.

4. Liability for the Common Areas

The landlord is charged with possession of the common areas and therefore may be liable in tort for negligent care of these parts of the premises. This responsibility covers injuries to both visitors and to tenants. Because the tenants are users rather than possessors of these areas they are generally not liable for disrepairs, except when they have caused the condition. Recently, negligent care of common areas has been expanded to include failure to keep them safe against intruders who assault tenants or their visitors in the building.

Illustration: Lil negligently maintained the common hallway and Tom was injured as a result. Tom may recover in tort from Lil.

Illustration: Lil negligently maintained the common hallway and a visitor of Tom was injured as a result. The visitor may sue Lil in tort, but probably has no cause of action against Tom, since Tom is not a possessor of the hallway.

Illustration: Tom negligently damaged a step in the common stairway and Lil failed to repair it. A visitor was injured as a result. The visitor may sue Tom for causing a dangerous condition but may also sue Lil for maintaining a dangerous condition.

Illustration: Tom or his guest was robbed at night while entering his apartment. If he can show that the assailant was able to enter the building because of faulty security (no guard) or faulty locks, he may be able to recover from Lil for his losses.

(*What are Common Areas*) Common areas are parts of the premises where no single tenant is entitled to exclude any other from use or enjoyment. Thus the entry ways and common stairs and halls are common areas. So also are rooms used by all the tenants, such as laundry rooms and shared bathrooms. Service systems such as the heating and plumbing are often regarded as common parts. And sometimes the exterior walls are treated as common.

a. Where the Tenant Has Made a Covenant to Repair

If the tenant has agreed to keep the common areas in good repair this may have an impact on the question of tort liability, as indicated in the following illustrations.

Illustration: If Tom is injured by a disrepair in the common area which falls under his own covenant for repair he cannot recover from Lil.

Illustration: If a visitor is injured by a disrepair falling under Tom's covenant to keep the common area in good repair, the visitor may now be able to sue Tom directly, (depending on whether or not privity of contract can be raised as a defense by Tom). The visitor can also sue Lil since the covenant by Tom is no defense (Lil cannot delegate her responsibilities away), but Lil may then cross-complain against Tom for indemnity based on the covenant.

5. Liability Based on a Covenant to Repair by the Landlord

If the tenant's injury is attributable to a disrepair which the lease obliged the landlord to correct, the modern view is to permit recovery by the tenant if he can show that he requested the repair and the landlord failed to make it. An older rule limited the tenant's recovery to the cost of repairs or permitted him to terminate the lease, but regarded liability in tort as either outside the damages intended by the parties or else as subject to the defense that once the tenant knew of the disrepair he had a duty to avoid any resulting personal injuries by either repairing or avoiding using the damaged component. In guest injury cases, privity of contract constituted an additional defense.

For a landlord to be liable in tort for breach of covenant to repair it is generally held that the covenant itself must be enforceable. Thus the breach of a gratuitous covenant to repair will not lead to personal injury liability. However, even without a binding covenant to repair, if the landlord voluntarily undertakes to repair and only worsens the condition by these acts, tort liability will follow.

Generally the covenant to repair is read as a covenant to repair within a reasonable time after notice by the tenant. It is not viewed as giving the landlord the duty (or the right) to enter the tenant's premises to inspect for disrepairs. Thus the landlord is liable only after notice and a failure to repair within a reasonable time thereafter.

a. Rights of Visitors

Occasionally it will be held that the landlord's liability for failure to comply with the covenant to repair is limited to the tenant (and perhaps the tenant's family). Generally, however, privity is not a defense, so that visitors as well as tenants may recover for personal injuries caused by disrepairs under these circumstances.

b. The Tenant's Liability to Visitors Under the Same Circumstances

The fact that the landlord has covenanted to repair does not mean that the tenant is not liable for injuries to visitors resulting from the disrepair. The tenant is still the possessor of the demised premises, owing corresponding duties to his visitors. Thus the visitor may have separate causes of action against both landlord and tenant, but the tenant may seek indemnity from the landlord, based on the covenant.

Illustration: Lil made a covenant to repair. The light switch is defective and Tom has notified Lil about it, but Lil has not repaired it. Tom's visitor received a shock when he touched the light switch. The visitor may sue Lil for breach of covenant to repair, and/or he may also sue Tom for failing to warn him about the switch.

6. Liability for Code Violations

Where a statute imposes a duty on the landlord to keep residential premises tenantable but also limits the tenant's remedies to quitting or repairing and deducting, it is generally held that no tort liability follows if the landlord fails to comply with the statute. However, some states hold that if the condition causing the injury violated some building, housing or health code, then the injured party may recover in tort from the landlord. The rationale is that such codes are safety-type statutes and that the tenant or visitor is in the class intended to be protected by them. Thus there may be recovery in tort for injuries following a code violation even though affirmative enforcement of the code is denied to the tenant.

Illustration: Lil's failure to insulate some wires violates a municipal code. Tom cannot make the repair himself and charge it to Lil merely because it violates the code. But if Tom is injured from the uninsulated wiring he may be able to recover from Lil in tort.

a. *Rights of Visitors*

The visitor also may be able to recover from the landlord for personal injury resulting from the code violation. At the same time the visitor may be able to recover from the tenant for negligent care of the premises.

Bernhardt, Real Prop. 3rd NS—8

Illustration: There is uninsulated wiring in Tom's apartment which violates the code, and a visitor is injured from it. The visitor can sue Lil for code violation, and also can sue Tom for failure to warn. As a possessor of land Tom owed duties to keep the premises safe for the visitor and Tom's failure to warn or to protect the visitor from the wire (or even to insulate the wire) makes Tom liable along with Lil.

b. Effect of a Covenant to Repair by the Tenant

If the tenant covenants to keep premises in repair and to comply with all codes, this may give the landlord a defense if the tenant is the one injured, or may permit the landlord to be indemnified by the tenant if a visitor is injured and recovers from the landlord. A tenant's covenant might also provide an additional theory of recovery on which the visitor may sue the tenant directly.

7. Hidden Defects

A landlord is liable in tort for injuries to the tenant which result from latent (hidden) defects in the premises which were known to the landlord and not disclosed to the tenant. This is a fraud theory of liability which means that timely disclosure is all the landlord need do to eliminate the liability. The duty is to disclose, not to repair the defect.

Generally the landlord must have actual knowledge of the defect before there is liability. But in a few states the landlord is liable even without actual knowledge if it can be said that he or she should have known. This imposes upon the landlord a duty to inspect, and expands the doctrine beyond its original fraud foundation.

Lack of actual knowledge by the tenant is all that should be required of him to recover for his injuries. But in some states discoverability by a reasonable inspection is a defense for the landlord. Consequently, there, the landlord's duty is only that of disclosing defects which the tenant cannot reasonably discover. There should also be a defense if the tenant actually discovers or is informed by the landlord of the defect prior to injury even though the leasehold has already commenced. The landlord's failure to disclose at the inception of the tenancy might permit the tenant to terminate (if caveat emptor does not apply) but would not let the tenant recover for personal injuries if he or she has not elected to terminate after discovery of the defect.

a. Rights of Visitors

Visitors are usually permitted to sue the landlord for failure of the landlord to disclose to the tenant the defect which led to injuries. (Presumably a timely disclosure to the tenant would have led the tenant to correct the condition and the visitor would not then have been injured). The tenant should be liable to the visitor only if it can be shown that the tenant was somehow negligent in failing to discover the defect. If the tenant were aware of the defect that fact would probably make the tenant liable rather than the landlord.

8. Landlord's Liability for Negligence

Just as the status of the plaintiff has been rendered irrelevant in many states, so also several states are

now concluding that the distinction between the ten-
ant/possessor and landlord/nonpossessor is not controlling in the tort field. It is being held in these
jurisdictions that a landlord is obliged to use due care
in maintaining the premises. The fact that the landlord is not in possession is taken as merely one factor
to be considered in determining due care.

9. Exculpatory Clauses

The tort liability of the landlord or the tenant to
members of the public may not be avoided by the use
of exculpatory clauses in their lease. Either may
indemnify the other against such liability but they
may not insulate themselves against it. Public policy
may also invalidate the attempt to exculpate a party
against liability for his own negligence towards the
other.

Illustration: Tom's lease recites that Lil shall not be
liable to him or anyone else for any negligent maintenance
of the building. The clause will not constitute a defense for
Lil in a tort action brought by Tom's guest for injuries due
to Lil's negligent maintenance of the common hallway.
The clause may also fail to protect Lil against a suit
brought by Tom on the same theory.

Illustration: Tom's lease recites that he will hold Lil
harmless against any liability imposed on her resulting
from the condition of the premises (an indemnity clause).
The clause will not constitute a defense for Lil against a
third party suing her in tort, but if the third party recovers
judgment against Lil, she may then proceed against Tom to
recover from him what she was required to pay to the third
party.

VI. TRANSFER OF THE TENANCY

A. THE DISTINCTION BETWEEN ASSIGNING AND SUBLEASING

An assignment of a lease is a transfer of the entire leasehold estate by the tenant to another (an assignee). A sublease is the leasing out of only a part of the tenant's estate by the tenant to another (a subtenant). Whether a transfer constitutes an assignment or a sublease is not determined by how the parties label the document. A court may declare that there has been an assignment even though the parties have called it a sublease, or vice versa. For a subletting to occur the tenant must retain some part of the leasehold estate. It is the original tenant's estate, measured in terms of time, which serves as the yardstick.

Illustration: Tom has a term with five years left to run. He subleases to Stan for 4 years. This is a true sublease, since it leaves Tom with a reversion of one year after Stan's term expires.

Illustration: Tom has a term with five years left to run. He purports to sublease to Stan one room on the premises for the entire five years. However, this is not a sublease, but rather a partial assignment. Tom has no reversion; he has transferred his entire estate (5 years) in part of his premises. It is the size of the estate, not the size of the property, which controls.

Illustration: Tom has a term with five years left to run. He transfers the entire balance of the term over to Ann, who agrees to pay Tom $50 more per month than Tom owes to Lil. This is an assignment despite the rent override since Tom has no reversion.

Illustration: Tom has a term with five years left to run. He transfers the entire balance of the term to Ann with a provision in the document that if Ann fails to perform any of her obligations then Tom may enter and terminate her estate. In some states this is treated as a sublease, and Tom is said to have a contingent reversion. Other states, however, taking the common law system of estates more seriously hold that this is an assignment because there is no common law estate such as a contingent reversion; thus the entire estate has been transferred to Ann. (Tom's power of termination is not a reversion. See Chapter 2, p. 39.)

A more modern view makes the assignment/sublease distinction depend upon the intent of the parties rather than the nature of the estate transferred.

B. THE RIGHT TO TRANSFER— RESTRICTIONS

A leasehold interest (i.e. a tenancy for a term or periodic tenancy) in land is a freely alienable estate. Thus it may be assigned or subleased by the tenant without the landlord's consent. However, it is lawful for the landlord to restrict the tenant's right to assign or sublet by a provision in the lease. The landlord has a sufficient interest in the property as to justify such a restraint on alienation, although there is a tendency to construe such restraints as narrowly as possible. Most such clauses are usually written as forfeiture restraints, purporting to terminate the tenancy at the landlord's election if the tenant has attempted to improperly transfer the leasehold estate. On restraints on alienation see Chapter 2, p. 76.

1. Landlord's Right to Be Unreasonable

Most lease provisions against transfer declare that the tenant shall not assign or sublet without the consent of the landlord. If the provision does not add that the landlord shall not unreasonably withhold consent most courts will not add such a requirement. However, some courts impose an obligation not to withhold consent unreasonably even though it does not appear in the lease. There is disagreement as to whether the landlord may condition her assent upon capturing whatever increase in rent the transferee has agreed to pay the transferor. Such a demand may be regarded as unreasonable unless the lease specifically permits her to do so. In jurisdictions which require a landlord to mitigate damages after a tenant abandons a duty to reasonably consent to transfers may be effectively imposed if an unreasonable refusal to approve a legitimate transferee led to the tenant's departing and then reproposing the same transferee in mitigation of his damages.

Illustration: Tom proposes to assign to Ann, but Lil unreasonably refuses to consent. Lil may be arbitrary unless the no-assignment clause requires her to be reasonable. However, if Tom now abandons and offers up Ann again, then Lil's second refusal to accept Ann may constitute a failure to mitigate damages, thereby ending Tom's rent liability in a state where Lil has a duty to mitigate damages.

2. The Effect of Consenting to the First Assignment

The Rule in Dumpor's case (1603) held that consent by a landlord to one assignment had the effect of waiving any right to prohibit subsequent assignments. Thus the assignee could subsequently assign without consent. This rule is generally inapplicable today either because it is judicially rejected or because the original lease provides that a consent to one assignment does not constitute such a consent to further assignments or because when the landlord does consent it is limited so as not to cover later assignments.

C. THE EFFECT OF AN ASSIGNMENT

1. The Effect of the Tenant

A tenant does not end his or her own liabilities on a lease by assigning it. Rights may be assigned but not duties. The tenant remains bound on all promises originally made to the landlord. (The tenant remains in "privity of contract" with the landlord despite the assignment).

Illustration: Tom assigned his lease to Ann, but Ann fails to pay rent. Even though Lil accepted Ann as an assignee Lil may still look to Tom for the rent based on Tom's original promise to pay.

2. The Effect on the Assignee

An assignment of the lease transfers the tenant's rights under the lease to the assignee, but it does not automatically also impose the burdens of the lease upon the assignee. The assignee is burdened with the tenant's covenants only if the assignee "assumes" these burdens, or if they are covenants which "run with the land". Burdens which run with the land are covered in more detail elsewhere. (See Chapter 6). If the assignee assumes the obligations of the lease then the landlord becomes a third party beneficiary of this assumption promise and there is a privity of contract between the landlord and the assuming assignee.

Illustration: Tom's lease contained a covenant to keep the premises insured, which under the law of the state is not a covenant that runs with the land. Tom assigned to Ann who did not assume. If Ann does not keep the premises insured Lil has no remedy against her. But since Tom remains liable upon his original promise to insure, Lil may seek relief against him.

Illustration: Tom's lease contained a covenant to keep the premises insured. Tom assigned to Ann who did assume. If Ann fails to insure Lil may now proceed directly against her on her assumption agreement. But Lil may also sue Tom on the original promise. (If Lil sues Tom, Tom may then sue Ann for breach of her promise to Tom to assume).

Illustration: Tom's lease contained a covenant to repair, which under the law of the state is a covenant that runs with the land. Tom assigned the lease to Ann who did not assume. If Ann does not repair Lil may sue Tom or Ann. Lil may sue Tom because there is privity of contract between them based upon Tom's original promise. But Lil may also sue Ann because the covenant ran with the land to Ann. (And probably Tom can sue Ann if he is the one Lil elects to sue first).

3. The Effect on the Landlord

When the tenant assigns the lease all rights thereunder are transferred to the assignee, whether or not the assignee assumes. Thus the assignee (rather than the tenant) may now enforce the covenants against the landlord.

Illustration: Tom's lease contained a covenant by Lil to insure. Tom assigned to Ann. Lil does not insure. Ann may enforce the covenant against Lil. If the covenant runs, the benefit has run to Ann. But even if the covenant does not run, the benefit of it has been assigned from Tom to Ann. Only Ann may enforce the covenant; Tom no longer has any standing to enforce it.

Illustration: Tom's lease contained a covenant by Lil to supply heat to the premises and also a covenant by Tom not to assign the lease without Lil's consent. Tom assigned his lease to Ann without Lil's consent. Ann may compel Lil to supply heat. The wrongful assignment permits Lil to terminate the tenancy, but if she does not do so, the assignment is valid and Ann receives the benefits of all covenants made by Lil to Tom which run with the land.

4. The Effect of a Second Assignment

An assuming assignee becomes like a tenant insofar as the duties owed to the landlord are concerned, and thus remains liable on the covenants of the lease even after a later assignment. But a nonassuming assignee is liable only on covenants which run with the land, and then only while in possession of the land. Once the nonassuming assignee assigns there is no risk of any future liability. (There is neither privity of contract nor privity of estate with the landlord).

Illustration: Tom's lease contained a covenant to insure the premises (which does not run with the land). Tom assigned to Ann who assumed, and then Ann assigned to Bob, who also assumed. If Bob does not insure then Lil may sue Tom or Ann or Bob since Lil is in privity of contract with all of them. Ann's liability on the assumption is not ended when Ann assigns, just as Tom's liability survived the first assignment.

Illustration: Tom's lease contained the same covenant to insure the premises. Tom assigned to Ann who assumed, and then Ann assigned to Bob who did not assume. If Bob does not insure then Lil may sue Tom or Ann, but not Bob.

Illustration: Tom's lease contained the same covenant to insure the premises. Tom assigned to Ann who did not assume, and then Ann assigned to Bob who also did not assume. If Bob does not insure then Lil's only remedy is against Tom.

Illustration: Tom's lease contained the same covenant to insure the premises. Tom assigned to Ann who did not assume, and then Ann assigned to Bob who did not assume. If the assumption agreement is valid then Lil can sue Bob (or Tom). But many states hold that there was no obligation for Bob to assume, since Ann was not personally responsible; thus Lil would be able only to sue Tom.

Illustration: Tom's lease contained a covenant to repair, which did run with the land. Tom assigned to Ann who did not assume and then Ann assigned to Bob who also did not assume. If Bob does not repair Lil may sue Tom or Bob, but not Ann. Tom is liable on the original promise (privity of contract) and Bob is liable because the covenant runs with the land and he now has the leasehold (privity of estate). But Ann is not liable because she never assumed (no privity of contract) and because she no longer has an interest in the land (no privity of estate).

D.   THE EFFECT OF A SUBLEASE

A sublease does not transfer the tenant's rights or duties to the subtenant. The tenant remains a tenant of the landlord and the subtenant becomes a tenant of the tenant, but not a tenant of the landlord. There is no legal relationship between the subtenant and the landlord (there is no privity of estate or privity of contract between them) and neither can directly enforce obligations against the other, at law.

Illustration: Tom sublet to Stan. The original lease contained a covenant to insure by Tom. If Stan does not insure Lil has no remedy at law against him. But Tom remains liable on his covenant to Lil and Lil may proceed against him. If Lil is entitled to terminate the tenancy for the nonrepair then a termination of Tom's leasehold will necessarily also terminate Stan's subleasehold.

Illustration: Tom sublet to Stan. Stan covenanted to insure. If Stan does not insure, Tom can enforce the covenant but not Lil, since the covenant was made to Tom, and there is no privity of contract or privity of estate between Lil and Stan, unless Lil can be treated as a third party beneficiary of Stan's promise.

Illustration: Tom sublet to Stan. The original lease contained a covenant to insure by Tom, and Stan assumed that obligation. If Stan fails to insure Lil may sue Stan. Lil is beneficiary of Stan's assumption agreement (there is privity of contract between them).

Illustration: Tom sublet to Stan. The original lease contained a covenant to repair by Tom, which is a covenant that runs with the land. Stan does not repair. Lil cannot sue Stan because even though the covenant is one that runs, it generally is held to run only with the estate (Tom's leasehold) and Tom has not transferred that estate to Stan. See Chapter 6, p. 224. Tom has carved out a smaller and different estate for Stan. Lil's only legal relief is against Tom, who is in both privity of estate and privity of contract with Lil. (However, Lil may be able to enforce the covenant against Stan as an equitable servitude, if Stan had notice. See Chapter 6, p. 226.)

CHAPTER FIVE

EASEMENTS

I. THE NATURE OF EASEMENTS

A. EASEMENTS AS DISTINGUISHED FROM POSSESSORY INTERESTS

"Owners" and tenants are usually regarded as having possessory interests in property. In general, possessors may act as they please upon their property and are entitled to exclude everyone else from it even though the presence of others would not directly injure them. (The word "owner" has been surrounded by quotation marks because a person may "own" an easement; the term is used here to refer to a person holding a possessory freehold estate in the land. "Tenant", of course, refers to a person holding a possessory nonfreehold estate in land).

The holder of an easement, i.e. a dominant tenant (represented by "Dita" in the illustrations) does not have possession of the property, but only, at best, a privilege to make some special use of it. Thus possession of the property subject to an easement is always in someone else, i.e., a servient tenant (usually "Steve" in the illustrations).

(*Absence of Right to Exclude*) Possession includes the right to exclude others from the property: since

169

an easement is a nonpossessory interest it does not carry with it the right to exclude others or to stop them from also enjoying the property. (An "exclusive" easement may sometimes permit others to be excluded by virtue of granting to the dominant tenant the exclusive right to make a designated use of the property).

Illustration: Steve, owning property in fee simple, granted a right of way across it to Dita. This gives her an easement, not a possessory interest in Steve's property. She may use the road but she may not stop others from also using it, except to the extent that their use interferes with her use. But Steve, as possessor, may exclude all others (except Dita) from crossing his property, even though their crossings constitute no real injury to Steve. As possessor Steve may also continue to use the road himself, so long as he does not interfere with Dita. Had Steve "leased" or sold the road to Dita, thereby transferring full possession to her, she would have been able to exclude Steve and all others from using the road during the term of the lease, without the need to show that such acts interfered with her use of the road.

Illustration: Laura leased her property to Tom for 10 years, and the lease restricts Tom to residential uses of the property. Tom still has a possessory interest in the property, and not just an easement. While Tom's possessory interest is limited, that does not retain in Laura the untransferred possessory rights. (Otherwise Laura would be entitled to run a business on the property so long as she could show that it did not interfere with Tom's residential use of it.) Because Tom has possession, he may exclude all others (including Laura) from the premises.

(*"Right" and "Privilege" as Used in This Chapter*) Technically, the freedom to perform an act without penalty (e.g. to walk across land, to fish, etc.) should be referred to as a privilege rather than a right. A right, strictly, is the ability to demand that others perform or not perform acts (the right to be paid, the right to exclude). However, where common language is to the contrary the word "right" will be used in the text to refer to what should more properly be called a privilege (the "right to fish", a "right of way"). See Restatement of Property, sections 1–10.

B. EASEMENTS AS DISTINGUISHED FROM OTHER NONPOSSESSORY INTERESTS

1. Profits

A profit gives the holder thereof the right to remove some part or product of the soil. The common law profits were: (a) Turbary—the right to remove turf for use as fuel; (b) Piscary—the right to fish; (c) Estovers—the right to cut timber for fuel; (d) Pasture—the right to have animals graze. Contemporary interests in land which are sometimes called profits are the right to mine coal or other minerals, or to drill for oil or gas, or to cut timber. Generally a profit carries incidental easements with it, e.g., the right to mine coal carries the incidental right to enter into the mine.

For many purposes there is no material legal difference between easements and profits. Both generally come under the same rules. Under the new Restatement Third, easements and profits (along with covenants running with the land) are all treated as "servitudes" and generally made subject to the same rules.

2. Natural Rights in Land

By virtue of possession alone a possessor may be entitled to make certain demands upon his neighbors regarding their use of their land, which in a sense gives him some "rights" in their lands. But no person acquires an easement in other land merely by virtue of owning or possessing some property himself. It is always necessary for the existence of an easement that some special act of creation occur.

Illustration: Martin owns lot 1 and Nora owns the adjacent lot 2. Merely by virtue of owning lot 1, Martin can make Nora stop excavating on lot 2 if that would have the effect of removing the natural support her lot provides to his lot. See Chapter 15, p. 387.

Illustration: The owner of a downstream lot may be entitled to enjoin the owners of upstream lots from either polluting the stream or from taking more than a fair share of its water. See Chapter 14, p. 380.

3. Licenses

Easements may be categorized according to their duration in the same manner as estates are. Thus there may be, for instance, an easement in fee simple, an easement for life, or an easement for a certain term. However, there is no easement equivalent to the tenancy at will. When a use of land is made terminable at the will of the servient tenant, it is called a license rather than an easement. The distinction between a license and an easement is that the former is terminable at will and the latter is not.

A license may be defined as a revocable nonpossessory interest in land.

II. TYPES OF EASEMENTS
A. APPURTENANT OR IN GROSS

An easement is appurtenant when it was created to benefit and does in fact benefit the possessor of land with regard to her interest in the land. The easement is in gross when the benefit to its holder is personal to her rather than in connection with her land.

Illustration: Steve granted to Dita the right to swim in a pond on Steve's property. Dita is not a neighbor. This is probably an easement in gross. Dita may enjoy swimming in the pond regardless of what property she owns or whether she owns any property at all.

Illustration: Dita owned a large parcel of land adjacent to a stream; she sold off that part of the property directly contiguous to the stream, but reserved the right to cross from her property to the stream. In this case her easement is appurtenant. It was created to benefit Dita's use of her own retained parcel. Once she sells the retained parcel she will have no interest in the privilege of going from it over Steve's property to the stream.

Appurtenant means that the easement is connected to the dominant tenant's land. It does not mean that the dominant and servient parcels are adjacent to one another. An easement may be appurtenant even though the two parcels are quite distant.

Illustration: Steve granted to Dita the right to flood his property; Dita is an upstream owner far removed from Steve. Dita may still have an easement appurtenant even though the parcels are separated if this privilege is one which Dita enjoys as a possessor of her land.

(*No dominant tenement when the easement is in gross*) When an easement is appurtenant there is always some land held by the dominant tenant which is benefitted by the easement. It is called the dominant tenement. When an easement is in gross, there is no land which of itself receives the benefit of the easement; there is only a person who is benefitted. Thus when an easement is in gross there is no dominant tenement although there is always a dominant tenant.

(*Profits*) A profit may be appurtenant or in gross according to the same criteria as apply to easements.

Illustration: Steve granted to Dita the right to mine coal on his land. This profit is probably in gross since Dita may enjoy the privilege of mining regardless of what property she owns.

Illustration: Steve granted to Dita the right to drain water from a lake on Steve's land in order to irrigate Dita's land. This is probably a profit appurtenant since it is enjoyed by Dita only insofar as she continues to own the land to be irrigated.

B. AFFIRMATIVE OR NEGATIVE
(OR SPURIOUS)

An easement is called affirmative when it entitles the dominant tenant to do something which affects the servient tenement which would otherwise be unprivileged. It is called negative when it entitled the dominant tenant to prevent the servient tenant from doing an act on the servient tenement which would otherwise be privileged.

Illustration: Steve granted a right of way to Dita. Without this easement Dita would be guilty of trespass if she walked across Steve's land; i.e., it would be an unprivileged act. With the easement, however, Dita may cross without being liable for trespass; i.e., it is now privileged. Persons who do not have an easement of way are under a duty not to trespass; having such an easement ends the duty not to trespass. Dita here has an affirmative easement.

Illustration: Steve granted to Dita an easement of view over his property. Without this easement Steve would be privileged to erect buildings on his property, even if they blocked Dita's view. But now that Dita has the easement, Steve no longer has the privilege of building so as to block her view. Now Steve has a duty not to so build, and Dita has a right to demand there be no building. Dita here has a negative easement.

(*Spurious Easements*) When some affirmative obligation is purportedly imposed upon a servient tenant, it may be called a spurious easement, which is to say that it is not an easement at all and its enforcement must be found under some theory other than easement law. Courts do not permit private parties to create "novel interests" in land, reserving that power to themselves and legislatures.

Illustration: Steve agreed with Dita that he would plant and care for a tree on his property. This does not give Dita an easement in Steve's property. A true negative easement permits Dita to restrain, not compel Steve with regard to some act. Nor is this an affirmative easement, since Dita is not by its terms privileged to enter Steve's property to plant or care for the tree herself.

III. CREATION OF EASEMENTS AND LICENSES

A. BY EXPRESS WORDS—GRANT AND RESERVATION

A possessor of land may give another person an easement in his or her property. The appropriate way to do this would be by a deed granting the easement to the other, e.g. "I grant to you a right of way across my lot". When an owner of land transfers it to another he may wish to retain certain rights in it, usually for the benefit of other land still held by him. The appropriate way to do this would be by deed granting the land but reserving an easement in it, e.g. "I grant lot 1 to you, reserving a right of way across it from lot 2 to the road." The new Restatement of Property provides that words of contract (as well as words of conveyance) may create an easement. Restatement of Property Third (Servitudes), § 2.1 (hereafter "Restatement of Servitudes). Thus an agreement providing for one party to have a right of way over the property of the other would be as effective as a deed.

At common law it was important that the grantor "reserve" rather than "except" the easement, since only physical parts of the property could be excepted. It was also important for the grantor to reserve the easement for herself rather than in favor of a third party, which was prohibited. If she wished a third party to have the benefit of the easement to be reserved, she would reserve it to herself and then transfer it to the third party rather than attempt to reserve it directly in his favor at the outset. The new Restatement of Servitudes explicitly permits a servitude to be created for the benefit of a third party. Restatement of Servitudes, § 2.6.

1. Formalities and Failure to Comply With Them—Licenses

Whatever formal requirements exist in the jurisdiction for the transfer or creation of interests in land generally are applicable to the creation of easements. Usually a writing, a signature and a delivery of the document are necessary. When the parties attempt to create an easement but fail by virtue of a noncompliance with the statutory formalities, a license in favor of the grantee results. Thus the interest is a revocable one (subject to defenses of the licensee prohibiting immediate revocation, discussed in section VII of this chapter).

Illustration: Steve orally granted to Dita a right of way across his property for 10 years. The statute of frauds requires that grants of interests in land exceeding one year be in writing. As a result the grant was void and did not give Dita an easement. But it did create in her a license to cross Steve's land. This means that Dita is not trespassing when she does cross the land, but it also means that Steve may revoke her privilege to do so at any time. The license here is akin to the tenancy at will which arises when a grantee enters onto the property under a void deed. (See Chapter 4, p. 109.)

2. Formal Creation of Licenses

Not all licenses arise because of inadequate attempts to create an easement. A revocable privilege of use may be precisely what the parties intend.

Illustration: Steve delivered to Dita an instrument which said, "You may walk across my property until I change my mind." The document here, even though probably in compliance with all the formalities of conveyancing, creates only a license. The license results here because of the express intent to make the interest revocable.

3. Interests Which the Law Makes Revocable

Another interest in land which is labelled a license arises not from a futile attempt to create an easement or from an express declaration of revocability but rather because the parties have created an interest which courts insist on characterizing as a license.

Illustration: Steve invited Dita to a party at his house. This was a license, even if the invitation was written (and even if it declared itself irrevocable). The interest in land which arises by virtue of being invited to a party is too slight to be labelled an easement.

Illustration: Steve sold Dita a ticket to watch a sporting event on his property. Despite the enforceable contract underlying the ticket, there is nevertheless only a license, not an easement conferred on Dita.

B. BY IMPLICATION

When the parties are situated such that an easement could have been granted or reserved by express language between them, but in fact no such statement was made, under certain circumstances a court may decide that the parties impliedly created such an easement.

Illustration: Dita owned a large parcel of land with a house on the rear of it and a driveway running from the house over the front of the land to the public road. She sold the front half of the parcel to Steve without reserving a right of way over it. Since Dita could have reserved such an easement, and since it appears that such an easement would have been reserved had the parties thought about it, it is likely that a court will hold that there was an easement created by implied reservation under the circumstances. There is a writing between the parties (the deed) and the implication of the easement out of that writing satisfies the Statute of Frauds.

1. Severance of Parcels

Since an easement can be created by implication only where it could have been validly created by express language, and is to be implied out of the circumstances surrounding a written grant of land, the creation of implied easements is limited to situations where the grantor is granting only a part of the property he or she owns, or is dividing up the entire property among separate grantees. In either case there is a severance of an earlier ownership into multiple ownership. (In all except the final illustration here Owen began by owning a large parcel of land with a house on the rear half and a driveway running from it over the front half of the land to a public street.)

Illustration: Owen conveyed the rear half to Dita, retaining the front half. Under these circumstances it may be possible to imply the creation of an easement in favor of Dita's half and against Owen's half.

Illustration: Owen conveyed the rear half to Dita and the front half to Steve. Under these circumstances it may be possible to imply the creation of an easement in favor of Dita's half over Steve's half.

Illustration: Owen conveyed the entire parcel to Dita. Under no circumstances can an easement be implied over the lot of Owen's neighbor next door even if there is a driveway from Owen's house across it. No express language in the deed from Owen to Dita could have created in Dita an easement over the land or Owen's neighbor if Owen did not have such an easement already. Therefore no easement can be created by implication here. (If Owen already had an easement over the neighboring land, then the sale of Owen's lot to Dita would involve the transfer of that existing easement to Dita, not the implied creation of a new easement in favor of Dita.)

Illustration: Owen conveyed the front half to Steve, but for other reasons no easement in favor of the rear half was implied at that time. Later Owen conveyed the rear half to Dita. No easement can arise by implied creation out of this second conveyance regardless of the circumstances. It is too late; the severance of ownership has already occurred. Had Owen attempted to expressly create an easement in favor of Dita over the front half of the land when he conveyed it to her he would have failed, since the front half is now owned by a stranger to the Owen–Dita transaction, and neither Owen nor Dita has the power to create an interest in Steve's land without Steve's consent.

Illustration: Owen conveyed the front half to Steve but for other reasons no easement in favor of Owen's retained half was implied at that time. Later Owen conveyed the rear half to Dita, and even later Dita conveyed this rear half to Edna. If no easement was created against the front half at the time that the front half was first conveyed to Steve (and the ownership initially severed), then no easement against it can ever be created, by implication or by express language, through transactions involving the other half. Once the front half becomes separately owned it will require the assent of its owner (Steve) to impose an easement upon it.

a. *Implied Grant and Implied Reservation*

The implication may be of a granted or a reserved easement.

Illustration: Dita owned a parcel of land with a house on the rear and a driveway running from the house over the front part of the lot to the street. Dita sold the front half of the lot to Steve. If an easement is implied from the circumstances of this conveyance it will be implied that an easement of right of way over the granted parcel was *reserved* by Dita for her retained parcel.

Illustration: Steve owned a large parcel of land with a house on the rear and a driveway running from the house over the front part of the lot to the street. Steve sold the rear part of the lot (with the house) to Dita. If an easement is implied from the circumstances of this conveyance it will be implied that an easement of right of way over the front was *granted* from Steve to Dita along with the conveyance of the rear part of the lot.

Illustration: Dita and Steve owned adjacent lots. During the past few months, without asking, Dita drove across Steve's lot to get to a road, leaving a well-worn path visible on Steve's land, and then sold her lot to Ann. Ann has no easement over Steve's lot. Had Dita sought to expressly grant such an easement to Ann the attempt would have failed because she had none to convey and only Steve could create an easement in Ann at that time. There cannot be created in Ann's favor by implication, what could not have been created by express language.

2. Prior Use—*The Quasi–Easement*

An easement will be implied at the time of severance only if the use involved existed prior to the severance. Such a prior use can not be referred to as an easement because the owner of the use was also the owner of the property subject to the use, so that it did not exist as an independent interest in (another's) property. To indicate a use which would have been characterized as an easement had the properties been separately owned the term "quasi-easement" is employed. Thus, prior to the severance there must have existed a quasi-easement.

Illustration: Dita owned a parcel of land with a house on the rear and a driveway from it over the front half which she used to drive from her house to the street. Dita sold the front half to Steve. Since the driveway and use of it were in existence before Dita conveyed to Steve (as a quasi-easement) it may be possible to imply an easement in favor of Dita.

Illustration: Dita owned a parcel of land with a house on the rear. Dita sold the front half of the parcel to Steve and then began to drive across it, not having done so earlier. There was no quasi-easement in existence here before the conveyance and consequently a reserved easement in favor of Dita will not be implied.

3. The Characteristics of the Prior Use

Not every use which existed prior to a severance of ownership will be converted into an easement after severance. Courts generally use adjectives such as "apparent", "continuous", "permanent", "necessary", and/or "beneficial" to indicate the characteristics which the quasi-easement must be found to have if it is to be converted into an easement.

a. *Apparent*

Since the basis for implying the creation of an easement is an assumption that the parties would have done the same by express language had they considered the matter, it is generally required that the quasi-easement be apparent, so that such an inference can be drawn. However, apparent does not mean visible; uses which are discoverable by an inspection may be held to be apparent.

Illustration: When Dita sold the front half of her property to Steve there was a paved driveway running across it to Dita's house on the rear. Even though Dita was not actually driving over the road at the moment that Steve purchased, nevertheless the driveway is apparent and an easement of passage over it may be implied in favor of Dita.

Illustration: Owen owns two houses, with the rear house being connected to a public sewer by a sewer pipe running under the front house, to which the front house is also connected. Although the sewer pipe is underground, an inspection by a plumber would reveal that fact, and consequently the pipe may be held to be apparent. (The Restatement of Servitudes provides that underground utilities serving either parcel are not required to be "apparent or known" in order to be created by implication. Restatement, § 2.12.) Thus when Owen sells either house an easement over the front house in favor of the rear house may be implied.

b. Permanent—Continuous

Even though some use of the quasi-servient parcel may be occurring at the time of severance, there is no basis for implying that the parties would have created an easement to that effect unless there are indications that the use was a permanent one which would continue after the severance. Thus courts require that the quasi-easement be permanent or continuous. The Restatement of Servitudes refers to this as a requirement that the prior use be "not merely temporary or casual". Restatement, § 2.12.

Illustration: When Dita sold the front half of her property to Steve she, at that moment drove across it to reach her house on the rear half. However, there is no driveway or other indication of use. Since there is no evidence that this was a regular activity of Dita there is no basis for implying an easement of passage across the front half.

Illustration: Dita had a paved road running from her house in the rear across the front half of her property. When she sold the front half to Steve an easement of passage might be implied since a paved driveway indicates a permanent burden upon the servient front half in favor of the rear half.

c. Necessary—Beneficial

Since the creation of an easement by implication requires a court not only to confer an interest in property upon one party but, more significantly, to deprive the other party of an interest in property without his or her consent, there is a reluctance to do so unless some significant purpose will be served thereby. Courts will not imply the creation of an easement unless there is a real benefit to be gained by the prospective dominant parcel. They require that the easement be necessary or beneficial.

Many courts require strict necessity before they will imply the creation of a reserved easement, whereas mere convenience to the dominant parcel may be enough to justify an easement by implied grant. An easement by implied reservation gives the grantor an easement in the property granted even though, as the author of the deed, he or she had the full opportunity to expressly reserve it, and even though the deed often contains normal covenants of title warranting that there are no easements burdening the property. Thus there is a reluctance to imply reserved easements as readily as granted easements.

Illustration: Steve had a house on the rear of his lot connected to a driveway running across the front half to the street. Steve sold the rear half to Dita. Even though Dita could build a new driveway entirely on her property, running to a different street, nevertheless an easement (by grant) in favor of Dita may be implied in light of the cost involved to her of building the other driveway.

Illustration: Dita had a house on the rear of her lot connected to a driveway running across the front half to the street. Dita sold the front half to Steve. Dita could build a driveway to a different street running entirely on her own property but it would be expensive. Since Dita is now claiming that she impliedly reserved an easement across the property she sold to Steve, those courts which require absolute necessity will deny the existence of such an easement because Dita is able (even though at heavy cost) to gain access by other means.

C. BY NECESSITY

When a parcel of land is subdivided so that one part of it is left without access to a road then an easement of passage is implied across the other part or parts. There is a public policy against useless (landlocked) land which generates this implication. Consequently, the implication is not dependent upon the acts of the parties or the circumstances of the conveyance or any prior quasi-easement although it may depend on there being no expressly contrary language in the creating document. And such an easement endures only so long as the necessity lasts.

Illustration: Dita granted to Steve the front half of her land, leaving herself with a landlocked rear half. Even though there was no quasi-easement whatsoever before the severance there may now be implied an easement of access over Steve's land.

1. Implied From a Plat

If the buyer of a house in a newly created subdivision has been shown a map (plat) of the area which shows her house fronting on a public street, she has a legitimate expectation that the subdivider will construct the streets and open them for public use. This expectation will be enforced in the courts by creation of an implied easement of access in those streets shown on the map. Some courts imply such an easement in favor of the buyer over all of the streets in the subdivision (beneficial or full enjoyment rule) whereas others confine the easement to only those streets necessary for access from the property to the nearest public way (narrow or necessary rule). An intermediate rule makes the scope of her easement as extensive as may be necessary to protect the market value of her property. The Restatement of Servitudes provides that mapped descriptions of streets implies an easement to use the street and that mapping of parks, beaches, etc., implies the creation of servitudes in those lands to that effect. Restatement, § 2.13. For the implication of other servitudes from a general plan, see Chapter 6.

D. BY PRESCRIPTION

Analogous to the doctrine of adverse possession is the doctrine of prescriptive easements. Most of the rules and concepts applicable to adverse possession are applicable here as well. (See Chapter 1). Those principles will be mentioned only briefly here.

Adverse possession depends for its foundation upon statutes of limitations governing possessory actions. Since ejectment does not lie for adverse use, that statute of limitations is inapplicable, and the doctrine of prescriptive easements arises only by judicial analogy to adverse possession rather than as a direct result of legislation.

The original judicial rationale for the creation of prescriptive easements was the fiction that a use which had continued long enough had probably commenced through the grant of an easement which had since gotten lost. The failure of the possessor to object to the adverse use was taken as proving that long ago the possessor had given permission to the user. This theory has been generally abandoned, although in some cases a few of the standards of prescription derive from that old view (such as the requirement of "peaceable"). Today most states treat prescriptive easements under a strict analogy to adverse possession, only modifying the rules to make them conform to the special characteristics of easements.

The new Restatement of Servitudes § 2.17 proposes that prescriptive use include activities undertaken pursuant to the terms of "an intended but imperfectly created servitude", e.g. where lack of a writing defeated the creation of a legal easement but the intended beneficiary thereafter used the property as if she was entitled to do so.

(*Prescriptive Use Versus Prescriptive Possession*) Many activities can be viewed either as uses on the property or as possession of the property. Thus the long continuance of an activity may lead to a finding either of adverse possession or prescriptive easement. The controlling factor may be the behavior of the owner of the same property during the prescriptive period.

Illustration: Dita regularly grazes her cattle on Steve's land. This could ripen into an adverse possession of the property or a prescriptive easement to graze. Which it becomes will probably depend on whether Steve is making any use of the property himself during the same time period. If Steve is also using the property, then Dita cannot claim adverse possession since she is neither exclusive nor uninterrupted. But Dita can, under these same circumstances, claim a prescriptive right to graze. If Steve is totally absent from the land, and if it is grazing land primarily, Dita's same acts could lead to a finding of adverse possession.

1. Elements of Prescription

a. *Adverse, Hostile*

These requirements, borrowed from adverse possession, continue here with their same meanings, i.e., generally ignoring the user's state of mind but requiring that her activities be done without the permission of the landowner. In some jurisdictions an owner may establish that all uses are permissive by posting the property to that effect (which may be easier to do than attempting constantly to make recreational users leave). In some jurisdictions, on unenclosed and unimproved land the owner is presumed to have given permission to others to use it.

b. *Payment of Taxes*

Many states limit adverse possession to situations where the possessor has paid taxes during the period. However, since easements are rarely assessed or taxed separately this is not a requirement for prescription.

c. *Exclusive*

Since possession by its nature involves exclusivity it is a general requirement of adverse possession that the claimant be exclusive. Although it is frequently stated that a prescriptive easement also requires the user to be exclusive, this does not mean that no one else can be making any other use or the same use of the property during the prescriptive period. At most it means that the user claims a right special to himself or herself to carry on the use. Thus a person walking over the property under the claim that it is a public right of way may fail to qualify as a prescriptive user.

d. *Uninterrupted*

An adverse possession is interrupted by the actual (or judicial) taking of possession by the owner or someone else. But possession in another does not necessarily conflict with an adverse use and thus will not automatically interrupt a ripening prescriptive easement. Only the actual interruption of the use itself will interrupt.

Illustration: Dita persistently walked across Steve's property for 25 years. But during that time Steve also used the same property for various purposes (he walked across it, sat on it, etc.). Steve's use and possession of the property did not interrupt Dita.

Illustration: Dita walked across Steve's property until Steve erected a fence barring her. This did interrupt Dita if it occurred before the statute of limitations expired.

(*Ineffective Interruptions*) An interruption stops the ripening of prescription only when it is effective to interrupt the use. (Under the lost grant theory, however, even an ineffectual interruption could bar prescription by virtue of refuting the inference of a lost grant having been given by the servient tenant).

Illustration: Dita persistently walked across Steve's property. Steve built a fence to stop Dita, but Dita knocked it down and continued crossing. Steve did not interrupt Dita's prescription.

Illustration: Dita walked across Steve's property. There Steve informed Dita that she may continue to do so. This alone had no effect on interrupting the statute of limitations. Steve cannot eliminate the adverseness of Dita's use by unilaterally attempting to consent to it.

2. Prescriptive Easements as Appurtenant or in Gross

Depending upon the circumstances, a prescriptive easement can be either appurtenant or in gross.

Illustration: Dita persistently walked from her property across Steve's property to get to the road. There was probably created in Dita an easement appurtenant to her property.

Illustration: Dita persistently fished in a lake owned by Steve. Dita does not live near Steve and during the prescriptive period Dita changed residences several times. Here Dita probably has acquired an easement in gross.

a. Negative Prescriptive Easements

It is generally impossible to acquire a negative easement by prescription since no activity has been carried out by the alleged dominant tenant which was wrongful as to the servient tenant.

Illustration: Dita has looked out from her windows over Steve's land for 30 years; now she seeks to enjoin him from building so as to preserve a claimed easement of view. Dita will fail since her looking all those years was not wrongful as to Steve. As an owner of property Dita was privileged to look over other's property, and Steve could not have enjoined her from doing so. Her privileged act cannot ripen into a right to stop Steve from engaging in his privileged act of building; Steve comes under no duty to not build as a result of having failed to build in the past. However, in England there is a doctrine of "ancient lights" to the contrary. And under the new Restatement's use of prescription to cure imperfectly created servitudes, an oral grant of an easement of view by Steve coupled with 30 years of looking by Dita would ripen into a prescriptive easement.

Illustration: Dita erected a building on her land 25 years ago. The building is so heavy that if Steve had ever excavated on his adjoining land, the building would have subsided. However, Dita has not thereby acquired any easement of support. Steve has not had any cause of action against Dita for the past 25 years, and therefore he has lost no rights or privileges by not suing her. She was privileged to build her building and he was privileged to excavate. His failure to exercise his privilege for the past 25 years has not caused him to lose it nor has Dita's continued

exercise of her privilege for that time converted it into a
right to demand that Steve not exercise his privilege to
excavate; he is under no duty to support her building by
not excavating. On support see Chapter 15.

IV. TRANSFER OF EASEMENTS

A. TRANSFER OF THE BURDEN OF AN EASEMENT

An easement always involves a servient tenement,
i.e. property burdened by an easement. When that
servient parcel is transferred, the burden of the easement is transferred with it because an owner cannot
convey more than he or she has, thus the burden of
an easement always "runs with the land". (However,
this doctrine is subject to the operation of the recording acts. See Chapter 10).

B. TRANSFER OF THE BENEFIT OF AN EASEMENT

An easement appurtenant always involves a dominant tenement receiving the benefit, but an easement
in gross has no dominant tenement, (only a dominant
tenant). Thus the rules for transfer of the benefit of
an easement differ according to the nature of the
easement.

1. Transfer of the Benefit of an Easement in Gross

Originally the benefits of easements in gross were
held to be nontransferable. They were regarded as

conferring too slight a benefit compared to the burden to warrant the extensive clouding of title that transferability would entail. Because easements in gross of a commercial nature do have a significant benefit, the modern view is to permit them to be transferred.

2. Transfer of the Benefit of an Easement Appurtenant

The benefit of an easement appurtenant is transferred along with the transfer of the dominant tenement, unless the grant expressly excludes the transfer of the easement, i.e. it "runs with the land". The exclusion of the easement from the transfer of the dominant estate may have the effect of continuing the easement in the transferor or it may lead to the destruction of the easement.

Illustration: Dita had an easement of right of way across Steve's property, which easement was appurtenant to her land. When Dita sold her property the buyer obtained both the land and the easement appurtenant to it, even if the deed did not mention the easement.

Illustration: Dita had an easement of right of way across Steve's property which was appurtenant to her land. Dita sold her property, excepting the right of way from the grant. This had the effect of either extinguishing the easement entirely, or converting it into an easement in gross held by Dita. The result will depend upon whether or not the circumstances surrounding the original creation of the easement justify an inference that its creator intended to permit it to exist independently of the former dominant tenement.

Illustration: Dita had an easement of right of way across Steve's property which was appurtenant to her land. She purported to grant that right of way to Ann, without conveying her own land to Ann. This did not confer upon Ann the right to drive over Steve's property, for that would impermissibly change the nature of the easement from appurtenant to in gross.

3. Transferability as Affected by the Creating Language

It is possible for the parties to modify the foregoing rules by special language in the instrument which created the easement. An otherwise transferable easement may be made nontransferable, or an otherwise nontransferable easement may be made transferable.

Illustration: Steve's deed to Dita said: "I give you the right to walk from your property across my property. However, if you ever convey your property, this right will expire." Although this is an easement appurtenant, it is not transferable with the dominant tenement.

Illustration: Steve's deed to Dita said: "I give you the right to swim in my lake, wherever you reside. And you may transfer this right to other members of your family." Although this is a noncommercial easement in gross, it has been made transferable (under limited circumstances) here.

V. SUBDIVISION OF EASEMENTS
A. SUBDIVISION OF THE BURDEN

When the servient tenement is subdivided, each part of the property remains subject to the easement, except when the easement is located spacially such that some parts of the servient tenement are not affected. A servient owner has no greater power to extinguish an easement by subdividing the property than he or she does by transferring it. See p. 192.

Illustration: Steve's property was subject to an easement of passage across it from east to west. Steve subdivided his land into a western and an eastern parcel. Both parcels remain subject to the easement.

Illustration: Steve's property was subject to an easement of passage across it from east to west along its northerly boundary. Steve subdivided his land into a northern and a southern parcel. The northern parcel is subject to the easement, but not the southern parcel since that part of the property was never subject to the right of way.

B. SUBDIVISION OF THE BENEFIT

The distinction between easements appurtenant and in gross is applicable here, as it was to the transfer of benefits of an easement. See p. 192.

1. Subdivision of the Benefit of an Easement in Gross

In those jurisdictions where easements in gross are not transferable at all, or are transferable only when commercial, such benefits also may not be subdivided or apportioned in any case where they could not be transferred. In jurisdictions where transferability is allowed, there is no clear standard governing the subdivisibility of the easement. An exclusive easement is generally more readily subdivisible than a nonexclusive one and other terms in the grant may furnish additional guidance as to the intent of the parties. For prescriptive easements, a court must determine whether the original acquiescence of the servient tenant can be reasonably enlarged to encompass a use not shared by more than one dominant tenant.

2. Subdivision of the Benefit of a Profit in Gross

Some courts apply different standards to the subdivisibility of a profit in gross. In some jurisdictions a profit in gross is subdivisible if it is admeasurable, i.e. quantifiable. In others the Rule of Mountjoy's Case is applied to mean that a profit can be subdivided only when it will continue to be worked as a common stock.

Illustration: Dita has the right to mine 50 tons of coal a month from Steve's land. Since this is an admeasurable profit, some states will permit her to subdivide, so long as no more than 50 tons of coal are removed per month. In other cases, Dita may subdivide only if all of the takers mine the coal jointly and not through separate operations.

3. Subdivision of the Benefit of an Easement Appurtenant

The benefit of an easement appurtenant is automatically subdivided when the dominant tenement is subdivided unless either the terms of the original grant prohibit subdivision or the terms of the subdividing grants restrain the transfer of the benefit.

Illustration: Steve granted to Dita a right of way across his property. Dita subdivided her lot into three parcels, conveying them to Ann, Bob and Carl respectively. Ann, Bob and Carl all received rights of way across Steve's property.

Illustration: Steve granted to Dita a right of way across his property, but the grant limited Dita to a right of way from her existing house over Steve's property. Dita subdivided her land, among Ann, Bob and Carl with the house being on the part taken by Ann. Only Ann has a right of way.

Illustration: Steve granted to Dita a right of way across his property. Dita subdivided her lot among Ann, Bob and Carl, but in the deeds to Bob and Carl there is the following language "excepting the right of way across Steve's property." Only Ann has a right of way.

VI. THE SCOPE OF EASEMENTS

This section concerns the variations of activities which are permitted to the dominant and servient tenants with regard to the easement involved.

A. VARIATIONS BY THE DOMINANT TENANT

No grant or reservation of an easement ever sets forth with total precision the nature of the activity which the dominant tenant may undertake or restrain. Consequently it is frequently necessary for courts to determine whether some new activity is within or without the scope of the easement. Here follows a series of illustrations indicating some of the ways in which the benefit of an easement may be sought to be varied.

Location of the Benefit: Illustration: Dita has a right of way from her house over Steve's land. She seeks to relocate the house elsewhere on her property and still continue to use the right of way.

Enlargement of the Benefit: Illustration: Dita has the right to draw water from a stream crossing Steve's property in order to irrigate her land. She seeks to draw water to irrigate the parcel adjacent to her land as well.

Location of the Burden: Illustration: Dita has a right of way located along the northern boundary of Steve's property. She seeks to cross along the southern boundary of Steve's property instead.

Activity on the Dominant Tenement: Illustration: Dita has a right to draw water for drinking and bathing. She seeks to draw water for irrigation instead.

Activity on the Servient Tenement: Illustration: Dita has a right of way over Steve's property. She now seeks to drive rather than walk across the property, or to cross at night instead of day, or to cross twice a day instead of once a day, or to bring friends with her instead of crossing alone.

1. Standards for Determining Whether the Variation Is Allowable

a. When There Is Explicit Language

If the language of the easement is explicit as to any matter, then the dominant tenant is not allowed to deviate from what has been set forth in the document.

Illustration: Steve granted Dita a right of way 10 feet wide across the north end of his property. Dita cannot widen the path or relocate it even though Steve would be unable to show that such a change would cause him any harm.

Illustration: Steve granted Dita the right to draw water for drinking purposes only. Dita cannot use the water for any non-drinking purposes, even though Steve would not be injured by such a change.

b. When There Is No Explicit Language

When the language of the easement does not make plain whether the new activity is allowable or not, there is no single rule for resolving the question. Some authorities look at various factors, including the circumstances of the original grant, the consideration paid for it, and the prior and the subsequent use made of the servient tenement. Others follow a "rule of reason" which holds that unreasonable rights and unreasonable burdens will not be implied. Both approaches seek to fill in the gaps of the conveyance according to notions of what the parties themselves would have done had they considered the matter and acted reasonably about it.

Illustration: Dita has a right of way across Steve's property, by a grant which did not refer to a mode of transportation. Dita originally rode a horse across Steve's property but now seeks to drive a car instead. The Restatement would look at the circumstances of the grant (whether the parties had cars at the time, whether the road was paved), how much Dita paid for the easement, and whether a car was ever driven over the road before or after the easement was given. The rule of reason would ask whether driving a car is a reasonable activity for Dita and whether it would be unreasonably burdensome to Steve.

An easement arising by implication is the most difficult of all to interpret with regard to scope. In general, a court will look to the same circumstances as were employed to settle the creation question in order to determine the nature and extent of that easement.

c. When the Easement Is Prescriptive

There is no language involved in the creation of prescriptive easements, so that a different set of inferences must be drawn to determine the allowable scope of activity. The only factor to consider is the previous use, but courts agree that future uses are not limited to the precise original use. Rather, the prescriptive use is taken as a pattern in an attempt to gauge from the servient tenant's acquiescence in that use whether or not the same acquiescence would have occurred had the new use been made instead.

Illustration: Dita walked across Steve's property at 5 p.m. every day for 25 years. Now she seeks to walk at 6 p.m. A court might well infer that Steve would not have stopped Dita at 6 p.m. in the past based upon his failure to stop her at 5 p.m. Thus Dita may now walk at 6 p.m.

Illustration: Dita walked across Steve's property every day for 25 years. Now she seeks to drive a car instead. A court might well infer that Steve would have interrupted Dita's crossings had she driven instead of walked in the past. Thus Dita will not be allowed to drive.

2. Changes Caused by Development of the Dominant Tenement

It is generally held that changes in the use of the easement arising from the development of the dominant tenement are allowable if that development is normal or reasonable and if the new activity is reasonably required by the dominant tenant. This is based upon the assumption that the parties were themselves forward-looking and would have agreed in advance to such changes had they originally thought about it. However, while a reasonable servient tenant would probably agree to normal growth of the dominant tenement, it is also the case that he would probably not consent to any change which unreasonably burdened his own property, even if it were the result of normal growth of the dominant tenement.

Illustration: Steve granted a right of way to Dita at a time when Dita used her land as a farm. Now the entire area is becoming residential. Dita has built several houses on her property and seeks to use the right of way for access to all of the houses. Since this is a reasonable development of Dita's property, and since the right of way is reasonably required by the houses for access, and since this new use does not increase the burden on Steve, it should be allowed.

Illustration: Steve granted a right of way to Dita at a time when Dita used her land as a farm. Now valuable minerals have been found on Dita's land and on other properties nearby, and extensive mining activity is commencing. Dita seeks to use the right of way for trucks to carry out the ores. Even though this may now be a reasonable activity on Dita's land, nevertheless the noise and disruption caused by the trucks should permit Steve to enjoin this new use of his land. However, many courts look only at Dita's use, and do not consider the burden resulting to Steve from it. It is also held that the dominant tenant, rather than the servient tenant is the one obliged to keep the easement in repair (although injured third parties may be able to recover against the servient tenant, notwithstanding this rule, since he is the possessor of the land).

B. VARIATIONS BY THE SERVIENT TENANT

1. The Nature of the Dominant Tenant's Rights

The holder of an easement has rights of use rather than rights of possession. A dominant tenant may not sue in trespass or ejectment, being limited to a cause of action for unreasonable interference with the easement. This means that harm is a far more essential element in the protection of easements than it is in the protection of possession.

Illustration: Dita has a right of way over a road on Steve's land. Ann has started walking on the same road without anyone's consent. Dita can obtain relief against Ann only if she can show that Ann's activity unreasonably interferes with her right of way. But Steve can recover from Ann in trespass without the need to show any direct injury from Ann's activity.

2. The Nature of the Servient Tenant's Rights

By virtue of granting a particular use to a dominant tenant, the servient tenant does not give up the right to make the same use or to make any other use of the property, so long as these activities do not unreasonably interfere with the dominant tenant's use.

Illustration: Steve granted a right of way to Dita. Steve may still walk on the road himself, and may do any other act he pleases on the road, so long as Dita's right of passage is not unreasonably hindered.

a. Rights of Third Parties

Since the servient tenant retains the right to make all noninterfering uses of the property, he or she may permit others to make similar uses.

Illustration: Steve gave Dita a right of way across his property. Steve may also permit Ann to use the same road so long as this does not hamper Dita. (Both Dita and Ann are now dominant tenants.).

3. Variations Allowed to the Servient Tenant

A servient tenant should be allowed to engage in any activity upon his or her own land, including that part of it subject to the easement, so long as these acts cause no unreasonable interference with the easement. This should be the result even when there is express language in the grant to the contrary, although it is frequently not the case.

Illustration: Steve granted Dita the right to maintain a sewer across his land. Steve should be allowed to relocate the sewer, so long as Dita's use of the sewer is not thereby impaired.

Illustration: Steve granted to Dita a right of way across the northern boundary of his property. Steve should be allowed to relocate the road, despite the language of the grant, so long as Dita's rights of access do not suffer. Many cases are to the contrary, however, holding that an easement of located or defined dimensions creates rights to the space involved similar to possessory interests.

VII. TERMINATION OF EASEMENTS

This section deals with the various ways in which an easement terminates, thereby restoring the servient tenant to unburdened possession of his or her property.

A. TERMINATION BY VIRTUE OF LANGUAGE IN THE GRANT

An easement may be created for a limited or conditional duration. When the time passes or the condition occurs, the easement ends.

Illustration: Steve granted to Dita the right to cross his property for so long as she lives in the house next door. Once Dita moves, the easement ends.

Illustration: Dita's ten-year lease of a house included the right to walk across the adjacent lot also owned by the landlord, Steve. At the expiration of the lease, the easement incident to it also terminated.

Illustration: Steve granted to Dita the right to park her car in his garage. After a fire destroyed the garage and Steve elected not to rebuild it, Dita's easement ended, since implicit in the grant was the assumption of the continued existence of the structure which serves as the servient tenement.

1. Termination of Licenses

Since a license may be viewed as a revocable easement it will expire once it is revoked. However, when an interest in land is a license only because the parties failed to comply with the formalities requisite to the creation of easements (see p. 177) it is held to become irrevocable if the licensee expends time or money in reasonable reliance on the grant. Consequently it can no longer be terminated at the will of the licensor. The Restatement of Servitudes treats reasonable reliance both as creating an exception to the Statute of Frauds (§ 2.9) or as creating an easement by estoppel (§ 2.10).

Illustration: Steve orally granted to Dita the right to forever maintain a sewer pipe under Steve's land, and Dita thereupon built and installed the pipe. The grant led to the creation of a license because it was oral and not because the parties desired to create a revocable interest. But the expenditure of time and money by Dita makes the license irrevocable. Steve is now estopped to revoke the license.

Illustration: Steve executed a grant in writing to Dita which recited "You may drive across my property until I change my mind." Dita thereafter paved the road. Steve may still revoke, because the expenditure of money was not in reasonable reliance on any permanent grant. The grant here was that of a license because of express language of revocability in the document, and not because the parties failed to comply with the statute of frauds.

(*The Duration of Irrevocable Licenses*) A license that is held irrevocable because of estoppel may be terminated by the court once conditions have changed or the licensee has recovered the cost of her reliance.

B. MERGER

An easement always involves a separate dominant and a servient tenant. When the dominant tenant becomes the owner of the servient tenement, there is no longer any easement, since one generally cannot have an easement in his or her own property.

Illustration: Dita had a right of way across Steve's land. She then bought Steve's land. Now Dita has possession of Steve's land, which already includes the right to cross it. Therefore, it would be incorrect to say that Dita still has an easement.

Illustration: Dita had a paved right of way across Steve's land. She then purchased Steve's land and, later, sold her original parcel to Ann, without mentioning any right of way over her retained parcel in the deed to Ann. No easement was transferred to Ann since Dita did not have an easement in her own land, but one might have been created by implication if, at the time of the conveyance to Ann, there was an apparent, continuous and necessary quasi-easement. See p. 178.

(*Temporary Merger or Reseparation*) If the dominant tenant acquires only a temporary possessory interest in the servient estate, the easement is merely suspended until the possession ends. On the other hand, if the easement was extinguished due to a complete merger of the parcels, it is not revived if they are subsequently separated again, although it is possible that a new easement will be implied from the severance.

Illustration: Dita had a right of way across Steve's land. Dita then rented Steve's land for 5 years. For those years it would be incorrect to say that Dita had an easement, but when the term ended Dita's easement resumed.

C. RELEASE (ABANDONMENT)

An easement is formally extinguished by a release deed properly executed and delivered by the dominant tenant to the servient tenant. This transfers the easement back to the servient tenant, which then leads to a merger of the easement into the larger possessory estate. All of the formalities for the creation of easements apply to the release of easements.

An oral statement by the dominant tenant purporting to terminate the easement or transfer it back to the servient tenant is ineffective for lack of compliance with the statute of frauds. However, under principles somewhat similar to the abandonment and surrender of leaseholds (see Chapter 4, p. 121) rules have developed permitting the termination of easements by operation of law under certain circumstances.

1. By Words Alone

An oral attempt to end an easement, with nothing more, will not terminate it. This would be a clear violation of the statute of frauds.

2. By Nonuse Alone

Mere nonuse by the dominant tenant does not terminate an easement. The holder of a right in property need not exercise it to keep it alive. However, in some jurisdictions prescriptive easements are lost by a period of nonuse equal to the time required to create such easements.

3. By Words Plus Nonuse

An easement may be terminated by oral statements of the dominant tenant signifying an intent to abandon followed by nonuse of the easement. The nonuse makes up for the lack of writing if it continues long enough to substantiate the statement of intent. The duration of the nonuse should be however long is needed to verify the intent to abandon. The law is willing to permit the termination of easements in such cases because their destruction creates no void in ownership, but merely restores the servient tenant to unburdened, complete ownership.

4. By Words Plus Inconsistent Acts

An easement may be terminated by oral statements of the dominant tenant showing an intent to terminate followed by significant acts performed by the dominant tenant which are inconsistent with the continuance of the easement.

Illustration: Dita had a right of way across Steve's property. She declared to Steve that she did not intend to use the road any longer and then built a fence between the properties blocking her own access to the road. The easement is extinguished by the combination of Dita's statements and acts.

5. By Inconsistent Acts Alone

Sometimes the acts of the dominant tenant may be so permanent and inconsistent with the continuation of the easement that an intent to abandon may be inferred, and the easement is thereby terminated.

Illustration: Dita had an easement of view across Steve's property. She tore down her house and erected a permanent windowless building on her property. Even though she has made no statements, an intent to abandon may be inferred, and her easement is terminated.

6. By Words of the Dominant Tenant and Acts of the Servient Tenant—Estoppel

An easement may be terminated by oral statements of the dominant tenant followed by acts of the servient tenant in reliance on the statement. Acts of the servient tenant cannot, of course, prove an intent to abandon by the dominant tenant, but if these acts involve an expenditure of money, and if, as a result, the servient tenant would be unreasonably harmed were the easement to be reasserted, the dominant tenant will be held estopped. (This may be viewed as giving the servient tenant a parol license to terminate the easement, which becomes irrevocable by virtue of the reliance. See p. 204).

Illustration: Dita announced that she intended to give up her right of way across Steve's land. In reliance on this statement Steve erected a building across the road. Dita is now estopped to assert that the easement was never formally terminated.

Illustration: Dita stopped using her right of way across Steve's land and Steve plowed up the road. Dita is not estopped from claiming her easement here, because she made no statements inducing reliance by Steve and because Steve will not be harmed if the road is reopened.

D. ADVERSE USE

This section involves inconsistent acts of the servient tenant (or some other party) without any conduct or declaration by the dominant tenant. A dominant tenant has a cause of action for unreasonable interference with the easement. If this right is not asserted in a timely fashion it is lost, like all other rights in property. The rules applicable for adverse possession and prescriptive easements are appropriate here.

Illustration: Dita had a right of way across Steve's land. Steve erected a fence barring Dita from access for 25 years. As a result, Dita has lost her easement.

Illustration: Dita had a right of way across Steve's land. Steve himself walked across the same road for 25 years. Dita has not lost her easement here because Steve's acts were not wrongful as to her (unless they interfered with her passage).

Illustration: Dita had a right of way across Steve's land, but she has not used it for 25 years. This alone does not destroy her easement since Steve has not acted adversely to her during the period so as to jeopardize her interest. Her failure to assert a privilege over time does not lead to the loss of the privilege.

Although a minority view is that an easement in a building is destroyed by the servient tenant's intentional destruction of the building, the majority view is that termination occurs only when the destruction is accidental or where the structure had become so obsolete that the servient owner was forced to destroy it. This result is reached on the ground that continued existence of the building was an implied condition in the creation of the easement (i.e., "You may cross through my building so long as there is a building to cross through.")

E. INVALIDITY

Easements and profits, like other interests in land, may be held invalid as violating the rule against perpetuities, especially when they are in gross and therefore not tied to the duration of a dominant tenement (although both the Restatement of Servitudes (§ 3.3) and the Uniform Condominium and Common Ownership Acts (§ 2–103) propose that the rule not apply to servitudes or to the power to create them). The rule against restraints on alienation may also invalidate easements and profits, although public purposes such as historic preservation may be held to make the restrictions reasonable.

CHAPTER SIX

COVENANTS RUNNING WITH THE LAND

An interest "runs with the land" when a subsequent owner of that land is held subject to the burden or benefit of that interest. Thus an easement runs with the land since transfer of the servient tenement leaves the property still subject to the easement and transfer of the dominant tenement carries the benefit of the easement along with it. One property owner may have the right to walk across another's land because of an arrangement their predecessors in title made, which binds them regardless of whether or not they ever personally ratified the transaction. The burden of this easement (being unable to stop the other from walking) ran with the servient tenement, and the benefit of the easement (the privilege of walking) ran with the dominant tenement. When an easement is in gross and therefore lacking any dominant tenement, its benefit cannot run with land, although its burden may.

Covenants (promises) respecting land may run with the land in a way roughly similar to easements. To say that a covenant or promise runs with the land is to mean that a piece of property will remain burdened or benefitted by that covenant even though it

211

is no longer owned by the person who made or received that promise. The covenant remains, affecting the land despite changes in ownership.

Illustration: Prudence (the promissor) promised Peter (the promissee) that she would not sell liquor on her property. Prudence sold her property to Ann. If the requirements necessary for a covenant to run with the land are met, liquor may still not be sold on the property even though it is now owned by Ann rather than Prudence.

The important consequence of a covenant running with the land is that its burden or benefit will thereby be imposed or conferred upon a subsequent owner of the property who never actually agreed to it. Running covenants thereby achieve the transfer of duties and rights in a way not permitted by traditional contract law.

Illustration: Prudence covenanted with Peter not to sell liquor on her land. Prudence then sold her land to Ann, who did not make any such promise. Nevertheless, if the covenant runs, Ann is bound by it and may not sell liquor on the property. Ann thus is bound by a promise she neither made nor assumed. If, however, the covenant is not one which runs with the land, Ann is not bound by it.

I. COVENANTS COMPARED WITH OTHER DEVICES WHICH BIND REMOTE TAKERS OF PROPERTY

A. EASEMENTS

Since, as was mentioned, easements run with the land, had that concept been broader there might have been no need for the courts to create the rival concept of covenants running with the land. But the category of activities which may be characterized as easements has always been somewhat limited and courts resist attempts of parties to create and label new kinds of restrictions on land as easements. Restrictions which are too novel to qualify as easements, or which are "spurious" easements (see Chapter 5, p. 174) cannot be treated as easements. Thus if many kinds of agreements respecting land are to be made enforceable between remote owners of the property it must be based upon the doctrines of covenants running with the land, rather than the law of easements.

Generally, parties creating an easement will use conveyancing language, i.e., "I grant" or "reserve" and when creating a covenant use promissory language like "I promise" or "agree". However, a court is free to determine what the interest actually is independent of the creating language. (The Restatement of Servitudes merely recites, "A servitude may be created by contract or conveyance." § 2.1. For purposes of this Chapter and to avoid confusion, easements and covenants will be treated as distinct property interests, rather than as nominal categories of servitudes.) A duty to refrain from acting may constitute either a negative easement or a covenant, but an affirmative obligation can only be a covenant and not an easement. A covenant, whether affirmative or negative, can never be acquired prescriptively.

Illustration: Prudence promised Peter that (1) she would not construct any structures in her garden so tall as to block Peter's view, (2) Peter could enter the garden to smell the flowers, and (3) Prudence would regularly water the plants. In the above examples, (1) constitutes a negative easement of view, prohibiting Prudence from doing an otherwise privileged act, construction on her own land; (2) constitutes an affirmative easement, entitling Peter to commit an otherwise unprivileged act on Prudence's land, trespass; but (3) imposes a duty on Prudence to perform an act she would otherwise not be required to do, and so can only be a covenant since it does not qualify as an easement. Absent a writing, Peter could acquire by prescription only the rights to (2), since neither Prudence's continued refraining from construction nor continued watering would oblige her to continue if she had not promised to do so. Of course once granted, all of Peter's rights may be lost by prescription.

B. CONDITIONS

The burden of a condition runs with land in the sense that the owner of an estate subject to a condition cannot convey it free from that condition. However, the benefit of the condition is itself an interest in land, and does not run with any other land. It is transferable in its own right.

Illustration: Owen conveyed to Ann in fee simple, but subject to the condition that Owen could reenter and forfeit Ann's estate if liquor was ever sold on the premises. Ann, therefore, has a fee simple subject to condition subsequent. If Ann conveys the property to Bob, Bob will have the same estate subject to the same condition, and thus is restrained from selling liquor there. Owen has a power of termination which is itself a property interest. He may transfer this interest in land to some third person, whether or not he also conveys to that person any other property he also owns. Because of the harshness of the forfeiture remedy, a court may construe the restriction as a covenant if it is at all ambiguous. This will still permit it to run, but with a less drastic remedy.

C. ASSIGNMENT AND ASSUMPTION IN CONTRACT

Modern contract law permits rights to be assigned and duties to be delegated. However, the doctrine of covenants running with the land arose before contract law had accepted these notions and has endured despite their development. Contract law can reach similar results (as far as the transfer of rights and duties is concerned) only when the remote taker of the property agrees, whereas the rules of covenants running with the land do not require the assent of the successor owner of the property.

Illustration: Prudence covenanted that she would not put her land to a use which competed with Peter's business. Peter then sold his land and business to Ann. If the benefit of this covenant is one which does not run with the land, then the benefit will be transferred to Ann only if Peter assigns it to her. If the benefit of the covenant is one that does run with the land, it is transferred to Ann along with the property itself and without the need for any assignment.

Illustration: Prudence agreed to water Peter's lawn every day. Prudence then sold her property to Ann. If the burden of this covenant is one which does not run with the land, then Ann is bound to water Peter's lawn only if Ann "assumed" the covenant. If the burden of the covenant is one that does run with the land, then Ann is bound whether or not she assumed the covenant.

II. REQUIREMENTS CONCERNING THE NATURE OF THE COVENANT

Not every covenant can run with the land. This section deals with the requirements concerning the nature of covenants which are capable of running with the land.

A. THE COVENANT MUST INVOLVE ENFORCEABLE PROMISES

A covenant was originally a promise made under seal. Today, the requirement of a seal has vanished, but contract law has many important rules dealing with the enforceability of promises. (There must be consideration, there must not be an illegal purpose, etc.) A covenant which would not be enforceable between the covenanting parties themselves cannot run so as to bind their successors. Generally, promises which are to run with the land must be in writing, since they relate to real property. However, the doctrines of estoppel and part performance are applicable here to excuse the lack of writing in appropriate cases. Where the covenant is in a deed which was signed only by the grantor (known as a "deed poll"), it is enforceable against the grantee if the deed was accepted by her even though it was not signed by her.

B. THE PARTIES MUST HAVE INTEND-
ED THAT THE COVENANT RUN—
"ASSIGNS"

No benefit or burden of a covenant will run unless the parties have intended that it do so. If there is an intent that a promise not run, then it will not run even though it satisfies all of the other requirements for a covenant to run with the land. Generally there is no special manner in which the parties must manifest their intent that a covenant run or not run. However, Spencer's Case (1583) held that a covenant concerning something not in esse (not yet in existence) will not run unless "assigns" of the parties are specifically mentioned.

Illustration: Prudence covenants to build and maintain a fence between her and Peter's property. Since the fence does not yet exist, this covenant will not run to burden Prudence's successors under Spencer's Case unless Prudence expressly states that she covenants for herself and her "assigns" in the agreement. If the fence were already in existence, and this were simply a covenant to maintain it, any language indicating an intent to have the covenant burden her successors would be sufficient.

C. THE PROMISE MUST BE OF
THE RIGHT SORT—*TOUCH*
AND CONCERN

Courts limit the remote enforcement of covenants to promises which "touch and concern" the land. This requirement also arose in Spencer's Case, where it was said that a covenant which was "merely collat-

eral to the land" would not run even though the
parties intended that it do so. Another case held that
the covenant "must affect the nature, quality, or
value of the thing demised or the mode of occupying
it." A commonly cited standard is stated: that a
covenant will be deemed to touch and concern land
when the promissor's (or promisee's) legal relations in
respect to land are lessened (or increased), i.e. his or
her legal interest as owner is rendered less (or more)
valuable. However, it also has been noted in several
cases that this standard is more question-begging
than helpful.

1. Burden v. Benefit

To say that the covenant must touch land is confusing, because any covenant consists of two distinct
parts which may relate to land in different ways.
There is in every promise a burden (the obligation
cast upon the promissor) and a benefit (the advantage
received by the promissee or by some third person).
The question is not the unitary one of whether the
covenant touches and concerns land, but rather the
two-fold one of whether the burden of the covenant
touches and/or whether the benefit of the covenant
touches. Just as an easement may be appurtenant
(the benefit touches the dominant tenement) or in
gross (the benefit does not touch the land of the
dominant tenant), so also it is possible that only the
burden or only the benefit or both burden and benefit
may touch and concern land. In general, a burden
which can be performed only by the person who owns
or possesses the land will be said to touch and con-

cern that land; conversely only a benefit which will be appreciated by the current owner or possessor of the benefitted land will be said to touch and concern that land.

Illustration: Prudence covenanted with Peter that she would not sell liquor upon her land. She made this promise because Peter has moral objections to alcohol. The burden of this covenant touches Prudence's land, in that it deprives Prudence of one of the privileges of use which she as a landowner would otherwise have. But the benefit of this covenant does not touch land; furthermore, no one but the current owner or possessor of the land is capable to controlling whether liquor is sold or not sold there. If Peter sells whatever property he did own at the time he received the covenant from Prudence, it is not likely that his successor will care whether or not she sells liquor.

Illustration: Prudence covenanted to water Peter's lawn every day. The benefit of this covenant touches Peter's land in that the benefit is one to Peter's property rather than to Peter himself; the only person interested in having the covenant enforced would be the current owner of the lawn. But the burden of this covenant does not touch Prudence's land, since Prudence is capable of performing this covenant regardless of what property she owns, if any.

2. Money Covenants

Although the payment of money can be both made and appreciated by persons regardless of whether or not they own land, that does not mean that such covenants never touch and concern land. Where the money constitutes a substitute method of performing an act which would itself touch and concern land, the payment of money to have it performed will also touch. Thus, a covenant to pay for property insurance may be a substitute for a covenant to keep the premises in good repair (so long as the proceeds are to be used for restoration rather than personal enrichment of the covenantee). Similarly, a covenant to pay assessments in a private subdivision may be a substitute for a covenant to pay for the upkeep of the common areas (so long as the homeowner's association is so limited as to its use of the proceeds.)

3. Touching vs. Running

To ask whether a covenant runs is to ask two separate questions: (1) does the burden run to bind successors of the promissor; and/or (2) does the benefit run to avail successors of the promissee? These questions should be treated separately.

a. *Requirement for the Burden to Run*

One view is that for the burden of a covenant to run it should only be necessary that it (the burden) touch the land, and that there should be no additional requirement that the benefit also touch land. This "liberal" view has the virtue of simplicity and directness. It focuses only on the qualities of the interest involved to decide whether or not the burden runs. A second view is that the burden of a covenant will not run unless both the burden and the benefit touch land. This more restrictive view derives from the old English prohibition against easements in gross and the policy that one parcel of land should not be restricted unless some other parcel is equally benefitted. An additional consideration is that it is much easier to locate subsequent owners of benefitted land than it is to locate successors of nonowning beneficiaries of covenants in gross.

Covenant Not to Compete: Illustration: Prudence promised not to sell liquor on her land in competition with Peter's tavern. Many states hold that the benefit of such a covenant does not touch and concern land since it does not increase Peter's physical enjoyment of his land, but only the amount of money which he can make on it. However, the burden clearly touches and concerns Prudence's land, since it restricts her privileges of activity on it. Thus this may be taken as a situation where the burden touches and concerns the land, but the benefit does not. Under the first view the burden may run; under the second it may not.

Covenant to Insure: Illustration: Prudence promised to pay for insurance to keep Peter's premises insured. Many courts hold that the burden of Prudence's covenant runs only if Peter is obligated to use the proceeds to repair the premises and not for anything else. Such a requirement converts Prudence's promise to pay money into a promise to pay for repairs, or a promise to make repairs, which obviously benefits land. To hold that the covenant runs in such circumstances can be read to say that her burden runs only if his benefit touches!

b.   Requirement for the Benefit to Run

The position that the burden of a covenant will not run unless both benefit and burden touch and concern land does not necessarily dictate the same requirement for the benefit to run. Since the running of the benefit does not hamper the alienability or utility of the land to the same degree, it may be permitted to run even where the burden does not touch.

Illustration: Prudence covenanted to water a tree on Peter's property. This benefit touches and concerns Peter's property and so should run to and be enforceable by Peter's successors in ownership of that property, even though the burden imposed on Prudence by this covenant is not one which affects any land owned by Prudence.

Illustration: Prudence covenanted with Peter not to engage in any competing business on her land. In those states where the benefit of such a covenant is considered not to touch land then it will not run with the land when Peter transfers his interest in the land. Under no view does a benefit run where it does not touch or concern the land.

III. REQUIREMENTS CONCERNING THE PARTIES—*PRIVITY*

A. REQUIREMENTS CONCERNING THE ORIGINAL PARTIES TO THE COVENANT—*HORIZONTAL PRIVITY*

1. The Privity Necessary for the Burden to Run

England and many American jurisdictions require that the original parties to the covenant be in "privity of estate" with each other in order that the burden of their covenant run with the land at law. However, the meaning of privity in this context is not uniform.

a. Tenurial Relation

The most narrow notion of privity (required only in England and perhaps in Massachusetts) is that the covenanting parties have a tenurial relationship, such as probably exists today only in a landlord-tenant situation.

b. Mutual Simultaneous Interests

A slightly less strict view of privity requires that the covenanting parties both have interests in the same land. Thus they may be coowners of property, or they may be dominant and servient tenants with regard to some easement in the property.

c. Privity Through a Deed

A more liberal view of what may constitute privity is that there is privity between the grantor and grantee of an estate, so that a covenant contained in a deed satisfies this requirement.

d. Lack of Privity

The most liberal view on this matter does not require privity at all between the covenanting parties. Under such a standard, agreements between neighbors may run with the land, whereas they fail to do so under any of the privity tests mentioned above.

2. Not a Requirement for the Benefit to Run

Most states require that there be privity of estate between the covenanting parties only for the burden of a covenant to run with the land at law. It is frequently held that the benefit of a covenant may run even when the covenanting parties are not in privity of estate. The new Restatement of Servitudes, § 2.4, entirely eliminates the requirement of privity between the parties for the creation of a servitude. § 2.4. It also provides that prescription may cure the absence of privity where state law does require it. § 2.17.

Illustration: Prudence and Peter are neighbors who enter into an agreement that Prudence will not erect any structure on her land over 30 feet high. Because they are not in privity of estate, a court might hold that the burden of this covenant would not run at law to bind Prudence's successors, but that the benefit of this covenant would run so as to benefit Peter's successors.

B. REQUIREMENTS CONCERNING THE LITIGANTS—*VERTICAL PRIVITY*

1. Requirement for the Burden to Run

It is generally held that the burden of a covenant will run at law only to those who succeed to the entire estates of the covenanting parties. In such a case it is more accurate to say that a covenant runs with the estate rather than with the land.

Illustration: Peter conveyed land to Prudence with a covenant in the deed that Prudence would not erect any structure over 30 feet high. Prudence then rented her property to Tom. The burden of the covenant does not run at law so as to bind Tom because he has not succeeded to Prudence's entire estate. (Prudence had a fee simple; Tom has only a leasehold estate in the property).

Illustration: Peter conveyed land to Prudence with a covenant in the deed that Prudence would not erect any structures over 30 feet high. Prudence then conveyed the same land to Ann. The burden of the covenant runs to bind Ann who has succeeded to Prudence's entire fee simple.

Illustration: Peter conveyed two acres of land to Prudence with a covenant in the deed that Prudence would not erect any structure over 30 feet high. Prudence then sold one of these acres to Ann. The burden does run to Ann, who has succeeded to Prudence's entire estate (a fee simple) in a part of the property. The division of the land geographically does not constitute a division of the estate.

Illustration: Prudence covenanted in a lease with her landlord Peter that she would keep the premises in repair. Prudence assigned the lease to Ann. Ann is bound, since the assignment transfers Prudence's entire leasehold estate to Ann.

Illustration: Prudence covenanted in a lease with her landlord Peter that she would keep the premises in repair. Prudence sublet the premises to Stan. Stan is not bound at law, since a subtenant does not succeed to the tenant's entire estate.

2. Not a Requirement for the Benefit to Run

Many states require vertical privity only for the burden to run at law. For the benefit to run, such privity is usually not required.

Illustration: Prudence covenanted in a deed from Peter not to erect any structure over 30 feet high. Peter then rented his property to Tom. Tom may enforce the covenant even though he has not succeeded to Peter's entire estate.

Illustration: Prudence covenanted in a lease with her tenant, Peter, that she would supply heat to his apartment. Peter then sublet to Stan. Even though Stan is only a subtenant, not having succeeded to Peter's entire leasehold estate, he may be able to enforce the covenant against Prudence.

IV. THE RUNNING OF COVENANTS IN EQUITY—*EQUITABLE SERVITUDES*

A. THE POLICY UNDERLYING EQUITABLE SERVITUDES

The rules of law governing the running of covenants are sufficiently difficult as to often defeat the attempts of parties to write covenants which will be enforceable against successors. In England, where the requirement of privity is limited to tenurial situations, no owner of property is able to sell it with enforceable restrictions in the deed. And in the United States, neighbors often cannot make enforceable agreements. One of the reasons that these rules of law have survived despite their undesirable effects is that an alternative enforcement device has long been available—enforcement in a court of equity.

In 1848, the English Court of Chancery decided *Tulk v. Moxhay,* which involved a covenant in a deed by the grantee to maintain a garden and a fence on the granted property. The grantee-covenantor then sold the property to the defendant who sought to ignore the covenant as against the grantor-covenantee. Since the original covenanting parties did not occupy a landlord-tenant relationship, there was no horizontal privity, and the covenant would therefore not run at law to bind the successor. Notwithstanding, the covenant was held enforceable against the subsequent owner, through creation of the doctrine of equitable servitudes.

Two reasons were given in *Tulk* why the covenant should bind the defendant. One reason was that if the covenant were not enforceable against successors then the grantee-covenantor would be able to sell the land for appreciably more than he had paid for it when it was first subject to the covenant. Thus a notion of unjust enrichment was involved. The other reason was that if the defendant, knowing of the original covenant, were able to take the land free of the covenant, he would thereby be interfering with an advantageous contractual relationship of the grantor-covenantee. Thus an idea of wrongful interference with contractual relationships also was involved. These two policies led the Chancery Court to determine to enforce the covenant against the successor of the covenantor.

The covenant was enforced against the successor to the covenantor in *Tulk* on the theory that the making of the covenant gave the covenantee an equity in the covenantor's property, which equitable interest remained with the property and bound any subsequent taker with notice of it. The analogy here to easements is obvious. Had the grantor reserved an easement in the property, it would be an interest in the grantee's property which would remain as a burden on it throughout all of its transfers, i.e. it would run with the land. The covenant in *Tulk* could not technically be called an easement at law, since it would be "spurious", requiring the servient tenant to perform an act on his own property. But it was enough like an easement for a court of equity to treat it according to the rules governing easements. Thus it became an easement in equity, i.e., an equitable easement or equitable servitude. As such it would run with the land.

B.   THE RULES CONCERNING
EQUITABLE SERVITUDES

1.   Applicability of the Rules for Covenants to Run at Law

The legal requirements of privity and touch and concern have limited or different application when equitable enforcement is sought.

a.   *Horizontal Privity*

Under *Tulk v. Moxhay* there is no requirement of privity between the original parties for a covenant to be enforceable against subsequent takers in equity.

Illustration: Prudence covenanted with her neighbor not to use her premises for business purposes. Prudence then sold to Ann who knew of the covenant. Although Peter could not enforce the covenant against Ann at law, it is enforceable against her in equity.

b.   *Vertical Privity*

Succession to the entire estate of the covenanting parties is not a requirement for equitable enforcement of a covenant.

Illustration: Prudence covenanted with Peter not to use her land for business purposes. Prudence then leased the property to Tom who was aware of the covenant. Peter may enforce the covenant in equity against Tom even though Tom has not succeeded to Prudence's fee interest.

Illustration: Prudence covenanted with her landlord, Peter, not to use the premises for business purposes. Prudence then sublet her property to Stan who was aware of the covenant in the head lease. Peter may enforce the covenant in equity against Stan, even though Stan took by way of sublease rather than assignment (and even though there is no privity of estate between a landlord and subtenant).

c. Touch and Concern

Touch and concern is subject to the same diverse constructions in equity as in law. (See Chapter 6, p. 217). In England, the burden of a covenant is not enforceable, even in equity, unless the benefit of the covenant also touches and concerns land. However, in the United States, it is often not required that the benefit touch and concern land for either the benefit or the burden to run. But where the burden does not touch and concern land, and is not an obligation to pay money, it probably does not run.

Illustration: Prudence covenanted that she would not compete on her land with Peter. Prudence then sold her property to Ann who was aware of the covenant. In many jurisdictions, the benefit of such a covenant is deemed not to touch and concern the covenantee's property, although its burden does touch and concern the covenantor's land. In England, the fact that the benefit does not touch means that the burden would not bind Ann, even in equity. But in the United States, Ann would probably be bound by an equitable servitude.

Illustration: Prudence covenanted with Peter that she would not compete on her land with Peter. Peter then sold his land to Bob. Unless there was an intent on the part of Peter and Prudence that only Peter himself would have the benefit of this covenant, Bob can probably enforce the covenant against Prudence, even though the benefit does not touch and concern land, either because the covenant will be allowed to run in equity or on the ground that it was impliedly assigned to Bob.

Illustration: Prudence covenanted with Peter that she would maintain Peter's garden. Prudence then sold her property to Ann who was aware of the covenant. Since the burden does not touch and concern land, Ann probably is not bound.

Illustration: Prudence covenanted with Peter that she would maintain Peter's garden. Peter then sold his property to Bob. Bob probably can enforce the covenant against Prudence, since the benefit of this covenant touches Bob's land.

2. Special Equitable Requirements

Although the traditional legal requirements for a covenant to run are eliminated or attenuated in equity, in their stead are some special requirements which equity adds before it will enforce a covenant against a remote taker.

a. Notice

Equity will impose the burden of a covenant only upon a successor to the covenantor who takes with notice of the covenant. Generally, the notice may be actual or constructive (i.e., charged to a person by virtue of the recording acts). This requirement derives from the fact that the servitude involved is an equitable rather than a legal interest which under the common law system of priorities, would be defeated by a subsequent legal interest taken without notice (the bona fide purchaser doctrine).

b. Negative Nature of the Covenant

In a few jurisdictions equity will not enforce affirmative covenants, i.e. covenants which require the covenantor to perform an act. Only negative covenants—(those which prohibit the covenantor from acting in a certain manner)—are enforceable. However, most courts do not make this distinction and will enforce either kind of covenant.

V. ENFORCEMENT OF NEIGHBORHOOD RESTRICTIONS

This section covers the problems which neighboring owners have in enforcing restrictions against one another where the original developer of the property inserted similar restrictions in all or most deeds but is no longer there to enforce the restrictions itself.   In all of the illustrations in this section, "CG Company" will refer to the common grantor, a corporation (thus sometimes referred to as "it"), who sold off all of the lots in strict numerical order to alphabetically listed buyers.

A. ENFORCEMENT BY LATER GRANTEES AGAINST EARLIER GRANTEES— *RUNNING OF BENEFIT*

Where a prior grantee has made a covenant restricting his or her lot, it is fairly easy for a later grantee from the same common grantor to enforce that covenant. The benefit of that earlier covenant touched the common grantor's retained land, and then ran with that part of it which was later conveyed to the subsequent grantee.

Illustration: CG Company conveyed lot 1 to Ann, who covenanted to restrict it to residential purposes. CG Company then conveyed lot 2 to Bob. Bob may enforce the covenant against Ann. Ann's covenant benefitted CG's retained land, which included lot 2. The benefit of Ann's covenant ran with lot 2 when it was conveyed to Bob.

B. ENFORCEMENT BY EARLIER GRANTEES AGAINST LATER GRANTEES—ALTERNATIVE THEORIES

A prior grantee may sometimes enforce restrictions against a subsequent grantee from the same common owner under one of three different theories depending upon whether the covenant involved was one made by the common owner, the subsequent grantee, or the prior grantee.

1. Enforcement of a Covenant Made by the Common Owner to the Prior Grantee—*Running of the Burden*

Where the common owner covenants with the prior grantee to restrict all retained property for the benefit of that first lot conveyed, the burden of this covenant fastens itself upon all of the common owner's retained land and then runs with it to bind subsequent grantees. This theory does not apply to subsequent grantees of land which was not in the original subdivision at the time the covenant was made because that land, being owned by someone else at the time, was probably not intended by the covenantor to receive the benefit of her covenant.

Illustration: CG Company conveyed lot 1 to Ann and covenanted that it would restrict all of the land which it still owned to residential purposes. CG Company then conveyed lot 2 to Bob. Ann may enjoin Bob from putting his lot to nonresidential use, since CG's covenant burdened lot 2, and the burden ran if Bob took with notice of CG's covenant. If lot 2 was not part of the subdivision when Ann covenanted, Bob may not enforce it against her.

2. Enforcement of a Covenant Made by the Subsequent Grantee to the Common Owner— *Third Party Beneficiary*

A prior grantee may enforce a covenant made by a subsequent grantee to the common owner if it can be shown that this covenant was intended for his or her benefit, as a third party beneficiary. Since the prior grantee is not the promissee or a successor to the promissee (having taken property before the promise was made), this is not a case where it can be claimed that the benefit of the covenant merely ran with the land to the prior grantee. Third party beneficiary theory does not involve either part of the covenant running with land; rather it requires a showing that the covenant was intended to benefit someone who has previously purchased property.

Illustration: CG Company conveyed lot 1 to Ann. Then CG Company conveys lot 2 to Bob, who covenanted that he would restrict his land to residential purposes for the benefit of all other lots in the subdivision. Ann may enforce Bob's covenant as a third party beneficiary of his promise. She is an immediate beneficiary of his promise, and is not required to show in this case that either the burden or the benefit of Bob's covenant runs.

When Third Party Beneficiary Theory Applies Many covenants in deeds are explicit as to the burden, but fail to recite what property is intended to receive the benefit. When the person seeking to enforce such a covenant is a prior grantee in the tract, it becomes necessary to show that "impliedly" he or she was intended to be a third party beneficiary of the covenant. In some states (perhaps due to the old common law prohibition against reserving conditions in strangers), this is not allowed; in others the theory will be applied whenever there is adequate extrinsic evidence to support it.

Illustration: CG Company conveyed lot 1 to Ann. CG Company then conveyed lot 2 to Bob who covenanted to restrict his land to residential purposes but the covenant did not state what land received the benefit of the covenant. Witnesses testify that CG told Bob that the covenant was intended to benefit all other lots in the subdivision and that Bob agreed. Under these circumstances some courts will permit Ann to enforce the covenant, even though she is not expressly designated as a beneficiary of the covenant.

3. Enforcement of a Restriction Where the Prior Grantee Has Covenanted With the Common Owner—*Implied Reciprocal Servitudes*

In some states it is held that when a grantee of land covenants to the common grantor that the land just granted will be restricted in some manner, there is at the same time implied a reciprocal restriction upon the common grantor's retained land in favor of the lot just granted. Thus there is created an "implied reciprocal servitude" burdening the retained land and running with it so as to bind subsequent takers with notice.

Illustration: CG Company conveyed lot 1 to Ann who covenanted in her deed to restrict her land to residential purposes. CG Company conveyed lot 2 to Bob without such a restriction. Ann may be able to limit Bob to residential purposes anyway, based upon an implied reciprocal of her own covenant. A court might hold that when Ann covenanted with CG, CG impliedly reciprocally covenanted back to Ann that its retained land would be also restricted. The reciprocal burden which then attached to lot 2 ran with the land to Bob, if Bob took with notice.

(*Reliance by the Prior Grantee*)   Some authorities say that reciprocal servitudes may be implied only when the prior grantee purchases in reliance and expectation of there being like restrictions imposed on subsequent lots. It is this reliance which furnishes the basis of the implication of a reciprocal covenant by the common owner.

C.   THE SIGNIFICANCE OF A COMMON PLAN

A neighborhood scheme, or common plan, has diverse significance in different jurisdictions.

1.   In Order to Find Notice

A common plan may satisfy the jurisdiction's requirement of notice. Recording a map or plat showing uniform restrictions may constitute record notice. The mere physical existence of uniform structures or landscaping may generate inquiry notice as to the cause of such uniformity.

2. In Order to Apply Third Party Beneficiary Theory

Under this view, no covenant is enforceable by any prior grantee unless there is a common plan. Without a common plan, only subsequent grantees may enforce the covenant. The Restatement of Servitudes provides that each lot within the general plan is impliedly benefitted from all servitudes created by the general plan. § 2.14(a).

3. In Order to Imply Reciprocal Servitudes

Under this view, (and also under the new Restatement) no burden will be imposed against a subsequent grantee based upon an implied reciprocal covenant unless there is a common plan. Without a common plan only express covenants of the subsequent grantee will be enforced.

4. In Order to Burden Benefitted Lots

Under this view any lot deprived of a benefit because of the failure to imply a reciprocal covenant in its favor due to the lack of a common plan may be held to be no longer burdened by that covenant.

Illustration: CG Company conveyed lot 1 to Ann, lot 2 to Bob, and lot 3 to Cindy. There are building restrictions in the deeds to Ann and Bob but not in the deed to Cindy. A court finds that there is no general building plan in the neighborhood. As a result no restriction will be implied against Cindy's lot under an implied reciprocal theory. The consequences of Cindy's lot being unburdened by any restriction means that Bob's lot does not receive the benefit it would have received had Cindy's lot been burdened. As a result it might be held that Bob's lot is also not burdened (since it is not benefitted). Thus Ann is unable to enforce the restrictions against either Bob or Cindy under this view.

Illustration: CG Company conveyed lot 1 to Ann with a restriction in her deed, then conveyed lot 2 to Bob with no restriction, and finally conveyed lot 3 to Cindy with a restriction similar to Ann's. Ann can enforce the restriction against Bob if a court will imply a reciprocal of her covenant to CG against Bob, (which may depend on the existence of a common plan); Ann can also enforce the restriction against Cindy, either under the same implied reciprocal theory or if she can show that she should be treated as a third party beneficiary of Cindy's promise to CG (which also may require the existence of a common plan). Bob can enforce the restriction against Ann as a successor to CG whose retained lots received the benefit of Ann's covenant, which then ran with lot 2 to Bob (although it may be necessary for him to show a common plan in order to enforce such a restriction when his own lot is not similarly restricted); Bob can also enforce the restriction against Cindy under a third party beneficiary theory, but not under an implied reciprocal argument, since he did not make a promise himself from which a reciprocal may be implied nor can he claim to be the beneficiary of any reciprocal implied from Ann's covenant to CG. Cindy can enforce the restriction against Ann as a successor to CG's lot 3, which was benefitted by Ann's covenant; Cindy cannot enforce the restriction against Bob, since he never made a covenant himself and it is most unlikely that any court would treat Cindy as the third party beneficiary of any reciprocal implied against Bob from Ann's promise or would imply a reciprocal obligation on Bob retroactively from Cindy's subsequent promise to CG.

D. ENFORCEMENT BY THE NEIGHBORHOOD ASSOCIATION

If the common owner intends to create a home-owner's association and to grant to it the power to enforce the common restrictions, one way to accomplish that purpose is to convey a parcel of land to it (e.g., for a community club house) and then to have all deeds recite that the restrictions are for the benefit of that parcel. If the association has not yet been created, the designated parcel may still be benefitted by the deed restrictions prior to the creation of the association and the benefit of the deed restrictions will run to it when it receives the parcel. Absent ownership of a benefitted parcel, the association may still be able to enforce the restrictions as assignee of the original covenantee, but in the absence of a benefit touching and concerning its land, it may have difficulty imposing liability on successor owners in jurisdictions which require more than merely that the burden touch and concern in order for it to run.

Once the common grantor has sold all of the land in the subdivision (and perhaps assigned enforcement of the covenants to the association) it is likely that a court will hold that the benefits of the covenants have run past it and that it can no longer enforce, release or modify them.

E. EFFECT OF OMISSION
IN LATER DEEDS

If the restriction has been properly created and recorded at the outset, the failure of an owner to mention it in a later deed to the property is irrelevant. The land involved is burdened (or benefitted) whether or not the deed says so. A proper record search of the chain of title will give notice of the restriction.

VI. TERMINATION OF RESTRICTIONS
A. TERMINATION RESULTING FROM ACTS OF THE PARTIES TO THE COVENANT

1. Restricted Duration

If the covenant states its existence will be for only a limited time, e.g., for 20 years or until termination, modification or renewal by a majority vote of property owners, expiration of that time period works a termination of the restriction. Statutes may also limit the possible life of such interests.

2. Release

It is possible for the promisee or beneficiary to release the promissor from the obligations of a covenant. This may be viewed as a release (the retransfer of a property interest) or as a rescission (the cancellation of a contract), but in either event a writing is required. The release only binds the releasor. If others are also able to enforce the covenant they are not bound by the release.

Illustration: CG Company conveyed lot 1 to Ann with a covenant that it would restrict all retained lots to residential use. CG Company then conveyed lot 2 to Bob and obtained a residential covenant from Bob that he would restrict his parcel to residential use. Later CG Company releases Bob from his covenant. Ann can still stop Bob from putting his property to commercial use. The release ended Bob's obligations to CG, but Bob was also under a duty to Ann, based upon CG's covenant to Ann, which ran with the land to bind Bob. CG's release could not affect Ann.

3. Merger

Covenants are destroyed when the benefitted and burdened parcels are merged under one ownership in the same way that easements terminate by merger of the dominant and servient tenements.

4. Abandonment

A common owner who initially includes restrictions in the deeds but then ceases to do so for the remaining lots may be deemed to have abandoned the idea and the lack of a common plan may make unenforceable those covenants which were created. Furthermore, even when covenants were included in all deeds, widespread and tolerated noncompliance by the owners may have the same effect.

5. Prescription

A covenantor (or successor) who refuses to honor the covenant may be sued (by the covenantee or her successor), and such suit is, like all others, subject to the statute of limitations.   Therefore, a covenant which has been repudiated for too long, may be lost by prescription.

6. Estoppel

Covenants may be terminated by estoppel in the same fashion as easements. This defense, like those which follow (including changed conditions), is strictly equitable and may merely prohibit enforcement by injunction without necessarily prohibiting a (legal) damage remedy.

7. Laches

Equitable relief will be denied when the plaintiff seeking to enforce a covenant has waited too long, and when delayed enforcement would cause harm to the owner of the burdened property.

8. Unclean Hands

Equitable relief will be denied to the owner of a benefitted parcel who has himself violated a similar covenant imposed on his land.

9. Acquiescence

Equitable relief will be denied to the owner of a benefitted parcel who has permitted too many other owners of similarly burdened lots to break their covenants.

B. TERMINATION RESULTING
FROM EXTERNAL ACTS

1. Changed Conditions

Most courts will not enforce a covenant (at least in equity) when the neighborhood conditions have so changed as to render the benefits of the covenant insubstantial.

Illustration: At the time that Prudence agreed with Peter to restrict her adjacent property to residential purposes the entire neighborhood was residential. Now the neighborhood has so changed that her house is the only residential structure remaining on the block, and her lot would be worth considerably more if it could be put to commercial use. Under the circumstances the slight benefit to Peter may no longer justify the heavy burden imposed on Prudence, and a court of equity might not enforce the covenant against her.

Most courts limit the defense of changed conditions to situations where the changes have occurred within rather than outside the neighborhood borders. External changes are insufficient to entitle the border lots to ignore the covenants applicable to them, lest this start a domino series of violations.

The fact that the zoning classification of the parcels permits other uses does not by itself constitute a changed condition, so long as the zoning ordinance does not prohibit the uses permitted under the covenant.

2. Governmental Acquisition

If the government acquires the burdened property by eminent domain, it takes it free of all private restrictions. As a result compensation may be owed to the covenantee as well as the covenantor, similarly to what occurs when property subject to a lease or an easement is so taken.

When the government disposes of the property by tax sale (for failure of the owner to pay the property taxes) courts are split as to whether the new owner remains subject to preexisting restrictive covenants.

B. TERMINATION RESULTING FROM INVALIDITY

Covenants which violate the rule against restraints on alienation may, like easements and profits, be held invalid. This may also be so with regard to the rule against perpetuities, although that doctrine is less likely to be applied to servitudes. Covenants which restrain trade in violation of the antitrust laws (e.g. covenants not to compete, tying arrangements forcing members of a subdivision to join and pay for common recreational facilities whether or not they desire to do so) may also be held invalid. Modern rules against unconscionability are increasingly being applied to agreements affecting land. See Restatement of Servitudes, § 3.7. Restrictive covenants which interfere with constitutional rights or anti-discrimination statutes by way of prohibiting minority groups (or the poor or families with children) from residing in the community are also generally invalid.

*

PART TWO

CONVEYANCING

Introduction

This part is concerned with the various problems which arise incident to the transfer of interests in land. Landlord-tenant law could be regarded as a branch of conveyancing, since it involves the transfer of a leasehold estate from landlord to tenant, but since the problems involved there generally deal far more with the relations of the parties once the conveyance has occurred (once the lease has been executed), it has been treated as a separate topic. Likewise the creation and transfer of easements could also be treated as a question of conveyancing, but there, too, the conveyancing aspects are fairly incidental to other issues. Adverse possession is not a question of conveyancing at all, since the title acquired by the adverse possessor is an original title and is not one derived from the former owner.

CHAPTER SEVEN

REAL ESTATE BROKERS

I. THE ROLE OF THE BROKER

A. THE ECONOMIC FUNCTION OF BROKERS

Most real estate sales are completed with the assistance of brokers, for financial rather than legal reasons. Property may be conveyed without utilization of a broker, but generally both buyer and seller find it convenient to have a broker or brokers assist them. Unlike many other retail industries, the broker (a "she" in this chapter) does not carry her own inventory of real estate, buying from owners (males) and then reselling to purchasers (females); rather the broker acts as agent for one or both parties without ever taking title herself.

In most cases, it is the seller who retains the broker, and that is the assumption made in all of the illustrations in this chapter. For rental properties, it is usually the landlord who retains the broker. Occasionally, a broker is retained by a buyer or tenant, although she may still receive her fee from the other side.

B.   WHO MAY FUNCTION AS A BROKER

A broker is a person who is licensed as such by the regulating state agency.   In order to obtain her license, she was required to possess certain minimum academic credentials (e.g. some college education), to pass a qualifying exam and to satisfy appropriate character and fitness requirements.   In addition she may be required to comply with continuing education requirements imposed on her profession.

Real estate salespersons hold inferior licenses, entitling them to perform broker services only under the auspices and supervision of a licensed broker.

Engaging in brokers' activities without a license may trigger criminal or civil liability and may give another party a defense against paying a commission otherwise due.   There is a "finder" exception, permitting an unlicensed person to recover compensation (if promised) for introducing a buyer and seller to one another, but doing more than that, e.g. participating in the negotiations, makes one a broker rather than a finder, and requires a license.

C.   THE SERVICE BROKERS PERFORM

A broker is retained to locate potential buyers for a property owner who wants to sell his property.   The broker becomes the seller's agent, not to offer the property for sale to buyers (who thus could accept an offer made by the broker on the seller's behalf and thereby form a sales contract) but rather to solicit potential buyers to make purchase offers to her principal, the seller, which he then may accept or reject.

This chapter covers the contract between the seller and the broker. The contract between the seller and the buyer is covered in the next chapter. The two contracts are often confused. For instance, an owner of property may employ a broker and agree to pay her a commission if she can find someone who will offer the seller $100,000 for his house. If she does find such a person, the seller is not required to sell to that particular buyer (one is always free to reject an offer) but the seller may owe the broker a commission since she has performed her part of the contract.

D. OTHER LEGAL OBLIGATIONS IMPOSED ON BROKERS

1. Discrimination

Federal and state civil rights and licensing statutes prohibit brokers from discrimination in their rendering of services or in advertising (e.g., "whites only signs"), from "racial steering": (refusing to show members of minority races homes in other communities), and from block busting (attempting to trigger panic sales by spreading rumors in white neighborhoods that minorities are flooding in). Sanctions may include both damage liability and loss of license.

2. Practicing Law

Brokers may not practice law, through either the rendering of legal advice or the drafting of contracts, deeds, mortgages, etc. for their clients. However, in many jurisdictions brokers are permitted to fill out simple legal forms incidental to the services they have rendered as brokers in a transaction.

3. Antitrust

Brokers may not conspire to fix their prices and thereby eliminate competition among them. Agreements to set the same commission rates, or the refusal of a local multiple listing service to admit "discount brokers" will generally violate federal or state antitrust statutes.

II. LISTING AGREEMENTS AND COMMISSIONS

The employment contract between a broker and her principal is called a listing agreement. The seller not only employs the broker, but authorizes her to act as his agent in showing (listing) the property to potential purchasers. If there is no agreement between the seller and broker, the broker may have trouble collecting a commission after a sale she has put together. Some states require that listing agreements be in writing, although the original statute of frauds provisions relating to land do not technically apply, since only an agency or employment contract is involved.

A. TYPES OF LISTINGS

Traditionally listing agreements are classified according to the circumstances under which the seller must pay a commission to the broker:

1. Open listing. A broker under such a listing earns a commission only if she is the "procuring cause" of the purchaser, and not otherwise. Thus she is entitled to no commission if the buyer is found by the seller or by someone else. Procuring cause is a question of fact. In some states it is sufficient if the broker was the first person to call the property to the attention of the buyer or to someone connected with her; in other states the broker must play a much more significant role in order to qualify as the procuring cause.

2. Exclusive Listing. If the broker need not be procuring cause in order to earn a commission, then she has an exclusive listing and will earn a commission even if the buyer is found by some other broker. If the seller remains free to find a buyer himself without commission liability, it is called an "exclusive agency" listing. If the commission is owed even when the seller is the one who located the buyer, it is an "exclusive right to sell" listing.

B. EARNING A COMMISSION

Under most listing agreements, a broker earns her commission when a "ready, willing and able purchaser" has been presented to the seller. The adjectives "ready, willing and able" are usually not defined, but they refer to a person who desires to purchase the property on terms acceptable to the seller and who is capable of performing his commitments under a sales contract (e.g., paying the price when due either out of his own pocket or having the creditworthiness to borrow the necessary funds).

1. Lesser and Contingent Offers

Once an offer has been presented which exactly matches the terms set forth in the listing agreement, the broker has earned a commission, whether or not the seller accepts the offer. But it is rare for such perfect offers to be made. If the offer is for less than the amount of the seller's asking price, no commission is yet earned, since the purchaser has not shown herself willing to purchase on the seller's terms. However, if the seller accepts the offer, the broker is then entitled to her commission.

If the buyer's offer is contingent, e.g. upon getting a mortgage loan or being able to sell her own house first, she is clearly not yet ready to purchase and no commission is yet due. Even if the seller accepts the offer, it remains unknown whether the buyer will complete the deal. Thus until the contingency is lifted by satisfaction or waiver no commission is earned by the broker.

2. Completing the Sale as a Condition Precedent

The fact that a broker earns her commission on finding a ready, willing and able buyer means that she is not required to see that the sale is actually completed in order to be entitled to be paid. She may demand her commission from the seller even though the buyer subsequently defaults. However, some states impose completion of the sale as a condition in residential contracts on the ground that unsophisticated sellers expect that to be the case. Furthermore, the parties themselves are always free to include such a condition in the listing agreement.

a. Closing as a Condition or Calendar Event

Many sales contracts between sellers and buyers contain provisions revising payment of the broker's commission rights (valid if also signed by the broker) and providing for its payment at the close of the sale. A court may then be required to determine whether such a provision was intended to abrogate the broker's earlier entitlement to a commission for having produced a ready, willing and able buyer or whether it merely postponed the time of payment of an earned commission to a later date.

III. BROKER LIABILITY

Brokers are involved in such complicated legal relations with sellers and buyers that they are frequently involved in litigation with them. The more common legal theories behind such lawsuits are listed below.

A. CONTRACT

The listing agreement is usually written as a bilateral contract between the broker and the seller in order to prevent the seller from revoking it just prior to completion by the broker. However, in order to make it bilateral, the broker must make some promise to the seller. She cannot promise success since that is too unpredictable, but she can promise to use diligence or best efforts to find a buyer. Lack of diligence may then subject her to liability, perhaps equal to the harm suffered by the seller because a timely sale was not made.

B. LICENSING STANDARDS

Licensing statutes frequently set standards of conduct which brokers must meet if they are to retain their licenses. Courts may also treat such statutory rules as grounds for imposing civil liability when the broker's violation causes harm. Thus lack of "honesty", a common statutory standard, may lead not only to suspension or revocation of a broker's license, but may also subject the broker to economic liability to the party harmed.

Illustration: The broker tells the seller that the buyer has offered only $90,000 but tells the buyer that the seller insists on receiving $100,000. The broker pockets as a "secret profit" the $10,000 difference between the two amounts. She may lose her license and may also be liable to one or both parties for this breach of a statutory standard.

C. NEGLIGENCE AND FRAUD

As professionals, brokers are held to a high standard of care and will be liable for their malpractice when their conduct falls below the appropriate standard of care. A broker clearly owes a duty of care to her principal (the seller), but lack of privity between her and the buyer may limit her liability to the buyer to cases of fraud or deceit.

Illustration: The broker failed to advise the seller to insist that the buyer's promissory note be secured by a mortgage and failed to advise the buyer to test the soil for contamination before buying, causing harm to both parties. She will be liable to the seller if a jury decides that due care required her to give him such advice. But in many states, she will be liable to the buyer only if the buyer can show that the broker knew of the contamination and intentionally concealed it or failed to disclose it to her.

D. AGENCY

An agent owes fiduciary duties of loyalty, integrity and good faith to her principal. Thus, as agent of the seller, the broker is prohibited from putting the buyer's interests or her own interests above the seller's. She may not side with the buyer against the seller in the negotiations. Furthermore she is absolutely prohibited from acquiring the seller's property for her own account unless her involvement in any such acquisition is fully disclosed to him beforehand.

1. Whose Agent Is the Broker

It has been assumed in this chapter that the broker is the agent of the seller on the ground that he is the one who has retained her and will pay her commission, which are the usual grounds for concluding that an agency relation exists. But the broker may then put her listing into a "multiple listing file" for distribution to all other brokers in the community who belong to the same service. By so doing the Broker agrees to split her commission with any other broker who finds a purchaser for the property. A buyer will generally assume that the "showing broker" with whom he has been working is his agent, while the "listing broker" is agent of the seller. But since the showing broker is receiving his share of the commission from the seller and since he has received his authorization to act from the listing broker who is an agent of the seller, the showing broker is more probably a subagent of the seller rather than an agent of the buyer. Despite what the buyer thinks, the showing broker's duties of loyalty, etc. are owed to the seller!

CHAPTER EIGHT

CONTRACT OF SALE: VENDOR–PURCHASER

When title to land is transferred pursuant to an agreement of sale there is customarily a time lag between the date of the execution of the contract and the date of its consummation. A sales contract is created when the seller and buyer both sign an agreement wherein the seller promises to convey and the buyer promises to pay; the contract is consummated when the seller actually delivers a deed to the buyer and the buyer actually pays the price to the seller, which is usually referred to as the closing of escrow. (On escrow, see Chapter 9, p. 291). This chapter is concerned with the relationship of the parties in this interim period, during which time they are generally referred to as vendor and purchaser ("Van" and "Pearl" respectively in the illustrations in this chapter).

I. FORMATION OF THE RELATIONSHIP—THE STATUTE OF FRAUDS

The vendor-purchaser relationship arises once the parties have entered into a binding contract for the sale of real property. For the contract to be binding, there must be a manifestation of intent to be bound, consideration, identification of the parties, specification of the price, and since the contract involves a promise to transfer an interest in land and a promise to pay for an interest in land. Thus it is subject to the Statute of Frauds, i.e., there must be a written memorandum identifying the parties, the property and the terms of the contract and which is signed by the party to be charged.

As with other contracts subject to the Statute of Frauds, even an oral agreement for the sale of land may be enforceable in equity (for specific performance) and sometimes at law (for damages) if there exists an estoppel (inducing detrimental reliance) or if there has been part performance. Courts disagree as to what constitutes sufficient part performance to take a case out of the Statute. The situations which may or may not be deemed as adequate part performance are: payment of all or part of the price; delivery of possession to the purchaser; delivery of possession and payment of all or part of the price; delivery of possession and the making of improvements by the purchaser. These have been listed roughly in order of increasing acceptance by the courts as situations where the lack of a writing will not be held fatal. In all of these situations, the acts tend to prove that a contract was made, since they would hardly have been undertaken otherwise.

A. DISCRIMINATION BY THE SELLER

Federal and state statutes generally prohibit sellers from refusing to sell to particular buyers because of their race, color, religion, national origin, handicap, sex, age, marital status or presence of children. Owners of single family homes are sometimes exempted from some or all of these requirements, and commercial properties may be regulated differently than residential ones. A seller violating these standards may be forced to comply (i.e., sell) and/or pay damages to the aggrieved buyer.

II. MARKETABLE TITLE

Because of the special nature of land, the question of title to any particular parcel has always been a more important and more difficult question than is generally the case with regard to title to personal property. The variety of permissible estates in land, the fact that ownership may be subject to leases, easements or restrictive covenants or adverse possession, plus the mechanical difficulties surrounding the transfer of land all contribute to make the condition of the vendor's title a matter of great concern to any prospective purchaser. This subsection is concerned with the problems generated between the parties when the vendor's title is subject to some difficulty.

A purchaser of land generally offers to buy it prior to having made any investigation of the title. The reason that this is not foolhardy activity is that the doctrine of marketable title permits the purchaser to withdraw from the contract if the title is in fact unmarketable. Thus there is implied in every contract for the sale of land (unless specifically disclaimed) a requirement that the vendor's title be marketable. Otherwise, every offer to purchase would have to be made explicitly contingent on the condition of the vendor's title.

A. WHAT IS MARKETABLE TITLE

A marketable title is a title which the vendor in fact does have, which is not subject to any encumbrance, and is not subject to any doubt. Thus a title is unmarketable if: (a) the vendor lacks all or part of the title alleged; or (b) the title is subject to an encumbrance; or (c) there is a reasonable possibility that (a) or (b) is the case.

1. Title Actually Held by the Vendor

Unless the contract indicates otherwise, the purchaser is entitled to receive an undivided fee simple absolute to all the property being purchased. If the vendor does not have such a title the purchaser may withdraw from the contract. The vendor is often said to lack a marketable title in such cases, although it could also be said that the vendor merely has a marketable title to less than what he promised to convey.

Illustration: Van and Pearl signed a contract for the sale of Van's land. Then it is discovered that Van does not own an undivided fee interest, but is only a joint tenant (or tenant in common) with some other person. Pearl is no longer obliged to complete her purchase.

Illustration: Van and Pearl signed a contract for the sale of Van's 40 acres. Then it is discovered that Van has title to only 25 of those acres. Since Van lacks a marketable title to the 40 acres he agreed to convey, he may not enforce the contract.

Illustration: Van and Pearl signed a contract for the sale of Van's land. Then it is discovered that Van has only a life estate in the land, rather than a fee simple. Pearl is not bound to purchase.

Illustration: Van and Pearl signed a contract for the sale of Van's land. Then it is discovered that Van's fee simple is subject to a condition subsequent, providing that his estate will be forfeited if liquor is ever sold on the premises. Since this is not a fee simple absolute, it is not a marketable title.

Illustration: Van and Pearl signed a contract for the sale of Van's land. Then it is discovered that Van had previously given Anne an option to purchase the land, which has not yet expired. This means that Van's title is not marketable. (Were Pearl to accept his deed, she would be compelled to sell the property to Anne if Anne exercised her option.)

Illustration: Van and Pearl signed a contract for the sale of a piece of land. Then it is discovered that Van has no title whatsoever to that parcel. Having no title, Van has no marketable title.

2. Title Free From Encumbrances

An encumbrance is a right or interest in the property held by some third person which diminishes the value of the estate but does not negate the existence of the estate itself. A marketable title is held to be one which is not subject to any encumbrances. Thus in most cases the existence of an encumbrance renders the title unmarketable unless the contract allowed for it at the start.

a. Easements

Illustration: If Van's title is subject to an easement his title is deemed unmarketable and Pearl may withdraw from the contract (unless the contract itself called merely for a title subject to that easement).

(*Exception for Visible Easements*) In many states an exception to the requirement of marketable title is implied for easements which are open and notorious, particularly utility easements. It is assumed that the purchaser observed these easements at the time that he or she offered to purchase and was willing to accept them.

b. Covenants and Servitudes

Illustration: If Van's title is subject to a restrictive covenant or equitable servitude then his title is not marketable and Pearl may withdraw.

(*Exception: Superfluous and Obsolete Covenants*) If the covenant merely compels the owner to do what the law itself requires (as where both a covenant and zoning ordinance impose the same prohibition against commercial activity), or if the covenant is now so obsolete as to be no longer enforceable, (see Ch. 6, p. 242) then its existence on paper may be held not to render the title unmarketable.

c. Leases

Illustration: If Van's title is subject to an existing lease, his title is unmarketable, even if the lease is economically advantageous.

d. Money Obligations

Illustration: If Van's title is subject to a mortgage, a judgment lien, an assessment lien, a mechanic's lien, or any other monetary charge, his title is unmarketable so long as such charge remains.

3. Title Free From Doubt

It is not required that the purchaser actually prove that the vendor's title is bad. A title is deemed unmarketable if there is any reasonable doubt concerning its marketability.

Illustration: In Van's chain of title there is a deed from Ann Smith to Paul C. Jones. However, the next deed in the chain is signed Paul Jones, rather than Paul C. Jones. There is the risk that Paul is not the same as Paul C., which—if true—means that Paul had no title to convey. Pearl is not required to prove that Paul is not Paul C., only that there is some doubt.

Illustration: In Van's chain of title is an old mortgage which was released of record, but the acknowledgement on the release was defective. Since this raises some doubt as to whether there is still a mortgage on the property, the title is not marketable.

Illustration: Although the records do not indicate that Van's grantor ever actually had title to the property, Van has, in fact, been in open, notorious, exclusive, continuous, etc., possession for the past 50 years and therefore probably has acquired a good title by adverse possession. However, since Van has never obtained a judicial declaration on this issue, it cannot be said that his title is free from all doubt.

4. Circumstances Not Affecting Marketability

Title to property may be marketable even though the property itself is undesirable. Property in poor physical condition, e.g., subject to termite infestation, flooding or bad soil conditions may nevertheless have a marketable title. Zoning and similar governmental restrictions on the use of property do not affect the marketability of the title (although in some cases an existing zoning or code violation may be treated as a title defect).

B. THE EFFECTS OF TITLE BEING UNMARKETABLE

1. Vendor's Right to Cure Defects

The vendor has no obligation to produce a marketable title until the time set for the closing of escrow (the completion of the contract). Thus the purchaser is not entitled to withdraw at the instant that some title defect is discovered. In many states the purchaser is required to give notice of the defect early enough so as to give the vendor an opportunity to cure. If the contract does not make time of the essence, the vendor's time to cure may extend a reasonable amount of time beyond the date set for closing or settlement. If the contract does make time of the essence, the vendor is required to cure the defect by the date set for the closing of escrow, unless the purchaser failed to give adequate advance notice of such defect, or has otherwise waived the clause.

Illustration: On January 1, Van and Pearl entered into a contract for the sale of Van's property to be consummated on March 1. On February 1, Pearl discovered that Van's title is subject to an easement. Pearl may not withdraw on February 1, but instead should notify Van at that time of the defect.

Illustration: On January 1, Pearl and Van entered into a contract for the sale of Van's land, to be consummated on March 1. On February 1, Pearl discovered that Van's title is subject to an easement, and gave Van notice to that effect. If by March 1, Van has removed the easement, Pearl cannot withdraw from the contract since Van has a marketable title as of the date required.

Illustration: On January 1, Pearl and Van entered into a contract for the sale of Van's land, to be consummated on March 1. On February 1, Pearl discovered that Van's title was subject to an easement and notified Van. Van commences diligently to have the easement removed, but had not succeeded by March 1. If time is not of the essence, a court may hold that Pearl is not yet released from her contract, and that Van has a reasonable time to clear his title. If time is of the essence, then Van's failure to have a marketable title on closing day entitles Pearl to withdraw.

Illustration: On January 1, Pearl and Van entered into a contract for the sale of Van's land to be consummated on March 1. On February 1, Pearl discovered that Van's title was subject to a mortgage and so notified Van. Van took no action to remove the mortgage prior to March 1st, but instructed the escrow agent to utilize a portion of the purchase price deposited by Pearl to pay off the mortgage in order to convey a title to Pearl free of it. Unless specifically prohibited by the terms of the contract, it is generally permissible for the vendor to use the purchaser's funds to remove monetary liens even though, technically, this gives the vendor use of purchaser's money an instant before he is in a position to transfer good title to the purchaser.

2. Vendor's Right to Specific Performance With Abatement

If the defect in title is insignificant and only formal, a vendor may be able to obtain specific performance and compel the purchaser to pay despite it. However, there will be some abatement of the price for the deficiency.

3. Purchaser's Right to Withdraw

A purchaser who is not tendered a marketable title on the closing date is entitled to withdraw from the contract and recover any consideration paid to the vendor. As already indicated, there is no right to withdraw prior to the closing date, but if the title has not been cleared as of the date set for the completion of the contract (and if either time is of the essence, or if a reasonable amount of time has lapsed since the vendor first received notice of the title problems), then the purchaser may withdraw.

4. Purchaser's Right to Damages

A purchaser who withdraws from the contract because of an unmarketable title is also entitled to recover any down payment made to the vendor plus out of pocket expenses incurred in preparing to purchase. Many states also permit the purchaser to recover loss of bargain damages as well.

5. Purchaser's Right to Specific Performance

A purchaser willing to accept an unmarketable title may do so, and the vendor may not refuse to convey based on flaws in his own title. Thus the purchaser may have specific performance of the contract.

a. Specific Performance With Abatement

Generally, if the defect is small and quantifiable, a decree of specific performance against a vendor with a defective title will involve some abatement of the price. However, when the defect is a substantial one the purchaser may withdraw entirely or may enforce the contract without an abatement, but cannot force the vendor to sell at a drastically reduced price.

C. WAIVER OF THE RIGHT TO MARKETABLE TITLE

The right to marketable title is one that is implied in any contract for the sale of land when there is no language in the contract to the contrary. It is customary, however, for the parties to expressly state certain requirements (or lack thereof) concerning the state of the title.

1. Complete Waiver of Marketable Title

Where the parties are unsure as to whether the vendor has any title whatsoever (which often occurs where owners are merely buying up doubtful claims against their own titles), they may explicitly waive any requirement of marketable title. Sometimes this is done by calling for delivery of only a quitclaim deed but more frequently there is an express statement in the contract to the effect that there is no requirement of marketable title.

2. Waiver of Some Particular Defect

Since many technical burdens on property are not undesirable, a purchaser may be willing to buy restricted property. Such willingness is indicated by a provision in the offer or contract that title is to be "marketable except for * * *" The effect of this provision is to eliminate the purchaser's right to withdraw based upon the existence of the designated deficiency.

Illustration: Pearl's offer to buy Van's property stated that "title is to be free of all liens, except for recorded building restrictions uniform to the neighborhood". After this offer was accepted, a title search by Pearl reveals that Van's lot is subject to a set-back requirement similar to all other lots in the block. This restrictive covenant would normally make title unmarketable, but because of the special language of this contract Pearl cannot withdraw.

3. Insurable Title

If the contract of sale calls for an insurable title, then the purchaser will be compelled to accept the vendor's title so long as a title insurance company indicates its willingness to insure the title without making any exceptions to its coverage.

4. Waiver by Acceptance of the Deed—Merger

The right to marketable title is a contract right only. It permits the purchaser to decline to complete the contract if the proffered title is unsatisfactory. If the purchaser does not refuse to perform and accepts the vendor's deed there is no longer any right to marketable title and the purchaser has no action against the vendor based upon the original contract for a defective title. All of the contract provisions have been "merged" into the deed. Any rights the purchaser thereafter has against the vendor must depend on language in the deed, particularly title covenants. On title covenants, see Ch. 9, p. 298.

III. EQUITABLE CONVERSION AND THE RISK OF LOSS

Because land is regarded as a unique asset, the purchaser under a binding sales contract has always been able to obtain a decree of specific performance against an unwilling vendor. This equitable right has the effect of giving the purchaser an interest in the land itself (as well as personal contract rights against the vendor). Thus it is said that by the execution of the agreement the purchaser becomes the equitable owner of the land. The vendor retains legal title, but since his rights under the contract are to money (to receive the price), the title is really held only as security for payment.

The following sections cover some important consequences of the doctrine of equitable conversion. However, first note two limitations on its application. First, the doctrine does not relate to possession. Even after a binding sales contract has been executed, the vendor remains entitled to possession. The purchaser may not enter until the vendor has permitted her to do so or legal title has passed (i.e., the contract has been performed). Second, the requirement of a specifically enforceable binding contract means that merely the execution of an option to purchase or right of first refusal in favor of the "purchaser" does not constitute an equitable conversion. Only after an option or preemptive right is actually exercised thereby binding the purchase to a contract can an equitable conversion occur.

A. DEVOLUTION ON DEATH

In earlier times, title to real property passed on death to heirs, but personal property went to the next of kin instead. Thus, if an owner of land died having previously contracted to sell it, the doctrine of equitable conversion meant that his next of kin were entitled to receive the price, although his heirs would be required to execute the deed to the purchaser when payment was received. His heirs were not entitled to the money because the land had previously been converted from realty to personalty when the contract was signed. Similarly, the heirs of a dead purchaser could claim the title, whereas payment for it would be made out of the personal estate otherwise due to the next of kin. And a woman who married the vendor after he had contracted to sell his land could not claim dower since the legal title which he had was held to be in trust for the purchaser.

B. INJURIES TO THE PROPERTY

When a third party injures the property during the contract period, the doctrine of equitable conversion dictates that the purchaser is the party entitled to bring suit, and the vendor may sue only when the purchaser declines. (Damages for trespass, however, depend upon rights of possession rather than title, so that the issue of standing in a trespass action depends on who has possession. The execution of the contract does not by itself entitle the purchaser to possession). A purchaser may sue a vendor in possession for waste, and a vendor may sue a purchaser in possession for impairing the security.

C. CREDITORS

Once a binding contract for sale of the land has been signed, creditors of the vendor can go after the unpaid balance of the purchase price but not the property itself; it is the purchaser's creditors who may reach the property in satisfaction of their claims against her.

Once a binding contract for the sale of land has been signed, the vendor's creditors can seek recovery from the unpaid balance of the purchase price, but not the property itself. The purchaser's creditors, however, may reach the property in satisfaction of their claims against her.

D. RISK OF LOSS FOR INJURIES CAUSED WITHOUT FAULT

There are three views as to how innocent losses which occur during the contract period should be allocated between vendor and purchaser in the absence of a provision to the contrary in the contract.

1. Majority Rule—Risk on Purchaser

Under a strict application of the doctrine of equitable conversion, the purchaser is regarded as the equitable and, therefore, real owner of the property as of the date of execution of the contract. Thus he or she is held to bear the risks of both loss and profit on the property during the contract period and cannot withdraw from the contract merely because the property has been damaged prior to the close of escrow.

Illustration: On January 1, Pearl and Van contracted for the sale of Van's property, to close on March 1. On February 1, a fire, caused by neither party, destroyed the premises. Under the majority rule Pearl is still obliged to complete the contract and pay the entire price. She may not withdraw and Van may seek specific performance or damages, if Pearl fails to complete the contract.

2. Minority Rule—Risk on Vendor

The minority (or Massachusetts) rule holds that there is a failure of consideration if the vendor is not able to deliver the premises on the closing day in their original condition. This rule treats the continued existence of undamaged property as an implied condition of the contract. Under this rule the purchaser is entitled to withdraw or else obtain specific performance with abatement if the property is damaged during the escrow period.

Illustration: On January 1, Pearl and Van contracted for the sale of Van's property, to close March 1. On February 1, a fire caused $3,000 damage. Pearl may (on March 1) either withdraw or sue for specific performance with abatement of price by $3,000.

3. Uniform Vendor and Purchaser Risk Act

Some states have enacted the Uniform Vendor and Purchaser Risk Act which allocates a loss caused by innocent destruction during the contract period to the vendor unless the purchaser has taken possession. Thus it adheres to the minority rule (putting the risk on the vendor) except in cases where the purchaser has taken possession.

4. Contrary Agreements

The parties are free to allocate the risk of loss to one or the other through a special provision in the contract, regardless of which doctrine the court would apply in the absence of any contract provision.

a. Insurance Provisions

Either party can purchase property insurance to protect their interest in the property. If the sales contract provides that the purchaser will keep the property insured until the close of escrow, the provision could be read to thereby assign the risk of loss to her. However, since insurance law does not prohibit a purchaser from independently insuring her interest in the property even when the vendor bears the risk of loss or is also insured, or vice versa, carrying insurance or agreeing to do so does not automatically equal accepting the risk of loss.

Where the risk of loss is on the purchaser and it is the vendor who was insured, most courts will make him hold any insurance award in constructive trust for the purchaser and thereby require her to pay less for the injured property. Sometimes a comparable outcome is reached where the risk was on the vendor but the purchaser was the one insured.

IV. PERFORMANCE

Within the time specified in the contract, or within a reasonable time if none has been specified (and perhaps even when a time has been specified but the contract did not make "time of the essence"), each of the parties must do what he or she has promised to do. The vendor must deposit into escrow a deed which conveys a good title to the purchaser for delivery to her and the purchaser must deposit into escrow the entire price then due together with any notes and mortgages the parties have agreed to accept in lieu of cash.

A. INSTALLMENT LAND CONTRACTS

In the ordinary "marketing" contract considered so far, delivery of the deed and payment of the price are "concurrent conditions", both required to be done at the same time. However, the parties may employ an installment land contract instead, whereby the purchaser is required to pay the price in installments over an extended duration (e.g., 10 or 20 years) before the seller is required to deliver his deed to her. The purchaser has a right to possession in the meantime. Such an arrangement is in reality a form of mortgage financing by the vendor (and should be subject to mortgage law) since it is a contract only in form.

However, when taken literally, the contract form can have significant implications in terms of the vendor's right not to have a marketable title until the time of closing, and the remedies available to a vendor upon breach by the purchaser (see Section V(B) below).

Once escrow has closed and both parties have accepted what was given to them, the contract is complete and its terms no longer survive. If problems between the parties arise thereafter relief must be sought on some basis other than the contract.

Illustration: After escrow has closed and Pearl has taken possession of the property she discovers that her title is subject to an easement held by a neighbor, that the house is infested with termites, and that there is a leak in the roof Van installed when he built the house. None of these matters will justify a suit for breach of the sales contract. Depending on the facts and the legal doctrines in the jurisdiction, Pearl may be able to claim that the existence of the easement violates the title covenants in her deed from Van, that the termites were fraudulently concealed by Van, and that there is an implied warranty of fitness of habitability in the construction of new housing by Van, a commercial builder.

V. NONPERFORMANCE
A. BY THE VENDOR

A vendor who cannot or will not convey the required title to the purchaser is in breach of contract, and the purchaser has several remedies available to her. She may:

(1) withdraw, terminate the contract and recover all monies she has deposited into escrow or paid to

the vendor (together with a purchaser's lien on the property as security), or

(2) force the vendor to comply through an action for specific performance (with an abatement or reduction of the price for small defects in the title), or

(3) sue for damages consisting of her out of pocket expenses and benefit of the bargain damages, where permitted. Benefit of the bargain damages (the difference between the contract price and the market value of the property) are sometimes confined to cases where the vendor's breach is in bad faith, thus generally excluding those cases where he cannot perform because of an unmarketable title (and making marketable title a condition but not a covenant in the contract).

B. BY THE PURCHASER

A purchaser who does not pay the price within the time required is in breach of her contract and the vendor has several remedies available to him. He may:

(1) withdraw and terminate the contract, and be free to sell the property elsewhere, but perhaps being required to refund the purchaser's down payment to her, or

(2) force the purchaser to pay the price through an action for specific performance, although this remedy is hardly useful against a purchaser lack-

ing the funds to perform and is rarely necessary to a vendor seeking merely monetary relief, or

(3) sue for actual damages, consisting of any expenses he has incurred plus benefit of the bargain damages (the difference between the price he was to receive under the contract and the market value of the property), although this may be denied him if he has subsequently resold the property for a profit to a third party, or

(4) retain any down payment made by the purchaser as liquidated damages, if the contract so provides or if state law permits him to do so even without such a provision in the contract.

CHAPTER NINE

TRANSFER OF TITLE BY DEED: GRANTOR–GRANTEE

In order for title to pass from the owner of property (the grantor) to someone else (the grantee), it is necessary that the grantor properly execute and deliver an instrument which is effective to pass title.

I. INSTRUMENTS EFFECTIVE TO PASS TITLE—DEEDS

The Statute of Frauds requires that title to land be transferred by a written instrument. The instrument typically used to achieve this effect is a deed, a document which states that the grantor "grants" or "conveys" or "quitclaims" title to the grantee. Many recites have statutes setting forth preferred forms and language for deeds. Generally, three types of deeds are common in the United States.

A. THE QUITCLAIM DEED

Here the grantor says "I quitclaim (or release) the property to you". By these words the grantor makes no representation that she has any property to convey. The deed merely states that any interest which the grantor does have in the property described is to be transferred to the grantee. This form of deed is useful to one trying to quiet title to property by buying up adverse claims to it, since it does not impose any liability upon a grantor in the event that nothing in fact was owned or conveyed.

B. THE GRANT DEED (BARGAIN AND SALE DEED)

Here the grantor says "I grant (or convey, or bargain and sell) the property to you". In many states, by statute, there is implied from such language a representation that the grantor does own the property being transferred, or has not previously encumbered it or conveyed it to anyone else.

C. THE WARRANTY DEED

Here the grantor inserts in the deed certain covenants concerning the title, in addition to using operative words to transfer that title. The function of these covenants for title is discussed at p. 298.

II. PROPER EXECUTION OF DEEDS
A. SIGNATURE

The Statute of Frauds also requires that the deed be signed by the grantor. The common law earlier required a seal, but that is everywhere abolished now. There has never been any need for the grantee's signature or seal to appear on the deed.

B. CONSIDERATION

A conveyance is not a contract, and therefore consideration is unnecessary. A deed may be a gift deed. Modern deed forms commonly recite that a consideration was paid, but this is done to rebut any inference of a resulting trust (see Chapter 2, p. 57) or to qualify the grantee as a bona fide purchaser under the recording acts (see Chapter 10, p. 342). A properly executed and delivered deed passes title whether or not consideration was given for it.

C. CONTENTS

A deed should identify the parties, describe the property and the estate in it which is being conveyed, and contain words which work to transfer title to the grantee.

1. The Parties

The grantee should be named or adequately described (e.g., "to my present husband"). The grantee's name can be left blank to be filled in later but if the grantor dies before that occurs, the deed may be invalid. Unless grantor dies, it is usually presumed that the grantee is authorized to fill in the name he wants.

The grantor must sign the deed. If her signature was forged, the deed is entirely void. This is also true if her signature is genuine but was obtained by fraud (e.g., she was told that she was only signing an autograph book). However, if the fraud was collateral to her signature (e.g. the grantee falsely promised to pay the grantor), the deed is voidable but not void and a subsequent transfer of the title to a bona fide purchaser may defeat the grantor's later attempt to invalidate the conveyance. (In this chapter the grantor is female and the grantee is male). Where the grantor is not the sole owner, her signature alone will only convey her interest in the property. A complete conveyance may require the additional signatures of her spouse, a co-tenant, holders of easements, etc.

2. Description of the Property

The deed must contain language sufficient to let someone locate the property being conveyed. This can be done by way of reference to an official survey or a recorded plat map or by a metes and bounds description. Similarly, any part of the property being "excepted" (if an existing interest) or "reserved" (if a new interest) should also be similarly described.

a. The Federal Survey

Meridian lines (north-south) and base lines (east-west) running across the country furnish location points for many parcels. In between those lines are subsidiary range lines (north-south) and township lines (east-west) every six miles, creating 36 square mile townships. The townships are divided into 36 sections one square mile each, and numbered sequentially from the top right corner of the township across to the top left corner (1 to 6), then down one level and back across to the right (7 to 12), zigzagging back and forth to the bottom, as farmers sometimes drag a plow across the field without having to double back. These one square mile (640 acre) sections may be divided into 160 acre quarter sections (e.g., northeast quarter), and perhaps further into 40 acre quarter-quarter sections (e.g., the northwest quarter of the southeast quarter). A description generally reads from the smallest locator up to the broadest.

Illustration: "E ½ of NW ¼ of SW ¼, Sec 8, T 5 N, R 6 W, PB & M" refers to the east half of the northwest quarter of the southwest quarter (a rectangular parcel of 20 acres) of Section number eight. This square mile is between 4 and 5 miles west of range line 6 west and between 1 and 2 miles south of township line 5 north. The range and township lines are respectively 30 miles north and 36 miles west of the principle base and meridian lines in the state.

b. Plat Maps

Most land development occurs as subdividers take agricultural or range land out of acreage and convert it into smaller residential or commercial plots. For their own convenience as well as to comply with state subdivision law, they have surveyors prepare maps of these newly created parcels, which maps are then recorded and referred to in the deeds, e.g. "lot 23, of Block 15 of the New Pines Subdivision, as recorded in Volume 9, page 150, official records of Jones County." Maps of condominium projects ("vertical subdivisions") will usually include height as well as other dimensions.

c. Metes and Bounds

Any parcel, especially an irregularly shaped one, may be described by marking its perimeter through certain directions or calls, e.g. "beginning at intersection of Oak and Main streets then west 25 feet to the fence, then south 100 feet, then northeast approximately 120 feet back to the beginning." This triangle would probably be described with much more detail and precision in a real deed.

d. Inconsistent Descriptions

A "monument" (the tree or the fence) is inconsistent with a "course" or "distance" (25 feet) or an "angle" (west), when they do not all lead to the same place. For example, if one walking 25 feet west from the tree would get beyond the fence in the prior paragraph, the monument reference should prevail over the course reference. In between monuments and courses in terms of this hierarchy are map references. Lowest ranking are name or quantity references ("e.g., "known as Smith Ranch, being 1.03 acres"). (Where there is uncertainty between neighbors rather than between grantor and grantee, the doctrine of agreed boundaries may furnish a basis of resolution. See Chapter 16.)

e. Boundaries With Width

When a monument or boundary has width (as is true for any road or stream used in the description) there is a presumption that the deed refers to its center. The presumption does not apply in certain common sense cases such as: (1) where the recital is otherwise; (2) where the grantor's ownership itself goes only to the near edge; or (3) where the grantor owns the entire boundary and no land on the other side of it (which would leave her with a narrow strip running the length of the boundary.)

Illustration: " * * * and bounded on the north by the road" presumable means that the grantee's northern border is the middle of the road, rather than the near (south) or far (north) edge of the road. But if the grantor owns both sides of the road and no land north of the road, then the boundary would be taken to refer to the northern edge of the road rather than to its middle. If the grantor owned no part of the road, its southern edge would obviously be the boundary.

f. Water Boundaries

Where a river or stream is the boundary, it is presumed that the grantee takes title up to the middle of it. As the stream changes course over time, the party on one side may gain land (accretion) while the party on the other loses land (reliction) due to this alteration of the boundary line. If the change in the stream is sudden and dramatic (avulsion), the boundaries between the neighbors is not moved but remains where it was notwithstanding the stream change. (Other consequences of owning "riparian" land adjacent to a stream are covered in Chapter 14.)

3. Description of the Estate

If the deed is silent on the matter, it is presumed that it transfers a fee simple absolute to the grantee. The ancient words of limitation "and his heirs" are no longer necessary. Therefore, if a lesser estate is intended, special qualifying language must be added (e.g., "for 10 years" or "for life"). Similarly, the deed should describe how multiple grantees are to take, whether as tenants in common, joint tenants, etc., or else a tenancy in common will probably be presumed (unless the parties are married, which may lead to a different presumption). Where a non-possessory estate is intended, e.g., an easement, ambiguous language may compel a court to resolve the grant contrary to the private expectation of one of the parties. Where restrictions are involved, the deed should make explicit whether they are to function as conditions (leading to possible forfeiture for violation) or as mere covenants, enabling only injunctive or monetary relief. All of these matters are discussed more fully in their appropriate chapters, e.g., Estates, Concurrent Ownership, Easement, Covenants.

4. Words of Grant

The grantor must show that she intends to transfer something to the grantee. No technical words are necessary, but "I grant" or "I quitclaim" are common phrases. The grantor should avoid using words which indicate a death transfer (e.g., "I leave") or else the deed might have to function and comply with the formalities imposed on wills.

D. ACKNOWLEDGEMENT

Most states do not require that the grantor's signature be acknowledged (notarized) or witnessed. This is commonly a requirement for wills, but not for deeds. However, the parties may have the grantor's signature acknowledged in order that the deed may then be recorded.

E. RECORDATION

In most states a deed passes title on delivery, and failure to have it recorded thereafter does not defeat the previous passage of title. Recordation has important advantages to the grantee (see Chapter 10), but is not an element of transfer of title. Many deeds are delivered but intentionally kept unrecorded.

III. DELIVERY OF DEEDS

A deed is not effective unless and until it is delivered; only then does it operate to transfer title. Until that time the deed is merely a piece of paper, not yet having any legal effect. Delivery is the final act of the grantor, making the deed effective as a conveyance.

A. WHAT IS DELIVERY

There are no formal, physical acts required for effective delivery of a deed. Delivery is not the same as the manual handing over of the document, since a deed may be delivered even though it is not handed over, or alternatively, a deed may be handed over and yet not have been delivered. The physical acts involved are significant only as manifestations of the grantor's intent, which is the essential feature of delivery.

Delivery happens when the grantor properly manifests an intent that a completed or consummated legal act has occurred. The grantor must intend that—as a result of his or her binding act—the deed has operated to pass title. What distinguishes a will from a deed is that a will operates in the future whereas a deed operates in the present. (In the illustrations in this Chapter, "Grace" is the grantor, "Gene" the grantee, and "Ezra" the escrow agent.)

Illustration: Grace signs her deed and sets it down saying aloud to those present, "Now I have transferred my property to Gene." Even though Grace has not handed the deed to Gene it may be considered delivered. Grace's statement indicates that she regards the deed as having already been effective to pass title, i.e. that she has committed a binding legal act.

Illustration: Grace signs her deed and hands it to Gene saying, "Hold on to this deed for me because later I may want to deliver it to you to make you the owner of the property." There is no delivery here because Grace's statement indicates that she does not regard handing the deed to Gene as an act sufficient to make the deed effective to pass title.

There is a presumption that a deed has been delivered when it is in the possession of the grantee and a contrary presumption when the grantor retains possession. However, both presumptions are rebuttable, as the above illustrations indicate. There is also a rebuttable presumption of delivery when the grantor has notarized or recorded the deed. When a deed has been dated and delivered, delivery is presumed to have occurred on any date mentioned in the deed.

There is also a technical requirement that the grantee accept a deed proffered to him, but such acceptance is presumed whenever title would be bene-

ficial to him. Acceptance of the deed will be presumed to have occurred on the same date it was
delivered. In fact, it is not even necessary for the
grantee to know that any of this has happened, but it
does permit him to reject a deed when it would have
harmful consequences to him.

B. INTENT THAT THE DEED BE
PRESENTLY OPERATIVE

A deed is not delivered unless the grantor has a
present intent that the deed then operate to transfer
title. If the intent is that the deed should only
operate at some future time, there is no delivery,
although a delivery may occur in that future.

Illustration: Grace hands Gene her deed saying "The
property is now yours". There is a delivery, since her
intent is that the deed presently operate to transfer title.

Illustration: Grace hands Gene her deed saying "Record
this deed when I die and that will make the property
yours." The deed has not been delivered now, since Grace's
intent is that the deed operate to transfer title sometime in
the future instead of the present. Her statement indicates
a belief that recordation is essential for the transfer of title.
Although she may be mistaken in this respect, it nevertheless demonstrates that she has no present intent that the
deed operate to transfer title. She has not intended a
completed legal act.

Illustration: The granting clause in Grace's deed to Gene
recites: "To Gene on his 21st birthday." When Gene is 19
years old, Grace hands him the deed saying, "I now give
you an interest in my property." Grace has *presently*
delivered a *future* interest to Gene. The delivery satisfied
the present intent condition. Whether the future interest

is valid or constitutes an illegal springing interest is a separate estate question, not involving issues of delivery.

1. The Effect of Future Events When There Is No Intent to Make the Deed Presently Operative

The grantor must have a present intent that the deed be presently operative before there can be a delivery. Where the grantor's intent is that the deed operate only in the future, there is no delivery now. But when that specified future arrives, there may then be a present intent. At that later moment, therefore, the deed can be regarded as delivered. (Sometimes it is said that the grantor has then ratified the earlier physical acts of delivery).

Illustration: Grace handed her deed to Gene saying, "This deed will make you the owner of the property when you are twenty one." Grace later attended Gene's twenty first birthday party and congratulated him on his new ownership of the property. The deed may be regarded as delivered on Gene's birthday. It had not been delivered earlier when Grace handed it to Gene, since she then had no present intent. But on his birthday it was her intent that the deed then operate, i.e. there was a present intent. Since no particular physical acts are required, the deed was delivered that day even though Grace conducted no ceremonial handing over of the deed to Gene at that time.

2. When a Future Event Is the Grantor's Death

The idea that a future intent may later become a present intent does not apply where the grantor's intent is that the deed operate only on his or her death. Once the grantor dies, there can be no intent of any sort, and thus a deed cannot be delivered by a grantor after death.

Illustration: Grace handed Gene her deed saying "Record this deed when I die and you will then become the owner of my property." Grace's false belief in the necessity of recording means that there was no delivery of the deed when it was handed to Gene, for her intent is that it not yet operate to pass title. For so long as Grace is alive she will continue to have no present intent that the deed transfer title (since she does not want title to pass until her death). But once she dies she obviously has no intent whatsoever, and there can be no delivery. As a result, Gene will never obtain title.

Illustration: Grace's safe deposit box is opened on her death and there is found in it a deed to Gene with the following note, "This deed is for Gene, so that he will be taken care of after I am gone." There is no delivery. Grace's note indicates an intent that the deed not operate until her death. She had no present intent therefore, at any time while she was alive, to commit a binding legal act.

C. NO CONDITIONAL DELIVERY
TO A GRANTEE

If it is determined that there has been a valid delivery of a deed to a grantee, then any conditions which the grantor attempted to add regarding the delivery are held to be inapplicable and the delivery is treated as absolute. The rule in most states is that there can be no conditional delivery to a grantee.

Illustration: Grace hands her deed to Gene saying "I am delivering my deed to you now and the land is now yours but do not record the deed until after Christmas". Since there is an intent to make the instrument presently operative, there is a delivery. Delivery to a grantee is always absolute, and so Gene may record the deed immediately.

Under the rule prohibiting conditional delivery to a grantee, one of two results occurs whenever the grantor in fact hands the deed directly to the grantee stating some conditions: 1) The court may hold that there was a present intent to make the deed operative, so that there has been an absolute delivery, and the condition fails; or 2) the same court may hold that the existence of the condition negates any present intent, so that there was not a delivery. (In a case where the condition involved is the death of the grantor, neither result will conform to his or her actual wishes. A sympathetic court may attempt to avoid this dilemma by construing the deed to reserve a life estate in favor of the grantor.)

Illustration: Grace handed her deed to Gene, saying "Record this deed when I die." There are two possible outcomes here: 1) the court will hold that there was a present delivery, so that the condition of nonrecordation fails, making Gene the owner at once with the right to record the deed immediately or 2) the court will hold that Grace did not intend the deed to be operative until after her death, which means there was no present intent while she was alive, and no intent at all after she died, so that the deed remains undelivered and Gene receives nothing. (Observe that neither resolution effectuates Grace's real intent—that Gene take the property on her death.)

D. DELIVERY OF DEEDS TO PERSONS OTHER THAN THE GRANTEE

1. The Grantee's Agent

Delivery to an agent of the grantee is the same as delivery directly to the grantee, since any agent of the grantee is subject to control by the grantee and not by the grantor. The rule that conditions surrounding the delivery fail probably still applies.

Illustration: Grace handed her deed to Gene's wife saying "Please give this deed to Gene when he gets home, but tell him not to record it until next year". If Gene's wife is regarded as Gene's agent, this is the same as a delivery to Gene, and the condition concerning recording will fail.

2. The Grantor's Agent

The grantor may hand a deed to her own agent for delivery to the grantee at a later time. In such a case the legal delivery will occur when the agent delivers the deed to the grantee, if there at that time is a present intent on the part of the grantor.

Illustration: Grace handed her deed to her husband saying "Please give this deed to Gene when you see him at the party tonight, unless I change my mind." Grace did not change her mind and her husband handed the deed to Gene that evening while Grace watched. The deed was delivered at that point. Grace made her husband her agent by her reservation of the right to recall the deed. Her handing the deed to him was not a delivery, because the reservation indicated that she had no present intent to make the deed operative. But that evening, when her husband handed the deed to Gene, Grace's earlier future intent became a present intent, so that delivery then occurred.

Illustration: Grace handed her deed to her husband saying, "Deliver this deed to Gene when I die, unless I have changed my mind." Grace died and her husband thereupon handed the deed to Gene. There is no delivery. Grace's husband was her agent, and an agent's power terminates on the death of the principal. Thus he no longer had authority to hand the deed to Gene. At the moment he handed it to Gene it could not be said that Grace had any present intent to make the deed operative (since she was already dead).

3. Escrow

A deed may be handed to a third person who is agent of neither party. Such a person is called an "escrow" (or "escrow agent" or "escrow holder" or "escrowee"). A true escrow agent is not subject to the control of either party alone. The grantor places the escrow agent beyond his or her control by giving up the right to recall the deed out of the escrow. This device permits a valid conditional delivery to be made in the present to take effect some time in the future, even when the condition involved is death of the grantor. By waiving the right to recall the deed the grantor manifests an intent to perform a binding legal act. The escrow agent's authority therefore no longer depends upon the grantor's continued assent, and the delivery may be completed when the condition occurs. (In the four following illustrations the grantor has expressly waived the right to recall the deed.)

Illustration: Grace handed her deed to Ezra, saying "Deliver this deed to Gene on his 21st birthday." Ezra delivers the deed to Gene on his 21st birthday, and at that moment there is a delivery.

Illustration: Grace handed her deed to Ezra, saying "Deliver this deed to Gene on his 21st birthday." Grace died before Gene turned 21. Ezra delivers the deed to Gene on his 21st birthday. The delivery is valid, even though Grace is dead.

Illustration: Grace handed her deed to Ezra saying "Deliver this deed to Gene when I die." Grace dies and Ezra hands the deed to Gene. There is a valid delivery.

Illustration: Grace handed her deed to Ezra saying, "Deliver this deed to Gene when he is 21." However, Grace took the deed back from Ezra when Gene was only 19. Nevertheless, title passes to Gene on his 21st birthday. The return of the document to Grace is irrelevant since a binding legal act occurred when Grace irrevocably delivered her deed into escrow.

a. A Contingency Certain to Occur

In a few states no deed may be deposited into escrow except upon a contingency which is certain to occur. This rule has been condemned as confusing the requirement of an unconditional waiver of the right to recall with an allowable conditional event, as is better shown in the following illustrations.

Illustration: Grace hands her deed to Ezra saying, "Deliver this deed to Gene when I die, and I waive the right to recall it." Here all jurisdictions agree that Ezra may complete the delivery on Grace's death. There is no right of recall, and the event is certain to occur.

Illustration: Grace hands her deed to Ezra saying, "Deliver this deed to Gene when I die, but I reserve the right to recall it." Here all jurisdictions agree that Ezra may not complete the delivery on Grace's death. The event is certain, but the right of recall prohibits a transfer after her death.

Illustration: Grace hands her deed to Ezra saying, "Deliver this deed to Gene only if he outlives me, and I reserve the right to recall it." All jurisdictions agree that Ezra cannot complete the delivery if Grace dies first. The event is here uncertain, but there is also a right of recall, meaning that there is no true escrow.

Illustration: Grace hands her deed to Ezra saying, "Deliver this deed to Gene only if he outlives me, and I waive my right to recall it". Here, most jurisdictions hold that Ezra may complete delivery after Grace's death because she has put the deed beyond her control. But a minority hold that the uncertainty of the condition means that the deed cannot be delivered despite its unconditional delivery into escrow.

b. An Underlying Contract

In noncommercial cases (donative situations) a binding delivery may be made into escrow even though there is no contractual relationship between grantor and grantee, so long as the grantor waives the right to recall the deed. However, in commercial situations most states hold that the grantor may recall the deed from escrow prior to the date of closing unless there is an enforceable contract between grantor and grantee.

Illustration: Grace and Gene orally contracted for Grace to sell her property to Gene for $10,000. Grace deposited her deed into escrow with instructions that it be delivered to Gene if he paid the price within one month. But before the month had passed Grace revoked her instructions and recalls the deed. Most states hold that Grace could do so, since the oral contract of sale was unenforceable under the Statute of Frauds.

The rule is consistent with the minority view that there can be no conditional delivery into escrow where the condition is uncertain to occur, since payment by the grantee is never a certain event. But the rule may also be reconciled with the majority view, if it is assumed that no commercial grantor ever intends to waive the right to recall. Thus a commercial escrow may not be a "true" escrow because the escrow agent remains subject to the grantor's control up to the moment of closing, and must honor a grantor's demand to return the deed. The existence of a binding contract between grantor and grantee does not change the nature of the escrow but instead means that the grantor can be compelled to deliver a deed (by a decree of specific performance of the contract) regardless of his or her state of mind. Once a grantor signs a contract enforceable by specific performance (see Chapter 8, p. 268), there is no longer any right to change his or her mind.

Illustration: Grace executed a binding contract with Gene to sell her land to him. Grace then deposited her deed into escrow with proper instructions but later sought to recall the deed before the time for Gene to perform. Whether or not the escrow agent returns Grace's deed to her is irrelevant, since Gene can seek specific performance of the contract and compel Grace to convey regardless of her state of mind. This result would follow even if no escrow were employed. If Grace refuses to execute or deliver a deed to Gene, a court would compel her to do so and title will pass regardless of her intent.

c. Relation Back

Generally, a deed deposited into escrow passes title upon the second delivery, i.e. the delivery from the escrow agent to the grantee. But, when necessary, courts will say that the passage of title relates back to the first delivery, in order to do justice and to effectuate the intent of the parties.

Illustration: Grace delivered her deed to Gene into escrow and died before escrow closed. Her heirs claim that her title passes to them. However, in order to protect Gene, it will be held that the post-death delivery of the deed by the escrow agent to him relates back to Grace's earlier delivery into escrow, so that he is the legal owner in preference to Grace's heirs.

Illustration: Grace deposited her deed into escrow and Gene died before escrow closed. Here again it will be held that the second delivery relates back to the time of the first delivery, when Gene was alive, so that legal title passed to him and then descended to his heirs. This avoids any problems arising out of the fact that there is no living grantee named in the deed (which would void the deed).

Illustration: Grace deposited her deed to Gene into escrow but later gave a second deed to the same property directly to Alice, who knew of Gene. The doctrine of relation back operates to give Gene priority over Alice even though the delivery to her preceded the second delivery to Gene. (If Alice is a bona fide purchaser without notice, she may prevail under the recording acts. See Chapter 10, p. 342).

Illustration: Grace deposited her deed into escrow and then her creditors attempted to attach the property. Some jurisdictions hold that Gene prevails over the creditors by virtue of relation back, but others hold that the doctrine will not apply when innocent third parties are involved.

E. THE EFFECT OF DELIVERY AND NONDELIVERY

1. Delivery

Title passes once a deed is delivered. What subsequently happens to the document is unimportant.

The deed has performed its function and transferred title. Title is not retransferred by loss or recall or destruction of the deed.

Illustration: Grace delivered her deed to Gene, but later changes her mind and asks Gene to return it to her. Even if Gene does return the deed, title will remain with him. Grace's delivery transferred title to Gene. If the parties now wish to retransfer title back to Grace, Gene must execute and deliver his own deed to her; returning her deed is not an adequate substitute. Nor does the return of the deed undo its earlier delivery.

2. Nondelivery

Until a deed is delivered it is legally insignificant and has no effect on title. However, a grantor who has negligently permitted the grantee to possess an undelivered deed may lose on estoppel principles to an innocent purchaser of the property from the grantee.

Illustration: Grace executed a deed to Gene but did not deliver it. Gene obtained the deed without Grace's knowledge and recorded it. Grace still owns the property. Gene accomplished nothing by his acts, nor has he acquired any interest in land which he can transfer to a bona fide purchaser, even though he recorded the deed.

Illustration: Grace handed her deed to Ezra, saying, "Deliver this deed to Gene if he graduates from college." Gene did not graduate from college, but Ezra handed him the deed anyway. The deed has not been delivered. Grace remains the owner of the property.

Illustration : Grace handed her deed to Ezra, saying "Deliver this deed to Gene when I die." Ezra instead handed the deed to Alice on Grace's death. Alice is not the owner, because the delivery to her was unauthorized. Gene may compel Ezra and Alice to give the deed to him, since he has title and is entitled to the deed.

IV. COVENANTS IN DEEDS CONCERNING TITLE

The most common way for a purchaser of real property to obtain protection for the title being acquired is through some form of independent title insurance. This involves an institution agreeing to indemnify the grantee if title is not what it was represented to be. However, an older form of title protection derived from recourse directly against the grantor when the title was defective (much as the modern purchaser of defective chattels is free to return them to the seller). This section deals with the protection the law affords to an aggrieved grantee against a grantor or a former grantor. In a sense it carries forward some of the principles of marketable title (see Chapter 8, p. 258) beyond the contract stage and over into the deed.

A. DEGREES OF PROTECTION AVAILABLE TO THE GRANTEE

Depending upon the kind of deed employed a grantee may obtain extensive or nonexistent protection against defects in the title.

1. Under a Warranty Deed

The execution of a warranty deed by the grantor gives the grantee the greatest possible recourse against the grantor in the event of defects in title. Such a deed contains up to six covenants concerning title.

2. Under a Statutory Deed

Many states have statutes providing that certain covenants of title may be implied from the form of the deed used by the grantor. These covenants are narrower in scope than the covenants found in a full warranty deed and therefore afford the grantee less protection.

3. Under a Deed Without Warranties

If the grantor executes a deed containing no express covenants or warranties and also no statutory warranties, then the grantee has no protection against the grantor for title failures. There are no implied warranties of title in the sale of real property. The most typical form of warrantyless deed is the quitclaim deed.

B. THE SIX COVENANTS OF TITLE

A full warranty deed will usually contain all or most of the covenants contained in the following subsections. The first three concern the title now held by the grantor and are referred to as "present" covenants; the final three are intended to protect the grantee at a later time and are called "future" covenants.

1. Covenant of Seisin

This covenant states that the grantor "is seised of the premises". As the wording suggests, it warrants that the grantor has seisin, i.e. has possession under a claim of freehold of the property about to be conveyed, but it does not assert that the seisin is lawful.

2. Covenant of Good Right to Convey

Here the grantor says "I have good right to sell and convey the premises." It complements the covenant of seisin by protecting the grantee in a situation where the grantor has tortious or wrongful seisin of the property.

3. Covenant Against Encumbrances

This says "The premises are free and clear from all encumbrances." This supplements the above covenants in that a person may be seised and entitled to convey an estate which, however, is encumbered, i.e., one subject to a lien of some sort (tax lien, assessment lien, mechanic's lien, or mortgage), a lease, or a restriction on use (easement, restrictive covenant or equitable servitude).

Some courts create an exception to such a covenant for a visible easement on the ground that the grantee must have seen the easement and been willing to accept the title subject to it. (This is similar to the marketable title exception. See Chapter 8, p. 261). A few other courts extend this exception to include any encumbrance actually known to the grantee (e.g., through a preliminary title report), but this is a minority view. Generally, any encumbrance "assumed" by the grantee (e.g. a mortgage) is deemed to be thereby excluded from the covenant against encumbrances, as is also the case for encumbrances which are deemed beneficial to the grantee (e.g. a power line easement serving the parcel).

4. Covenant of Quiet Enjoyment

Here the grantor warrants that the grantee "shall quietly enjoy" the property conveyed. It is intended to protect the grantee against any eviction caused by the grantor, agents of the grantor, or paramount title.

5. Covenant of Warranty

Here the grantor covenants to "warrant and defend the grantee against the lawful claims and demands of all persons." This enhances the covenant of quiet enjoyment by obligating the grantor to compensate the grantee if the grantee is so disturbed.

6. Covenant of Further Assurances

In this covenant the grantor promises "to do, execute or cause to be executed or done all such further acts, deeds or things for the better, more perfectly and absolutely conveying and assuring the premises conveyed to the grantee as the grantee may reasonably request." By virtue of this covenant the grantor is obliged to transfer to the grantee any adverse interest which he or she subsequently acquires. (Much the same result is obtained under the doctrine of estoppel by deed. See p. 303).

C. SPECIAL COVENANTS

The six title covenants discussed above are general covenants, i.e. they are intended to cover all exceptions to the absolute warranties they make. However, it is possible for a grantor to make a special covenant—one which warrants only against a limited number of exceptions to the title. Statutory covenants are often of this sort.

1. Special Covenants of Right to Convey, Warranty and Quiet Enjoyment

A typical special covenant of this class would warrant that the grantor personally has not conveyed any interest in the property to any other person. Such a covenant would not be breached by the existence of an outstanding title in someone else due a conveyance made by a predecessor of the grantor.

2. Special Covenant Against Encumbrances

A typical special covenant against encumbrances asserts that the grantor has not personally permitted any encumbrances to burden the title. It does not warrant that previous owners of the property have also kept it free from them. Thus it is breached by an encumbrance only if that encumbrance was "done, made or suffered" by the grantor personally.

Illustration: Grace conveyed her property to Gene with a special covenant against encumbrances. Later it is discovered that the property is subject to an easement granted away by an earlier owner in the chain of title. Although the easement is an encumbrance, Grace was not its creator, and her covenant has not been breached.

3. Estoppel by Deed

Where the deed is a full warranty deed, or (in some states) at least contains a covenant of warranty, or (in other states) even if it contains no title covenants but at least is not a quitclaim deed, and the grantor subsequently acquires title or an interest in the property described in that deed, that interest passes immediately from the grantor to her grantee and she is thereafter estopped from later asserting that claim against her grantee. The after acquired title "feeds" the estoppel. This may force a title searcher to check whether the holder of interest in land purported to transfer it before the interest ever came to her. See Chapter 10, p. 328.

D. BREACH OF COVENANT

1. What Constitutes a Breach

In this section, the six covenants will be compared in terms of what adverse claims constitute a breach.

a. *Covenant of Seisin*

This covenant is breached if the grantor lacked seisin at the time of conveying. Technically, it is therefore breached even if the grantor owns the property but a potential adverse possessor (whose claim has not yet ripened) is on it. Also, technically, it is not breached where the grantor does not own but is rather wrongfully possessing the property, not yet qualifying as an adverse possessor (i.e., having a tortious seisin). The grantee need not be evicted from the land in order to claim a breach here; it is sufficient merely to show that the grantor was without seisin.

b. Covenant of Good Right to Convey

This covenant is breached if the grantor lacks the right to convey the estate which the deed purports to convey. Since one may have a right to convey without necessarily having seisin, lack of seisin is not itself a breach of this covenant. Like the covenant of seisin, a breach does not require that the grantee be dispossessed from the premises.

c. Covenant Against Encumbrances

This covenant is breached if there are in fact any encumbrances on the property when it is conveyed. There is no requirement that the encumbrance actually disturb the grantee.

d. Covenants of Warranty and Quiet Enjoyment

These covenants are breached if the grantee is later "evicted" by paramount title or act of the grantor or of the grantor's agents.

There is no breach of these covenants unless an eviction has occurred. Eviction includes the obvious case of true physical ouster, but may also be constructive, as where the grantee pays off a paramount lien in order to avoid an ouster, or where the grantee is compelled to tolerate the assertion and enjoyment by another of an easement across the property.

e. Covenant of Further Assurances

A breach of this covenant occurs if the grantor refuses to obtain a release of some encumbrance (where such could be done) or refuses to convey to the grantee some paramount interest later acquired.

2. When a Covenant Is Deemed Breached

The covenants may be divided into "present" and "future" covenants. Present covenants are breached, if ever, at the moment of the conveyance to the grantee; future covenants are breached only when an eviction occurs, and not before.

a. The Present Covenants

The covenant of seisin is breached at the moment of delivery of the deed if the grantor lacked seisin at that time. The covenant of good right to convey is breached at the moment of delivery if the grantor lacked the right to convey the property at that time. The covenant against encumbrances is breached at the moment of delivery if there is an encumbrance against the title at that time.

b. The Future Covenants

The covenants of quiet enjoyment and warranty are breached only when a paramount title or encumbrance is asserted so as to constitute an actual or constructive eviction or disturbance of the grantee. The covenant of further assurances is breached only when the grantor refuses to obtain or supply the necessary documents the grantee needs to perfect the title.

E.   WHEN COVENANTS ARE ENFORCEABLE BY A REMOTE GRANTEE

The distinction between present and future covenants controls which covenants "run with the land" so as to protect remote grantees.   Since a present covenant is breached immediately or never, it does not run; future covenants do run.   (See, generally, Chapter 6 on covenants running with the land).

1.   Covenants of Seisin and Right to Convey

These two covenants assert present facts about the state of the grantor's title.   Those facts are either true or not.   If true, the covenants have not been breached and will never be breached.   If untrue, the covenants have been broken at the moment of the conveyance and thus will not run thereafter.   There is however the possibility that the cause of action for breach might run, which is the rule in a minority of states.

Illustration: Grace executed a deed to Gene containing covenants of seisin and right to convey.   However, Grace had previously conveyed the same property to Ann.   Gene executed a deed of this property to Rita, but this deed contained no covenants.   Rita has no remedy against Grace or Gene, even though she in fact received no property.   She cannot sue Gene since he made no covenant.   And although Grace did covenant, her covenants do not run with the land so as to protect Rita (although a minority of states hold that Gene has impliedly assigned his cause of action against Grace to Rita.)

2. Covenant Against Encumbrances

This, too, is a present covenant and does not run with the land. If there is an encumbrance on the property at the time it is conveyed, the grantee has an immediate cause of action. But subsequent remote grantees may not sue for that encumbrance (if it still exists when they take) unless their own respective deeds contain covenants against encumbrances, or if the cause of action for breach of the original covenants has been assigned to them (which, in a minority of states is held to be done impliedly.)

Illustration: Grace conveyed her property to Gene with a covenant against encumbrances in the deed. However, it was subject to an easement. Gene then conveyed the property to Rita by a deed which did not contain such a covenant. Rita has no remedy. Her deed from Gene contained no covenant against the easement. And Grace's covenant did not run with the land to aid Rita.

3. Covenants of Warranty, Quiet Enjoyment and Further Assurances

These future covenants do run with the land and do therefore protect the remote grantee who actually suffers the injury when the breach occurs. Once these covenants are actually breached, they no longer technically run with the land. However, the cause of action arising from the breach is often thereafter treated as impliedly assigned from grantor to grantee, thus reaching the same result as if the covenant did run (although now subject to the statute of limitations, since a breach has occurred).

Illustration: Grace conveyed property which she did not own by a deed containing all six covenants to Gene. Gene later conveyed it to Rita by a deed without covenants. The true owner appeared and dispossessed Rita. Rita has no cause of action against Grace for breach of the covenants of seisin or right to convey since they were present covenants and did not run to her. But Rita may sue Grace for breach of the covenants of quiet enjoyment and warranty after she is evicted. If Rita is not evicted, then she has no cause of action against Gene or Grace since those of Grace's covenants which do run have not yet been breached. If Rita now sells the property to Sam, he will have no cause of action at all against Grace, since even the future covenants do not run once they are breached.

Illustration: Grace's property was subject to a mortgage when she conveyed it to Gene by full warranty deed. Gene then conveyed the same property to Rita by a deed without covenants. The mortgage was not paid, and the mortgagee foreclosed and evicted Rita from the property. Rita may sue Grace for breach of the covenants of quiet enjoyment and warranty, since those ran with the land and were breached when Rita was ousted. But Rita has no cause of action against Grace for breach of the covenant against encumbrances, since that was breached at the moment that Grace conveyed to Gene and did not thereafter run. Rita cannot sue Gene at all since he made no covenants to her.

F.   MEASURE OF DAMAGES

The covenants differ in their measure of damages. In general, however, the covenantor is never liable for more than the amount originally paid by the covenantee, i.e. restitution is the maximum amount owed.

1.   Covenants of Seisin and Right to Convey

When these covenants are breached the grantee is entitled to recover the price paid for the property (or so much of the property as the deed failed to truly convey). Courts differ as to whether the grantee may be allowed to retain the property or must tender a reconveyance to the grantor as a precondition to recovery.

2. Covenant Against Encumbrances

Encumbrances may be divided into monetary and nonmonetary ones. Where the encumbrance is a monetary one, e.g. a tax lien or mortgage, then the measure of damages is the cost of removing it, not exceeding the value of the land. If the encumbrance is non-monetary, e.g. an easement or restrictive covenant, then the measure of damages is the extent to which it reduces the market value of the land.

3. Covenants of Warranty, Quiet Enjoyment and Further Assurances

For total eviction, damages are the price paid; for partial eviction, damages are a proportionate amount of the price paid. In other states, the damages are based on the value of the land at the date of the breach, rather than the original price paid. Damages do not generally include the cost of improvements made by the grantee, although he may be able to make such a claim under an unjust enrichment theory or "innocent improver" statute. Where the grantee buys up the outstanding title or encumbrance, the measure of damages is the amount paid for it, not exceeding the amount originally paid to the grantor. Furthermore, the grantee may recover attorney's fees spent in protecting title against the superior claim.

4. Damages in the Case of Remote Grantees

Some courts limit the recovery of a grantee against a remote grantor to the amount actually paid to his or her immediate grantor, even though that is less than the amount received by the original covenantor. If a remote grantee is the beneficiary of several covenants of warranty made by different grantors in the chain of title, all may be sued, but the grantee is limited to only one full satisfaction. If an earlier grantor in the chain is sued but is himself the beneficiary of even earlier warranties, he has an action over against his covenantor.

Illustration: Grace conveyed the property to Gene by full warranty deed; Gene conveyed it by full warranty deed to Rita; and Rita conveyed it by full warranty deed to Sam. Gene paid Grace $10,000 for the property; Rita paid Gene $9,000, and Sam paid Rita $11,000. Now it is revealed that Grace never owned the property and the true owner appears and evicts Sam. Sam may sue Rita based on her covenants and recover $11,000. Or he may sue Gene based on the future covenants in the deed to Rita and recover $9,000 (the amount Gene received), or he may sue Grace on the future covenants in the deed to Gene and recover $10,000. (However, only one recovery is permitted to Sam, i.e. he may not collect $11,000 plus $9,000, plus $10,000 although he may obtain a judgment or judgments against all of the parties). If Sam recovers from Rita, she may have an action over against Gene or Grace; if Sam or Rita recovers from Gene he may have an action over against Grace.

V. DUTIES OF DISCLOSURE

The common law covenants of title refer only to the state of the title, not to the physical condition of the property conveyed. The common law implied no warranties of fitness or merchantability of the property. Despite the changes in the doctrine of caveat emptor which have occurred in the field of personal property, this basic rule still obtains in real estate today. However, vendors are now often held subject to greater disclosure duties and commercial vendors may be held subject to an implied warranty of fitness.

A. NONDISCLOSURE

In many states a vendor is now required to disclose any material defect known to him and not known to the purchaser. Failure to disclose permits the purchaser to rescind the contract or cancel the deed, sue for damages, or possibly recover for personal injuries suffered as a result of the defect. Similar duties may be imposed upon brokers, lenders, attorneys, escrow officers and inspectors with regard to defects actually known to them and perhaps even to defects they may have suspected or perhaps merely should have known about.

B. IMPLIED WARRANTIES IN SALE OF NEW HOMES

A growing number of jurisdictions are beginning to impose upon builder-vendors an implied warranty of the quality. Originally applied to only the builders of mass-produced homes, the doctrine appears to be expanding to include all those who build houses for sale to the public.

Many issues remain to be resolved. These include:

a) Statute of Limitations. Does the time to sue commence when the defect was created, when construction was completed, when title was transferred to the buyer, when some indication of the defect first surfaced or when the buyer finally discovered what the problem was?

b) Plaintiffs. May only the original purchaser sue, or may a remote one also sue? Will it depend on whether (and how long) the original buyer occupied the property? If a remote buyer is not automatically entitled to sue, may the original buyer assign any cause of action or potential cause of action he has as part of the sale to the remote buyer?

c) Defendants. In addition to the seller, may the buyer also recover from the prime contractor (in charge of the overall project), the subcontractor (who handled the particular feature), the materialman (who supplied the components), the architect, or the construction lender?

d) Damages. The probable measure of property damages is the cost of repairs or diminution of value, but are property damages the buyer's only remedy, or may he also recover for personal injuries?

e) Disclaimers. To what degree can a seller protect herself by appropriate language in the contract? Is this a matter for freedom of contract or should it be treated like fitness is treated in residential rental housing?

CHAPTER TEN

PRIORITIES: THE RECORDING SYSTEM

This chapter is concerned with the relative rights of successive transferees of interests in land from the same transferor. Priority problems arise when the transferor grants partial interests in property to successive transferees (as where the owner first gives a mortgage on the property to one person and then a mortgage on the same property to another person), or successively purports to transfer the entire estate to different persons (as where the owner first conveys the property to one person and then seeks to convey the same property to another person) or where there are successive transfers of partial and total interest in the same land (as where the owner first gives a mortgage to one person and then conveys the same property to another person). The relationship between the transferees is regarded as a question of priorities—who has the prior, i.e., superior interest. (In most of the illustrations in this section the transfers used are transfers of the entire estate, but the same principles of priority would generally apply to transfers of partial interests. In these illustrations the original transferor is usually assumed to be the owner of the property and is therefore designated

"Owen", the successive transferees are given names in alphabetical order.)

I. COMMON LAW PRIORITIES

At common law most questions of priority were determined according to time. The party who took first had the superior interest. ("First in time, first in right.") This was supported by the fact that after the owner gave his interest to the first party, he had nothing left to give to the second. The same principles applied to the resolution of priorities between equitable claimants, so long as the equities were otherwise equal. The one exception to these rules was that a prior equitable claim would be defeated by a subsequent legal claim in the hands of a bona fide purchaser (i.e. the earlier claim would lose priority).

Illustration: Competing Legal Claims. Owen delivered a deed to his property to Ann and later delivered a deed to the same property to Bob. Ann prevails over Bob in their competing claims to legal title, since Ann's claim came first in time. Ann has the legal title.

Illustration: Competing Equitable Claims. Owen executed a contract to sell his property to Ann and later executed a similar contract to sell it to Bob. Both claims are equitable, since Owen retains legal title (See equitable conversion, Chapter 8, p. 268). As between the competing equitable claims, Ann again prevails because her claim was first. Ann has the superior right to buy the property.

Illustration: Prior Legal and Subsequent Equitable Claim. Owen delivered a deed to Ann and later contracted to sell the same property to Bob. Ann's prior legal claim (based on her deed) prevails over Bob's subsequent equitable claim. Ann is not obliged to sell the property to Bob.

Illustration: Prior Equitable and Subsequent Legal Claim; Bona Fide Purchaser Doctrine. Owen contracted to sell his property to Ann and later delivered a deed of the same property to Bob. If Bob was a bona fide purchaser, paying value to Owen and being without notice of Ann, then he will prevail over her even though her claim was prior in time. (I.e., Bob not only has legal title, but he is also not obliged to honor the contract and sell to Ann.) This was the only case at common law where priority in time was not the sole controlling factor in determining questions of priority of right.

The common law principle of priority as based on time is logical but entirely unworkable. By saying that A prevails over B because she took first, whether or not this is known to B, means that there is no sensible way for B to purchase O's property. How can B be sure when he pays his money to O that O has not previously conveyed the property to A (a person B has never heard of)? A diligent search of the records regarding O's title is useless if the mere fact that A took first means that she prevails even though she has never recorded her deed. Thus, in order to justify payments of the price in reliance on what the public land records show, there must not only be a system of land records, but the common law priority system must be replaced by one equivalent to the bona fide purchaser doctrine protecting the second taker when he is without notice of the first.

Given such a system, the law does not need to mandate that every document be recorded in order to be effective. Rather, it provides: (1) if a document is recorded it will be effective as against the entire world (will give "constructive notice" of its contents to everyone) and (2) if a document is not recorded, it will be ineffective as against certain protected parties.

II. THE RECORDING SYSTEM— RECORDING STATUTES

Every state has created a system of public land records whereby all documents affecting titles to land may be recorded and viewed by others. Thus potential purchasers of land may check these records to ascertain whether their sellers own the land in question and/or whether they have previously conveyed to others any interest in it. Since such a search is useful only if all such documents have been recorded or if the searcher is not jeopardized by any previously executed document which was not recorded. Thus recording acts take the common law rule that a prior equity is defeated by a subsequent bona fide purchaser of the legal title and apply it to all conflicts, whether involving legal or equitable claimants or both.

A. VARIOUS RECORDING ACTS

1. Notice Acts

These statutes provide that an unrecorded instrument is invalid as against any subsequent purchaser without notice. These acts give protection to a purchaser of property who buys it without notice of prior unrecorded instruments affecting it.

Illustration: Arizona's statute provides (in part): "No instrument affecting real property is valid against subsequent purchasers for valuable consideration without notice unless recorded as provided by law * * *."

2. Notice–Race Acts (Race–Notice Acts)

These statutes provide that an unrecorded deed is invalid as against any subsequent purchaser who buys without notice of it and whose own instrument is recorded first. These acts give protection to purchasers of property who buy without notice of unrecorded claim if they also record their own deeds before the earlier unrecorded instruments are recorded.

Illustration: California's statute provides (in part): "Every conveyance of real property * * * is void as against any subsequent purchaser or mortgagee of the same property * * * in good faith and for a valuable consideration, whose conveyance is first duly recorded * * *"

3. Race Acts

A few statutes provide that an unrecorded deed is invalid as to any deed recorded before it. There is no requirement that the subsequent grantee be without notice in order to prevail. The sole question here is which deed was recorded first. Sometimes these statutes are worded in terms of priority, but in other cases they achieve this effect by making recordation part of the process of delivery, so that a deed will not pass title until it is recorded.

Illustration: Maryland's statute provides: "No deed of real property shall be valid for the purpose of passing title unless acknowledged and recorded as herein directed."

Illustration: Ohio's mortgage statute provides (in part): "All mortgages * * * shall be recorded * * * and take effect from the time they are delivered to the recorder. * * * If two or more mortgages are presented for record on the same day, they shall take effect from the order of presentation for record. The first presented must be the first recorded, and the first recorded shall have preference."

4. Period of Grace Acts

These statutes operate like notice statutes, except that a grantee is given a certain length of time to record before any sanction is imposed for nonrecordation. These acts were popular when travel to the recorder's office was difficult and time consuming, but modern communication and transportation methods have rendered them obsolete and they will not be considered further.

B. COMPARISON OF THE OPERATION OF THE VARIOUS TYPES OF STATUTE

This section will consist of a series of illustrations indicating those situations where different types of statutes achieve a different result.

1. Race v. Notice

Illustration: Owen deeded his property to Ann, who did not record it. Owen then deeded the same property to Bob, who was aware of Ann but recorded his deed anyway. In a notice jurisdiction, Ann prevails because Bob took with notice. But in a race jurisdiction, Bob would prevail because he recorded first.

Illustration: Owen deeded his property to Ann who did not record. Owen then deeded the same property to Bob who was without notice of Ann and who also did not record. Then Ann recorded. In a notice jurisdiction Bob prevails because he purchased without notice of Ann, but in a race jurisdiction Ann wins because she recorded first.

2. Race v. Notice–Race

Illustration: Owen deeded his property to Ann who did not record. Owen then deeded the same property to Bob who was aware of Ann but who recorded his deed anyway. In a race jurisdiction Bob prevails because he recorded first. In a notice-race jurisdiction Bob has recorded first, but since he did not purchase without notice, his prior recordation is not enough, and Ann prevails.

3. Notice v. Notice–Race

Illustration: Owen deeded his property to Ann who did not record. Owen then deeded the same property to Bob who is without notice. Ann recorded before Bob. Bob prevails over Ann in a notice jurisdiction, where the only requirement is that he purchase without notice. But he loses in a notice-race jurisdiction since he must not only purchase without notice but must also record first.

Illustration: Owen deeded his property to Ann who did not record. Owen then deeded the same property to Bob, who was without notice of Ann, and who also did not record. In this situation, where neither has recorded Bob wins in a notice state (he purchased without notice), but loses in a notice-race jurisdiction (he has not recorded first). In a notice-race jurisdiction the prior grantee prevails unless the subsequent purchaser records first. That has not happened here, and so the prior grantee, Ann, prevails. If, however, Bob now records before Ann does, Bob may yet prevail.

III. THE MECHANICS OF RECORDING AND SEARCHING TITLE

A. RECORDING A DOCUMENT

The process of recording a document affecting title involves the following steps.

1. Deposit of a Proper Document at the Recorder's Office

Recording begins when a duly executed, acknowledged and delivered recordable document is taken to the recorder's office (or other designated depository) in the county where the property is located.

To be accepted for recordation, the document must affect title. It can be consensually created, such as a deed, lease, or mortgage; a contract for the sale of land is generally although not always deemed to be recordable (depending on how seriously the doctrine of equitable title is taken) and an option to purchase land is generally not regarded as recordable. Such documents must generally also be notarized in order to be accepted by the recorder. Official documents arising out of legal proceedings relating to land, such as probate or quiet title decrees, judgment or tax liens, and lis pendens are also recordable.

The recorder's office looks only to the form of the document to determine whether to accept it. No governmental official ever passes upon its validity or effectiveness to pass a title, or investigates to determine whether the grantor truly owns the property involved. All such conflicts are resolved by way of litigation between claimants. The recorder's office merely serves as a library and the recorder's gate-keeping function is limited to determining what may be stored in that database.

2. Copying of the Document Into the Official Records

The recorder's office makes a copy of the entire document, usually photographically. This copy is then inserted into the current book of official records. These record books, consisting solely of copies of documents, are kept and labelled in strict numerical order. When one book is filled, a new book is started and is given the next number. Thus a typical document will appear in Volume 387, page 453 of the Official Records; the next document will appear in Volume 387, page 454.

3. Indexing of the Document

In addition to the official records, the recorder's office maintains a set of indexes, where informational entries concerning each document are made so that an orderly search for the document will disclose it. Most states have a grantor-grantee index, a set of books containing a reference to all documents recorded, in alphabetical order, according to the name of the grantor. The index will show first the name of the grantor, then the name of the grantee, then probably a description of the document and perhaps the property, and finally a reference to the volume and page in the official record where the document is copied. A grantee-grantor index contains the same information, but is organized according to an alphabetical list of grantees, rather than grantors. A tract index organizes all of the entries according to the location of the property rather than the names of the parties. Indexes (or "indices") are often limited as to time. Thus there may be one set of indexes covering all documents recorded between 1920 and 1950, another set covering 1950–60, and another for 1960–70, separate sets for each of the years of 1970, and finally a monthly, weekly and/or daily index for the current year.

Illustration: A deed of Blackacre from Owen to Ann, recorded in 1965, will be indexed in the grantor-grantee index for the decade 1960 under the name of Owen; it will be indexed in the grantee-grantor index for the same decade under the name of Ann; and it will be indexed in a tract index under Blackacre.

If the recorder's office fails to perform these tasks properly and fails to record or index or records or indexes a document in the wrong place, the document may fail to give constructive notice of its contents.

4. Return of the Document

Once the document has been fully recorded and indexed, it is returned to the depositor, since the copy is all that the recorder's office keeps.

B. SEARCHING A TITLE

1. Locating the Present Owner in the Grantee Index

A person searching a title (usually on behalf of the buyer) starts with a known name, i.e. that of the current seller of the property. If that person is truly the owner of the property, he will probably have taken title by a deed, which would be indexed under his name in the grantee index. Thus a search for Owen would start in the "O" volume of grantees, in the year Owen claims to have purchased the property or, if that is not known, in this year's grantee volume and then going back year by year until an entry is found.

2. Locating Prior Owners in the Grantee Index

From the first entry, the name of the previous owner can be ascertained, since it will appear opposite the named grantee in the grantor column. That name (e.g., Norma) will then be searched in the grantee volumes, usually starting with the date that she conveyed to the current owner and going back in time until her name appears as grantee from the owner before her. That owner's name is then searched in the grantee indexes, and the process continues with each name until the searcher arrives at an indisputable source, generally the government. At this point, the searcher may conclude that there is a complete chain of title.

a. *Stopping Short of the Original Source*

Many states have marketable title statutes or bar conventions that searches need go back only a set number of years, e.g., 60 years. Any title existing at that time is presumed valid and need not be further justified, although this can create problems when there are rival "roots of title" for different searchers to find.

b. Dealing With Gaps

Supplementary indexes may be necessary to fill in missing links. For instance, if a search shows that Norma received a deed from Michael, but no deed to Michael can be found, the next link may be found in the probate records if they are kept separately. These would show that Michael inherited the property from Lana by will and a return to the grantee index would then show Lana as a grantee twenty years earlier from Kurt, thereby permitting resumption of the search. A comprehensive recording system should include all records affecting titles in one place, but that is not always the case. Bankruptcy, tax matters and condemnation records are often stored separately.

3. Searching for Encumbrances and Other Interests in the Grantor Index

Once the searcher knows all names in the chain of title, his task is then to determine whether any of those owners encumbered or otherwise affected the title during their tenure on the property. This is accomplished by searching each name in the appropriate grantor index, usually during that person's ownership of the property, since any such event would appear in the indexes under that owner's name. Thus a mortgage or easement given by the owner or a judgment or lis pendens filed against the owner would be entered in the index showing the owner as grantor and the other party (mortgagee, dominant tenant, judgment creditor, or plaintiff) as grantee.

4. Following the Subsequent History of Such Encumbrances

In order to tell whether those defects on the title still exist, the searcher will then go through either the grantor or grantee indexes for the years thereafter. If they were canceled, there should be a document indexed under the owner's name as grantee and the interest holder's name as grantor, showing that the mortgage was paid, the easement was terminated, etc. If no such document can be found, then the interest still survives of record.

IV.   RECORD NOTICE— CONSTRUCTIVE NOTICE

The recording acts penalize only "unrecorded" documents. If an instrument is properly recorded it takes priority over subsequent claims, whether or not those claimants actually look for or see that instrument. When an instrument is properly recorded it is said to give "constructive" notice, i.e. subsequent claimants are charged with notice of its existence regardless of whether or not they have searched the records. The doctrine of constructive notice means that there is no profit in not searching the records since a claimant will be charged with notice of all prior recorded instruments independently of whether he or she has any actual knowledge of them.

Not every document which has been delivered to the recorder's office and copied into the records is held to be recorded and/or to have given notice within the meaning of the recording acts. This section covers the cases where documents have been mechanically copied into the records but may still be held to not be recorded or to not give notice. These situations are generally more readily understood by beginning with illustrations and then following each illustration with an analysis.

A. DOCUMENTS WHICH CANNOT BE LOCATED AT ALL

1. Misindexed Documents

Illustration: Owen conveyed his property to Ann who recorded but the recorder erroneously indexed the deed under the name of "Smith" rather than "Owen" in the grantor column. Owen then conveyed the property to Bob. Because of the misindexing Bob will not find the deed for Ann (since he will search out only the name "Owen" in the grantor-grantee index). For this reason many courts will hold that the deed to Ann was not recorded, since it was not indexed so as to give notice to any person checking out Owen's title. However, in some states where the statute provides that an instrument is deemed recorded when it is deposited in the recorder's office for recordation it is held that Ann will prevail since her deed is technically recorded even though it cannot be found. In jurisdictions holding for Bob it becomes the practical duty of all grantees to return to the recorder's office at a later date to check the proper indexing of their instruments. In jurisdictions holding for Ann, however, there are no practical steps for subsequent purchasers to take to avoid this hazard.

2. Wild Documents

Illustration: Owen conveyed his property to Ann who did not record. Ann then conveyed the property to Bob who did record. Owen then deeds the property to Carol who did record. Carol should prevail over Bob. Even though Bob's deed was recorded, the nonrecordation of the deed from Owen to Ann means that Bob's deed is not connected in the indexes to any name in the chain of title. (It will be indexed with Ann as Grantor and Bob as Grantee, but a purchaser from the apparent owner of record, Owen, will have no reason to think to look up either name in the index. And if the name Owen is looked up in the grantor-grantee index, nothing will be found). A wild deed is not deemed to give notice within the meaning of a notice act and is not deemed to have been recorded first within the meaning of a notice-race act.

B. DOCUMENTS WHICH CAN BE LOCATED ONLY WITH DIFFICULTY

1. The Late Recorded Document

Illustration: Owen purchased the property in 1930. In 1940, he conveyed the property to Ann who did not record. In 1950 Owen conveyed the property to Bob who did record, but who knew of Ann. In 1951 Ann recorded. In 1960 Bob deeded the property to Carol. The jurisdictions are divided as to whether Ann or Carol will prevail with a majority favoring Ann.

The argument for Ann. Ann's deed is not in the direct chain of title, but it can be found by an extensive search of the records. A normal search would investigate each owner only during the time period of his or her ownership, but if each owner is checked out for the time period following divestment of title up until the present, then the deed to

Ann will be found. (A normal search would investigate Owen only for the period 1930–1950, the years when he was owner of record, but if that search were extended to cover Owen from 1950 to the present then the deed to Ann would be found.) Under this rule a title searcher must check out each owner from the date of acquisition up to the present (rather than only up to the date of divestment).

The argument for Carol. The other rule is that a purchaser need check out an owner only during the time of record ownership, and no further. Thus the deed to Ann would not be found by such a search, and Carol therefore would not be charged with notice of Ann. Ann's deed would be held not to have been recorded within the meaning of the recording act.

2. The Early Recorded Document—Estoppel by Deed

Illustration: In 1949 Ann conveyed property which she did not then own to Bob. Bob recorded. In 1950 Owen (who did own the property) conveyed it to Ann. Ann recorded. In 1960 Ann conveyed the property to Carol. Carol recorded. In most states, the legal effect of the conveyance from Owen to Ann in 1950 was to immediately transfer the title to Ann and then from Ann to Bob under the doctrine (either judicial or statutory) of estoppel by deed. By virtue of her deed to Bob, Ann is estopped to assert that she had no title to convey to him, and any title subsequently acquired by her "feeds" the estoppel and inures to the benefit of Bob. Thus Bob has the title Ann obtained from Owen in 1951 unless Carol prevails under the recording acts. The courts are again divided.

The argument for Carol. Bob's deed has been recorded but it is not in the chain of title. For Carol to discover it, she would have to check out each owner in the index during a period of time prior to the time that the owner acquired title. This rule holds that Carol is not required to do this. She must check out Ann for the years 1950 to 1960 (the years of Ann's apparent ownership), but she is not required to check Ann out for the time prior to 1950. Consequently she is not charged with notice of what is in the records for Ann in 1949, and therefore has no record notice of Bob. Bob's deed is out of the chain of title.

The argument for Bob. The other rule reasons that by a more diligent search the deed to Ann could be discovered and therefore Carol should be charged with notice of it and of all deeds subsequently executed by Ann. In such a state, a purchaser must check out each name in the index from the date of divestment back in time to the commencement of the records (rather than merely back in time to the date of acquisition of title). Thus a search under Ann's name would begin in 1960 and go back in time to the origin of the records, rather than merely back to 1950 (when Ann became the owner of record).

3. Deeds Out

Illustration: Owen conveyed lot 1 to Ann by a deed which recites that Owen also gave Ann an easement over his retained lot 2. The deed was recorded. Owen then conveyed lot 2 to Bob without mention of the easement in favor of Ann, and Bob recorded. Bob's property will be held subject to Ann's easement if Bob can be charged with notice of the contents of Owen's deed to Ann. There is another division of opinion here.

The argument for Ann. The deed from Owen to Ann was properly recorded and would be revealed to Bob by a diligent search of the index. Bob should study the contents of any other deed executed by his own grantor to see whether it purports to convey his property or any interest in his property. Bob is thus charged not only with notice of the existence of the deed from Owen to Ann, but is also charged with notice that it gives Ann an easement over this property. Thus a purchaser in such a jurisdiction must check out all deeds executed by a common grantor, even though in the index they appear to relate to different property.

The argument for Bob. Under this rule Bob is charged with notice only of deeds in his own chain of title, and a deed to other property is not held to be within that chain. Once he learns from the index that the deed concerns other property he is not required to look up the deed itself to see if it also affects his own property. Thus he is not charged with notice of the grant of the easement. Under this rule it becomes Ann's obligation to see that her deed is doubly indexed so that it refers to both lots 1 and 2.

C. DOCUMENTS WHICH ARE READILY LOCATABLE BUT STILL DO NOT GIVE NOTICE

Through inadvertence the recorder may permit to be recorded some document which by law should not have been recorded (as is the case in some states for executory land contracts, or assignments of mortgages), or because the document was defectively executed (not signed or not acknowledged). The courts do not agree as to whether such a document gives notice to those searching the records. Some hold that such a document does not give notice, even to a searcher who actually sees it, while others hold that the purchaser who actually sees such a document is charged with the duty of investigating its validity. (As to the duty to inquire further, see p. 331).

1. Defective Documents

Illustration: Owen conveyed his property to Ann, but his signature is not acknowledged. Nevertheless the recorder accepts the document for recording and spreads it on the records, where the photographic copy makes it plain that the notarial acknowledgment is defective. Owen then conveyed the same property to Bob. In some jurisdictions Bob prevails even though in searching the title he actually saw Ann's deed, since the defect is held to defeat the contention that it has been recorded or that it gives notice. But in others Bob is charged with a duty (at least if he actually saw the deed) to investigate the circumstances in order to ascertain the nature of Ann's interest, and if a reasonable inquiry would disclose her interest then Bob is charged with notice, and Ann will prevail.

2. Nonrecordable Documents

Illustration: Owen contracted to sell his property to Ann. Although the local recording act does not authorize the recordation of executory contracts for the sale of land Ann nevertheless delivered the contract to the recorder who copied it into the records and properly indexed it. Owen then conveyed the same property to Bob. The result here is the same as in the previous illustration dealing with defectively acknowledged documents. In both cases the recording of an improper document is held not to give constructive notice, although persons who actually see it may sometimes be charged with notice of it or else with a duty to investigate further.

V. INQUIRY NOTICE

The doctrine of record notice, by virtue of charging a subsequent claimant with notice of all previously recorded documents within the chain of title, imposes on such a person the practical duty of searching the records. Since a purchaser will be charged with notice of what is in the records (and therefore made junior to whatever is there), every person intending to buy or encumber property must of necessity search the records first to ascertain the priority of his or her own claim. But the doctrine of notice may go even further in certain cases and impose upon the subsequent claimant the obligation of making a reasonable investigation outside of the records. When such a duty is imposed the subsequent claimant is charged with notice of what a reasonable inquiry would disclose. Thus a person may be charged with "inquiry" notice as well as actual or constructive notice of prior claims. The duty to investigate the validity of recorded but defective documents (see p. 330) may be considered as an example of the application of the doctrine of inquiry notice.

Inquiry notice is not applied in the same and absolute fashion as is constructive notice. First, it must be shown that some suspicious fact existed in order to generate the initial obligation to make an inquiry. And, second, it must be shown that a reasonable inquiry would have revealed the fact in question. Where an inquiry was actually made and did not lead to discovery of the relevant facts the inquirer is not necessarily protected since the trier of fact can conclude that the inquiry was too casual and should have been more diligent. If either component is lacking there is no imputation of notice.

A. NOTICE BASED ON INFORMATION IN THE RECORDS

1. References in Recorded Documents to Unrecorded Documents

Some courts require a purchaser to investigate references to other documents which appear in recorded instruments even though the documents referred to have not themselves been recorded. If a reasonable search would uncover the unrecorded document, then the purchaser is charged with notice of it and may not claim to be a bona fide purchaser without notice.

Illustration: Owen mortgaged his property to Mel but the mortgage was not recorded. Owen then conveyed his property to Ann (who knew of the mortgage) by a deed which recited "subject to the mortgage given to Mel" (and provided further information as to it). Ann later conveyed the property to Bob by a deed which also said "subject to the mortgage given to Mel". The reference in Bob's deed to Mel's mortgage might be held to create a duty on Bob to inquire further as to Mel's interest by virtue of its suspicious nature. If a reasonable inquiry and search would then reveal Mel's interest, Bob could be charged with notice of Mel's mortgage, and will be held to take the property subject to that mortgage.

2. References in Recorded but Unread Documents to Other Unrecorded Documents

It is not required that the suspicious fact be actually known by the subsequent claimant. That person may be charged with constructive notice of the fact by virtue of a properly recorded reference to it. The suspicious fact generates a duty to inquire whether it is actually known or merely constructively known.

Illustration: Owen mortgaged his property to Mel but the mortgage was not recorded. Owen then conveyed the same property to Ann (who knew of the mortgage) by a deed which recited "subject to the mortgage given to Mel" (and provided further information as to it). Ann recorded her deed. Later Ann conveyed the property to Bob by a deed which did *not* refer to Mel's mortgage. Bob did not search the records. Bob may be held to take the property subject to the mortgage. Owen's deed to Ann was properly recorded and therefore may be held to give notice of its contents. Bob could thus be charged with constructive notice of the reference to Mel. This is a suspicious fact and imposes a duty upon Bob to investigate. The fact that the reference to Mel was only constructively known by Bob would be irrelevant. He has the same duty to search as if he had actually seen the reference. Otherwise Bob would be better off by not searching the records, which is not a policy to be encouraged.

3. Indefinite References to Other Documents

In some states a reference in one document to some other document does not compel the purchaser to investigate if the reference is too indefinite (as to parties, date, nature of the interest, or description of the property involved). In such a case the purchaser who sees such a reference has no duty to investigate further.

Illustration: Owen mortgaged his property to Mel but the mortgage was not recorded. Owen then conveyed the property to Ann (who knows of the mortgage) by a deed which recited "subject to all mortgages, easements and other interests outstanding against the property". Ann recorded and later conveyed the property to Bob without mentioning the mortgage. Such an entirely indefinite reference (sometimes referred to as a "Mother Hubbard clause") should give Bob no duty to investigate. Therefore Bob is not charged with notice of Mel, and will take title free of the mortgage.

B.   NOTICE BASED ON POSSESSION OF THE PROPERTY

In most states a purchaser of property is charged with notice of any possessor's rights to the property. Thus a prior unrecorded grantee who has taken possession of the property prevails over subsequent purchasers even though nothing appears in the records. The effect of this doctrine is to compel a subsequent purchaser to inspect the land as well as search the records.

Illustration: Owen conveyed his property to Ann who did not record but who did take actual possession of the property. Owen then conveyed the same property to Bob who searched the records and found no mention of Ann. In most states Bob will be charged with notice of Ann, based on her possession, despite the absence of her deed from the records.

1.   The Information Charged to the Purchaser— Constructive Notice v. Inquiry Notice

A purchaser is usually charged absolutely with notice of the fact (when it is a fact) that someone is in possession of the property (constructive notice) whether or not an inspection of the property is made. If someone other than the owner is in possession, that is usually held to be a suspicious fact generating a duty to inquiry as to the possessor's rights (inquiry notice).

Illustration: Owen conveyed his property to Ann who did not record and did not take possession. Owen then conveyed the property to Bob who inspected the property. Since Bob had no notice of any suspicious fact, he had no duty to inquire. Thus Bob prevails over Ann.

Illustration: Owen conveyed his property to Ann who did not record but did take possession. Owen then conveyed the property to Bob who inspected the land and saw Ann there. Since Bob had actual knowledge of the suspicious fact that someone other than Owen was in possession of the property Bob had a duty to inquire further as to Ann's rights. If a reasonable inquiry would have revealed her unrecorded deed Bob will be charged with (inquiry) notice of that fact. Ann will then prevail.

Illustration: Owen conveyed his property to Ann who did not record but did take possession. Owen then conveyed the property to Bob who did not inspect the property. Since Ann is in possession Bob is charged with constructive notice of that fact. Bob's constructive notice generates the same duty to inquire as to her rights as did his actual notice of this same suspicious fact in the previous illustration. If a reasonable inquiry would disclose her claim she will prevail.

Illustration: Owen conveyed his property to Ann who did not record. Ann put a tenant, Tom, in possession, but told Tom that she was acting as Owen's agent in renting the property to him. Owen then conveyed the same property to Bob. In this case Bob may well not be charged with notice of Ann's interest. He is charged with notice of Tom's possession, and while notice of this suspicious fact may give him a duty to inquire of Tom as to his rights, a reasonable inquiry here might not lead to the discovery of Ann's interest, and therefore Bob might not be charged with notice of it. It would be a question of fact as to whether Bob must inquire of Ann as to whether she claims any interest in the property after Tom informs him that Ann told him that she was Owen's agent. If a jury concluded that Bob should make such an inquiry (and if it also concluded that Ann would respond honestly) then Bob will be charged with notice of Ann's interest. But if the jury concluded otherwise, then no notice of Ann's interest will be imputed to Bob.

2. Inquiry Notice When the Statute Requires Actual Notice

When the recording act of the state says that unrecorded documents are void only as to persons without "actual" notice of them, strict adherence to its text may limit the scope of notice and rule out constructive and/or inquiry notice based on possession. In some states a statutory requirement of actual notice is held to mean that the purchaser is not charged with notice of the possessor's rights unless these rights are actually known to the purchaser, i.e., there is no duty to inquire of the possessor even when there is actual notice of the fact of possession. In other states with similar statutes there is held to be a duty to inquire of a possessor, but only if the fact of possession is actually known to the purchaser, i.e. there is no initial duty to visit the land to look for a possessor. These two interpretations limit the doctrines of inquiry notice and constructive notice respectively.

Illustration: Owen conveyed his property to Ann who did not record but took possession. Owen then conveyed the same property to Bob who inspected the land and saw Ann, but made no inquiry of her. The recording act in the jurisdiction provides that an unrecorded deed is void against purchasers without actual notice. Under a restrictive view of actual notice Bob prevails since he has no obligation to ask her about her rights (no duty of inquiry notice). Under a less restrictive view, since Bob has actual knowledge of Ann's possession, he may be charged with notice of her rights if a reasonable inquiry of her would have revealed these rights. But even under this second view, Bob would prevail if he had not visited the property at all (and thereby acquired no actual knowledge of Ann's possession). For Bob to be charged with notice of Ann's rights in a case where Bob never looked at the land the statute must be read as not protecting any person with notice (whether actual or otherwise).

Illustration: Owen conveyed his property to Ann who did not record. Ann then rented the property to Tom who did not record his lease but who did take possession. Owen then conveyed the same property to Bob who searched the records but did not view the land. If the local recording act provides that any unrecorded deed is void only as to a purchaser without notice, Ann and Tom should prevail over Bob. Bob would be charged with notice of the rights of persons in possession when that possession is not consistent with the record title, which means notice here of Tom's possession and the fact that Tom claims a lease from someone other than Owen. These suspicious circumstances would create an obligation to investigate further and would probably lead to discovery of Ann's interest in the property. If the recording act referred to actual notice, Bob might prevail, since a court could hold that he had no such actual notice and the language of the statute created no duty to look.

3. When the Possession Is Not Suspicious

Possession gives a duty to inquire only when it is suspicious. If possession is perfectly consistent with record title, it is not suspicious, and there is no duty to inquire.

Illustration: Owen conveyed the property to Ann for life, remainder to Bob. Ann took possession, and recorded her deed. Bob conveyed his remainder interest to Ann, but this deed was not recorded. Later Bob conveyed his interest to Carol. Carol should prevail over Ann as to Bob's remainder interest. Although Ann was in possession, the records indicated that she held a life estate in the property and her possession therefore was entirely consistent with the records and was not suspicious. Consequently Carol had no duty to inquire of Ann regarding her rights. Carol has a remainder after Ann's life estate.

a. Landlord–Tenant Exception

Because it is so common for tenants to have rights above and beyond those mentioned in their original leases, many courts require that a purchaser inquire of the tenants despite the fact that their possession is consistent with the record title.

Illustration: Owen leased property to Tom by a five year lease which was recorded. Later Owen and Tom executed another agreement giving Tom an option to purchase the property, which was not recorded. Owen then conveyed the property to Bob who searched the records and saw Tom's lease but did not talk to Tom. Bob may be charged with notice of Tom's option, under the rule that a tenant must be asked as to his rights even though his possession is consistent with the records. Thus Bob must sell if Tom elects to exercise the option to purchase.

C. NOTICE BASED ON NEIGHBORHOOD CONDITIONS

Recall that in the section on deeds out, it was said that a purchaser may be required to check deeds to other properties conveyed by the same grantor to see whether those deeds included restrictions on the parcels retained by the grantor now being conveyed to this grantee. Recall also that in the chapter on covenants running with the land, a court may find that a restriction is implied against the grantor's retained land as an implied reciprocal restriction contained in a deed out to some other parcel. A court may hold that the purchaser of this lot has constructive notice of such restrictions because of a duty to read those deeds out and to appreciate that reciprocal restrictions may be implied, or alternatively hold that a purchaser who sees uniform building restrictions in the neighborhood is charged with a duty to inquire as to whether such restrictions also apply to the lot being purchased, either directly or reciprocally.

D. HARMLESS NOTICE

The fact that a party or predecessor may be charged with notice, or even have actual knowledge, of the claims of someone else under an unrecorded instrument, does not automatically lead to victory for the nonrecording claimant.

Illustration: Owen conveyed his property to Ann who did not record. Owen conveyed the same property to Bob who did record but knew of Ann. Bob then conveyed to Carol who was without notice, paid value and recorded. Carol prevails over Ann since she is a person protected by the recording acts. Bob was not protected because of his notice of Ann, but he nevertheless acquired an apparent title which gave him the power to divest Ann by conveying to a bona fide purchaser such as Carol. Carol prevails despite Bob's knowledge.

Illustration: Owen conveyed his property to Ann who did not record. Owen then conveyed the property to Bob who was without notice of Ann, paid value and did record. Bob then conveyed the property to Carol who knew of Ann, did not pay value and did not record. Despite all of these failings, Carol still prevails over Ann. Because Bob qualified as a purchaser for value without notice who recorded first, he divested Ann of her title under any recording act. He had a legal title, which he then transferred to Carol. Carol need not qualify under any recording act because she took from a real, not an apparent owner.

VI. PERSONS PROTECTED AGAINST PREVIOUS FAILURES TO RECORD

The recording acts rarely make unrecorded deeds absolutely void. The statutes declare instead that unrecorded deeds are void as against certain classes of people. Unless a subsequent taker falls within the category of protected persons the failure to record the instrument is harmless.

A. DIFFERENT CLASS OF PERSONS PROTECTED UNDER THREE DIFFERENT TYPES OF STATUTES

1. Persons Protected in a Race State

In a race state, the only persons protected as against unrecorded deeds are those who record their own deeds immediately. If a subsequent grantee buys without notice but does not record, the statute gives no protection against an unrecorded prior grant.

2. Persons Protected in a Notice State

In a notice state, the only persons protected as against unrecorded instruments are those who purchase without notice of them.

3. Persons Protected in a Notice–Race State

In a notice-race state, the only persons protected as against unrecorded deeds are those who purchase without notice of such deeds and who also record their own deeds before such previous deeds are put on the record.

B. PURCHASERS WITHOUT NOTICE

Except for race states, the only persons protected as against prior unrecorded deeds are those who take without notice of those documents. The question of notice is covered in the next section.

C. PURCHASERS FOR VALUE

Most states, either by statute or decision, do not protect subsequent takers of property who have not paid value for their interest. Only a person who pays value can be deemed to have "relied" on the records in a meaningful way. Since the recording system has been set up to encourage and protect reliance on the records, there is no reason to protect those who have not significantly relied.

Illustration: Owen conveyed his property to Ann who did not record. Owen then conveyed the same property to Bob, who searched the records and finds no reference to Ann. Bob paid Owen $10,000 for the property. Bob prevails over Ann because he is a bona fide purchaser who has paid value. Had Bob known of Ann he would not have paid Owen the money; he paid because the records did not indicate Ann's claim. If Bob were to lose to Ann, he would suffer a $10,000 loss because of Ann's failure to record her deed, since there was no way for Bob to discover her interest. Bob must prevail in order to protect the investment he made in reliance on the records.

1. Donees

A donee, or beneficiary of a gift deed, is not a subsequent purchaser protected by the recording acts, since no value has been paid, and therefore no detrimental reliance has occurred.

Illustration: Owen conveyed his property to Ann who did not record. Owen then executed a gift deed of the same property to Bob, who was without notice of Ann and who did record. Ann prevails over Bob since Bob is not a purchaser for value. He had not given up any money or things of value in reliance upon the records and therefore will not be injured if the property is not awarded to him.

Illustration: Owen executed a gift deed of his property to Ann who did not record. Owen then executed another gift deed of the same property to Bob who is without notice of Ann and who did record. Ann still prevails over Bob because Bob has not paid value. Ann's unrecorded deed is void only against subsequent takers for value, and Bob does not qualify. (Ann is not required to have paid value, since Owen had a title to convey to her. It is not a question of who has the better equities as between Ann and Bob, but rather whether Ann's legal title is to be divested by one who has not qualified under the recording act.)

Illustration: Owen conveyed his property to Ann who did not record. Owen died leaving Bob as his heir. Bob then conveyed the property to Carl who paid value, was without notice of Ann and recorded. Carl prevails over Ann. Ann's failure to record left Owen an apparent title and, therefore, the power to divest her by conveying to a bona fide purchaser. When Owen died, there was no title to descend to Bob, nor did Bob qualify as a bona fide purchaser (not having paid value), but the power to divest Ann did pass to him since he now appeared on the records as the apparent owner. His conveyance to a bona fide purchaser, Carl, is protected by the recording acts.

2. Cancellation of a Prior Debt

The cancellation of a prior debt in return for a conveyance is often regarded as the payment of value. A creditor who accepts a deed in satisfaction of the obligation is regarded as a purchaser for value in some jurisdictions but not in others.

3. Payment of Less Than Full Consideration

The courts do not require that the subsequent purchaser pay full consideration, so long as some amount in excess of a nominal consideration is actually paid. The amount appropriate varies from state to state.

4. Promise to Pay

Where the promise to pay can be cancelled, a court generally does not treat the promissor as having paid value. But if the promise cannot be cancelled, then its maker will be treated as having paid the amount promised.

Illustration: Owen conveyed his property to Ann who did not record. Owen then conveyed the same property to Bob in return for Bob's promissory note for $10,000 (the full price of the land). Before Bob has paid any part of the note

Ann appears and asserts her claim. If the note is made payable to Owen and Owen still has it, Ann should prevail, since Bob will have the defense of failure of consideration on the note if he does not get the land, (especially if the deed contains covenants of title. See Chapter 9, p. 298). If, however, the note is negotiable and has been negotiated to a holder in due course (who takes free from the defense of failure of consideration) then the note cannot be cancelled and Bob will have to pay it. So he should prevail over Ann.

5. Payment of Part of the Price—Alternative Solutions

When a part of the price has been paid prior to the discovery of an unrecorded prior deed, then the payor should be given protection according to the amount paid and other circumstances. This can be done by either (a) dividing the land, if possible, or (b) giving the subsequent purchaser the entire property with the balance of the price going to the prior unrecorded grantee, or (c) giving the prior grantee the property and giving the subsequent purchaser a lien on it for the amount actually paid. The result should generally depend upon the circumstances, as illustrated below.

Illustration: Partition. Owen conveyed two acres of vacant land to Ann who did not record. Owen then conveyed the same two acres to Bob for a price of $10,000. After Bob had paid $5000 of the price Ann appeared. A possible remedy in this case would be to give Bob one acre and to give Ann the other. By giving Bob one acre and excusing him from further payment he receives all of the protection he needs (if each lot has the same value).

Illustration: Title to the Subsequent Purchaser. Owen conveyed his one-family house to Ann who did not record. Owen then conveyed the house to Bob for a price of $10,000.

Bob paid $7,000, took possession and made improvements before Ann appeared. Under these circumstances an appropriate remedy would be for Bob to be given title to the entire house (and not just 7/10ths of it) but to require the balance of the price to be paid to Ann rather than to Owen.

Illustration: Title to Prior Purchaser. Owen conveyed his property to Ann who did not record. Owen then conveyed the same property to Bob for a price of $10,000. Bob had not taken possession nor made any improvements when Ann appeared, and had paid only $1000 on the price at that time. An appropriate remedy under these circumstances would be to hold that Ann has title to the entire property but must pay back Bob his $1000.

The result may also depend on whether a deed has yet been delivered to the purchaser. In a few jurisdictions, payments made by a purchaser under a contract for the sale of the property are not protected because title has not yet passed; this poses serious problems to purchasers under long term installment contracts who are obliged to pay the price over ten or twenty years before receiving deeds.

D. ENCUMBRANCERS

Persons who take encumbrances on property for value are generally protected by the recording acts. A mortgagee who loans money and takes a mortgage to secure the debt in reliance upon the records is entitled to have that reliance protected.

Illustration: Owen conveyed his property to Ann who did not record. Owen then borrowed $10,000 from Bob giving Bob a note and mortgage on the same property to secure the debt. Bob's mortgage should be protected as against

Ann's unrecorded deed, i.e. Bob should be held to have a mortgage upon Ann's land. (Bob does not contend that he owns the property, since he took only a mortgage, not a deed. Ann's contention is that she owns the property free and clear of the mortgage since it was not Owen's to mortgage.) Bob's loan was made in reliance on the records and Bob therefore should be protected to the extent of his reliance.

1. Where the Encumbrance Is Not Taken in Reliance on the Records

Where a creditor loans money and takes back an unsecured promissory note, there is no reliance on the land records at that time since the creditor does not seek the property as security. If, later, the creditor requests that the debtor secure the existing note with a mortgage there is no reliance on the records at this time either since the money has already been advanced. Therefore there is never any reliance upon the records, and the subsequently secured creditor is not protected against prior unrecorded deeds.

Illustration: Owen conveyed his property to Ann who did not record. Owen then borrowed $10,000 from Bob and gave him an unsecured promissory note. Later Bob requested that Owen secure the note with a mortgage on the property and Owen did so. Then Ann appeared. Ann should prevail, i.e. her property will not be subject to Bob's mortgage because Bob did not give value in reliance on the records. He was not relying on the records when he loaned the money, for he sought no land as security. And when he did seek the land as security he was not giving up any new value, since he had already loaned the money.

Illustration: Owen conveyed his property to Ann who did not record. Owen then borrowed $10,000 from Bob and gave him an unsecured promissory note. The note fell due, and Bob agreed to extend it only if Owen secured it by a mortgage on the property, which Owen did. Many states will now hold for Bob, since value was given for the mortgage, i.e. the extension of time. (Bob gave up his right to collect immediately). Ann owns the property, but it is subject to Bob's mortgage.

E. CREDITORS

1. General (Unsecured) Creditors

Unsecured general creditors are not protected as against prior unrecorded conveyance. This is because these persons have not given value in reliance on the records.

Illustration: Owen conveyed his property to Ann who did not record. Owen then borrowed money from Bob and gave him a promissory note. Bob can claim no interest in the property as against Ann, since he did not make the loan in reliance on the records. (However, it should be added that even without Ann, Bob's unsecured note gives him no interest in the property. That is what is meant by "unsecured").

2. Judgment and Attachment Creditors

Most states provide that a creditor who obtains a judgment may have it recorded, whereupon it will become a lien on all real property owned by the judgment debtor. If the creditor has attached any property prior to judgment, the judgment lien will relate back to the date of the attachment (and prior to the judgment the attachment will create an attachment lien on the property). In most states such lien creditors are not protected by the recording acts, because they have not obtained their liens in reliance on the records.

Illustration: Owen conveyed his property to Ann who did not record. Bob then obtained a judgment against Owen based on nonpayment of an unsecured promissory note and recorded the judgment so as to make it a lien on Owen's property. As between Bob and Ann, Ann will prevail, i.e. her property is not subject to the lien of Bob's judgment. At no time did Bob pay value in reliance on the records. He did not so rely when he originally loaned Owen the money, since he took an unsecured note. Nor did he so rely when he sued Owen or obtained his judgment. And when he obtained his lien through recording the judgment, he gave no new value in reliance on the records. Thus Bob does not qualify for the protection of the recording acts.

3. Execution Purchasers

Although most states do not protect the judgment creditor, if that creditor thereafter obtains execution on the judgment and has the property sold to satisfy the judgment, the person who purchases it may be a purchaser for value within the meaning of the recording acts.

Illustration: Owen conveyed his property to Ann who did not record. Bob then obtained a judgment against Owen, levied execution on the property and conducted an execution sale of it to Carol for $10,000. Carol will prevail over Ann since she paid value in reliance on the records. It is true that Bob obtained no lien on property and had no property on which technically he could execute. But nevertheless he had the apparent right to do so, and could transfer a good title to a bona fide purchaser for value in the same way as Owen could transfer a good title to such a person despite his earlier conveyance to Ann.

Courts are divided as to whether a judgment creditor becomes a purchaser for value when he bids in his judgment at his own execution sale. Some hold that there is no new value being given and thus do not protect him. But others hold that the creditor thereby gives up the judgment in return for the property, which is regarded as paying value. A further reason for protecting such a creditor is that otherwise the most likely candidate for bidding at the execution sale will be virtually excluded.

VII. LIMITATIONS OF THE RECORDING SYSTEM

Not all interests in land derive from written instruments, and not all written instruments affecting interests in land are recordable. The sanctions for nonrecordation apply only to interests arising from written instruments and to the failure to record instruments which by statute are entitled to be recorded.

A. INTERESTS NOT ARISING OUT OF WRITTEN INSTRUMENTS

1. Adverse Possession and Prescriptive Easements

Adverse possession and prescriptive easements give an original rather than a derivative title and are not therefore referable to any writing. Consequently there is no requirement that the holder of such an interest record any document and there is no sanction for nonrecordation.

Illustration: Paul possessed Owen's land for 25 years, satisfying all of the elements of adverse possession. Owen then conveyed the property to Ann, who searched title and found no record of Paul (and did not see Paul in possession). In a contest between Paul and Ann, Paul prevails since he did not claim a derivative title under any recordable document and therefore is not penalized for failure to record.

Illustration: Dita adversely walked across Owen's land for 25 years, acquiring thereby a prescriptive easement of right of way. Owen then conveyed the property to Bess, who searched title and found no record of Dita's easement. Bess' title will be held subject to Dita's easement, since her interest was not one which was created by a recordable instrument.

2. Easements by Necessity

An easement of necessity is created out of the public policy that parcels should not be landlocked. Typically it arises when a large parcel is subdivided leaving the inner portions without access. See Chapter 5, p. 185. The courts are divided as to whether a subsequent purchaser without notice takes free of or subject to the easement.

Illustration: Dita conveyed away all of her property to Steve except for one landlocked parcel which she retained under circumstances which entitle her to claim an easement of necessity against Steve. Steve conveyed his property to Ann who searched his title and found no record of an easement in favor of Dita. In some jurisdictions Dita will be held to have an easement over Ann's property on the ground that her easement was not one created by a recordable document. But other courts will rule in favor of

Ann, saying that Ann should not be penalized for Dita's negligent manner of conveying her property.

3. Easements by Implication

Easements are created by implication when a parcel of land is subdivided under circumstances which permit a court to infer that one of the subdivided parcels was intended to be burdened for the benefit of the other even though no easement was created by any express language in the deed. See Chapter 5, p. 178. The courts are divided as to whether a subsequent purchaser of the servient parcel who is without notice takes free of or subject to the easement.

Illustration: Dita owned two houses which shared a common sewer line running from the rear yard over the front yard to a public sewer. She conveyed by the front house to Steve under circumstances which would lead a court to imply an easement reserved in her favor. Later Steve conveyed his house to Ann who found no record of the easement in the records (and saw no physical evidence of the pipe on the land). In some jurisdictions Ann will be held to hold her property free of the easement because she took without notice of it, but in others it will be held that Dita still has an easement since it was not a recordable interest in land.

B. INTERESTS ARISING OUT OF NON-RECORDABLE OR EXCEPTED INSTRUMENTS

Recording statutes may provide that certain documents need not be recorded in order to protect those persons in whom an interest in property is thereby created. This is commonly the case for short-term leases. And in many states court decisions have held that certain documents affecting title to property are non-recordable, e.g. executory sales contracts. The failure to record such a document therefore does not penalize the persons taking under it.

Illustration: Massachusetts has a notice act which applies to deeds of fee simple, fee tail or life estate, and to leases of more than 7 years. In Massachusetts, Owen leases his property to Tom for 5 years by a written lease which was not recorded. Owen then conveyed the property to Ann, who made a title search and found no record of Tom (and also did not see Tom in possession of the property). Ann still takes subject to Tom's lease, since Tom has an interest which was not required to be recorded and therefore is not penalized for not having recorded.

Illustration: Owen agreed to sell his property to Ann under a written contract of sale. Under the laws of the state, such a contract is not a recordable document. Owen then conveyed the same property to Bob, who searched title, etc. Bob should take subject to Ann's contract, since Ann cannot be penalized for not recording what was non-recordable. (However, it is also possible to argue that nonrecordable documents do not come under the recording acts at all, leaving the common law to control such situations. As a result Ann would lose since her prior equity is defeated by a subsequent bona fide purchaser of the legal title).

CHAPTER ELEVEN

TITLE INSURANCE

I. SEARCHING TITLE

A prudent purchaser of land (Pearl in the illustration in this chapter) will have her vendor's (Van) title searched prior to the settlement or closing of escrow in order to ascertain that it is marketable. The search is commonly made by an attorney or professional abstractor who then guarantees the accuracy of the search. Thereafter, if a title defect is discovered, the purchaser will be able to recover on this guarantee of good title given by the searcher (referred to hereafter and in the illustrations as a title company).

A title insurance policy cannot eliminate existing defects in a title. If a title company searches a title and discovers a defect, it can only write its policy of title insurance so as to show that defect as an exception to coverage. (While this listing of found defects is made for the title company's protection, some courts impose an affirmative obligation of the company to disclose them to the insured.) What is insured is the accuracy of the search, not the perfection of the title. A title policy guarantees to its owner that the title company has found no defects in title other than those it has disclosed.

Illustration: In searching the title of Van's property for Pearl, the title company discovers that it is subject to a recorded easement. Unless something is done to eliminate that easement, the title company will only issue a policy of title insurance to Pearl showing that her title is subject to the easement. But the policy will guarantee that there are no other defects on the title besides this easement (if no others were discovered). The company will not thereafter incur any liability because of the easement, but if it later turns out that the title was also subject to a previously recorded mortgage (not shown in the title policy), the title company will be liable for that.

Illustration: In searching Van's title on behalf of Pearl's bank, which intends to make a mortgage loan to her, the title company discovers an existing recorded mortgage. Thereafter, it can offer to insure the bank's mortgage only as a "second" mortgage, inferior to the existing mortgage. But it can insure that the bank's mortgage will not be a "third" i.e., subject to any other mortgage, if the search reveals that there is no other mortgage of record. See Chapter 12, p. 370.

II. PRELIMINARY TITLE REPORTS AND TITLE INSURANCE

Prior to the closing of escrow, a purchaser will often obtain a preliminary title report from the title company showing the then current condition of the vendor's title. If it is satisfactory, escrow is closed and the purchaser receives a title insurance policy from the same company guaranteeing that the title described in the preliminary report now vests in her. If there are defects in the vendor's title, the purchaser may either accept them or arrange to have them eliminated prior to settlement. She may also agree to subject the title to new encumbrances.

Illustration: Pearl's preliminary title report shows that Van has a marketable title to his property. Under the circumstances she will close escrow and receive a policy of title insurance showing that the same marketable title is now vested in her. This is usually accomplished by Pearl instructing the escrow agent to close the escrow when it is able to issue such a policy to her, and a last-minute search of the records then being made by the title company. It is common for the same company to both close the escrow and issue the title policy in such a situation.

Illustration: Pearl's preliminary title report shows that Van's title is subject to a recorded height limitation, which is common to the neighborhood and acceptable to Pearl. Under the circumstances, she will instruct the escrow agent that she will accept a title policy showing title vested in her subject to that restriction.

Illustration: Pearl's preliminary title report shows that Van's title is subject to a mortgage, which is not acceptable to Pearl. Under the circumstances she will instruct her escrow agent to close escrow only when a title policy can be issued that does not list the mortgage as an exception. The escrow agent can accomplish this by diverting a part of Pearl's purchase price from Van to his mortgagee to pay off the mortgage (so long as Van agrees), thereby eliminating the mortgage from the title and the title policy.

Illustration: The preliminary title report shows Van's title to be clear, but Pearl is borrowing part of the purchase price from a bank and has promised to give it a mortgage as security. Under the circumstances Pearl will instruct the escrow agent to obtain a title policy showing title vested in her subject to the bank's mortgage, and the bank will issue escrow instructions stating that its loan funds may be disbursed only when a title policy is issued to it showing that it has a valid first mortgage on the property.

III. TITLE RISKS

A. COVERED RISKS

Many title insurance policies not only guarantee the accuracy of the record search but also insure against certain "off record" risks of nondelivery, forgery and incompetence.

Illustration: The chain of title for property was A to B, B to Van, Van to Pearl. All of these deeds were recorded. However, the deed from A to B had never been delivered (or A's signature was forged or A was incompetent to execute a deed at the time). Because of this fact, B never acquired a title to the property nor, therefore, did Van or Pearl. If Pearl's policy insures that she has title, the title company must indemnify her for any loss despite the fact that there was nothing in the records to reveal this problem. In such a case, her title policy does perform a true insurance function.

B. EXCLUDED RISKS

Many risks inherent in the recording system are generally excluded from coverage by title policies. These exclusions or exceptions are by and large a direct response to the cases where the recording system does not protect a purchaser despite her diligent search of the records.

1. Grantee's Knowledge of Failure to Pay Value

Most policies exclude title defects which are unrecorded but known to the purchaser or which will succeed against a purchaser who has not paid value. Since the recording system protects only the bona fide purchaser for value and without knowledge, a title company declines to take the risk of an unrecorded interest prevailing because of the purchaser's failure to qualify for such protection.

Illustration: Prior to conveying the property to Pearl, Van gave a mortgage to Walt which was not recorded. Even though it is not recorded, Pearl will take subject to the mortgage if she either actually knew of it or did not pay value for the deed from Van. Since there is no way for the title company to find out about this mortgage, because it is not recorded, it cannot afford to insure Pearl against it, and therefore effectively excludes it from coverage.

2. Defects Discoverable by Investigation Outside the Records

Title policies also generally exclude from coverage risks which can be ascertained only from a physical inspection of the premises, e.g., questions involving boundaries, surveys, adverse possession, mechanics liens or rights claimed by persons in possession. The title company usually limits its coverage to those risks which it can ascertain from a search of the official records, and requires the purchaser to handle external considerations. (Since these risks are not completely unascertainable, additional coverage against them may frequently be purchased from the title company by paying a higher premium.) The title company's primary skill is in searching the official records and it generally seeks to limit its exposure to matters discoverable from such searches. Furthermore, since the purchaser of property has usually inspected it personally, such exclusion reduces the cost of the policy by eliminating an unimportant risk. Where coverage against such matters is desired, it can be purchased (in the form of an endorsement), in which case the company will physically inspect the premises. Since mechanics liens relate back in time to when a work or improvement was first commenced, the title company will look for signs of construction, etc. to determine whether there may be any such liens which may later be filed and still take priority over the insured's interest.

Ownership of property is now everywhere subject to innumerable governmental restrictions, such as zoning, subdivision, environmental and eminent domain ordinances and regulations. Such laws are not entered into the official records (which are organized on a name, rather than a neighborhood basis), and therefore will not be found by a conventional record search. While most of these restrictions do not make title legally unmarketable, title insurance companies prefer to avoid disputes with their insureds by specifically excluding them. A person interested in such matters must generally go to all of the relevant agencies to find out about such restrictions.

3. Subsequent Defects

A title policy excludes defects arising subsequent to its issuance, since its search is only of past records and it cannot know or control what will happen to the title in the future. (In that sense it is quite different from most other forms of insurance.) Because of this limited coverage, there is only a one-time premium rather than an ongoing obligation to pay for continued coverage.

IV. RELIEF UNDER THE POLICY

A. TITLE COMPANY OPTIONS

A title insurance policy usually gives the title company the option of paying the purchaser for the loss resulting from the defect (up to the policy limit) or acquiring or resisting the adverse claim. The policy usually also provides that the company will be subrogated to any rights the purchaser has against third persons because of the title defect.

Illustration: After issuing its policy insuring Pearl that her title is clear, it is discovered that a neighbor claims an easement across her property. The title company may: 1) compensate Pearl for the loss of value of her property due to the easement; 2) purchase the easement from the neighbor, so as to make Pearl's title conform to what was stated in her policy, or 3) contest the validity of the neighbor's claim. If Pearl holds a warranty deed from Van, the title company may seek to recover from Van as subrogee to Pearl's rights under her title covenants.

B. DURATION OF COVERAGE

The protection of a title policy usually lasts only for so long as the insured purchaser owns the property. It does not run with the land to protect the next purchaser, who is therefore required to purchase his or her own title policy. The original purchaser's protection usually ends when she disposes of the land, but if she retains some interest or need thereafter, the coverage will continue.

Illustration: Pearl sold her property to Quentin, taking back a mortgage on it to secure part of the price. It turns out that Pearl never owned the property contrary to what her title policy said. This fact has made her mortgage worthless, and she may recover from her title company even though she no longer owns the property. If Pearl gave Quentin a deed with title covenants and faces liability to Quentin based on those covenants her title policy may protect her in that regard as well.

CHAPTER TWELVE

MORTGAGES *

I. THE SIGNIFICANCE OF A MORTGAGE

A. SECURED AND UNSECURED DEBTS

Most debts are unsecured, i.e., nothing backs them up besides the debtor's promise to pay. (A promissory note, without more, creates only an unsecured debt; it is merely written evidence of the debtor's unsecured promise to repay an obligation.) It is also possible for an obligation to be secured; the debtor may, in addition to promising to pay the debt, also promise that if he does not pay, the creditor may satisfy the debt out of some designated assets (the "security") owned by the debtor. An instrument containing the debtor's promise that the creditor may look to real property as security in case of default is commonly called a mortgage; in such cases the debtor is referred to as the mortgagor (Mort in the illustrations), and the creditor as the mortgagee (Marie).

Illustration : Mort borrowed $50,000 from Marie and signed two documents. One, the note, said (in essence): "I promise to pay you $50,000 by (date)" The other, the mortgage, said (in essence): "If I do not pay you back the

* This topic is included under Conveyancing since most mortgages are executed in conjunction with the purchase of land.

$50,000 then you may have (or sell) my house in order to
satisfy the debt."

B. THE ADVANTAGE OF HOLDING
A MORTGAGE

Unsecured creditors must always take judicial action in order to recover when they are not paid. If
successful, they obtain money judgments, which are
not money but merely judicial declarations that the
debtor owes the creditor. If the debtor fails to pay
the judgment, the creditor must go further and have
the sheriff seize and sell either the judgment debtor's
property (execution) or any debts owed to the debtor
(garnishment) and then use the proceeds to satisfy
the judgment. By taking security, the mortgagee
avoids the risk of there being no assets available to
satisfy the judgment. At the outset of the transaction, real property is pledged (hypothecated) as security in case the mortgagor defaults.

C. THE PECULIARITIES OF
MORTGAGE LAW

When a chattel is employed as security, a loan
transaction may be quite simple: the chattel is given
in pledge to the creditor and returned if the debt is
paid or kept if it is not paid. The paperwork is often
short and uncomplicated. When real property is
used as security, however, the parties must comply
with the rules of conveyancing and estates in land.
When the law of future interests was more strictly

applied, extreme care was required. A simple debtor's promise to convey his home or his house to his creditor if he failed to pay his debt would probably be treated as an attempt to create an illegal springing interest, and therefore be void.

1. The Fee Simple Subject to Condition Subsequent

The device which ultimately came to be employed was the fee simple subject to condition subsequent, the condition being the unusual one of payment (rather than nonpayment) of the debt. The mortgagor executed an immediate conveyance of his property to the mortgagee, but subject to the condition that if he repaid the debt on time then he could reenter and terminate the mortgagee's estate (or sometimes made a conveyance of a fee simple absolute with a covenant by the mortgagee to reconvey upon payment of the debt). This arrangement gave the creditor title for the life of the loan, so that the debtor could not dispose of and thereby impair the creditor's security. Furthermore, if the debtor failed to pay, the creditor's title automatically enlarged into a fee simple absolute without the need for any judicial action. See Chapter 2, p. 36.

2. The Equity of Redemption

The fee simple subject to condition subsequent gave the debtor no right to pay late. Once "law day" passed, the creditor had a fee simple absolute and the debtor had no legal remedy to compel his creditor to accept late payment. But equity courts gave the delinquent debtor the right to obtain a decree permitting him to pay late and thereby "redeem" himself from his default (his *equity of redemption*). Such an arrangement was regarded as fair to the creditor, who received interest for the delay, and necessary to avoid a forfeiture by the debtor when the value of the security exceeded his debt.

3. Foreclosure

Once creditors knew that their debtors would be entitled to pay their debts late, they needed to know how long that privilege would last, and were forced to bring suit in equity courts to impose time limits on this right. Upon petition by a creditor (brought after the debtor was already in default), the chancellor would issue a decree providing * * * that if the debtor did not redeem within a certain period of time, he would be thereafter "foreclosed" from being able to do so.

Early foreclosure decrees merely had the effect of making the mortgagee's title irredeemable if the debtor did not redeem in time. Later these decrees came to be known as strict foreclosure. Although the extra time did help the debtor somewhat, there would still be a forfeiture to him if the value of the property exceeded the amount of his debt. In order to avoid such an unjust enrichment of the creditor, courts of equity then began to decree that after the time for redemption had passed there would be a public sale of the property, from which the creditor would receive only that part of the proceeds necessary to retire her debt (plus interest, etc.) and the surplus paid to the debtor. The creditor is thereby made whole and the debtor's "equity" in the property is saved to him.

Today, many states permit creditors to conduct foreclosure sales without first filing judicial foreclosure actions. These sales, known as nonjudicial foreclosure sales, private sales, sales by advertisement, etc., generally require enabling language in the loan documents (a "power of sale" clause). The sales are usually subject to significant state regulation, such as mandatory waiting periods (during which time the debtor may pay the arrearages and thereby cure the default and reinstate his loan) and notice and publicity requirements.

4. Mortgagor Protection Rules

a. *Deficiency Rules*

If a foreclosure sale fails to produce sufficient funds to satisfy the debt, the mortgagee may seek to have a deficiency judgment entered against the mortgagor for the balance due under the promissory note, or may bring an independent action on that note. There is a risk that the mortgagee will underbid at the sale in order to obtain the property cheaply and then seek to hold the mortgagor for a large deficiency. To avoid this, some jurisdictions require a presale or postsale hearing on the value of the security sold, and limit any deficiency judgment to the difference between the debt and this value, regardless of the fact that the property may have been sold at foreclosure for considerably less. Other jurisdictions force the mortgagee into some form of election of remedies, limiting her to either recovery of the property or judgment for the debt, but not both. Some states accord a further right of redemption to the mortgagor after the sale (based upon the amount bid rather than the amount formerly due) as a deterrent to underbidding, a process generally referred to as statutory redemption (to be distinguished from the equity of redemption). Statutory redemption is the right to pay to the foreclosure purchaser, after the sale, the amount s/he paid for the property at the sale. Equity of redemption is the right to pay the creditor the amount of the debt before the sale. Other states entirely prohibit deficiency judgments in those sales which are not subject to statutory redemption, or for certain kinds of property (such as single family residences or family farms). Special protection against deficiency judgments is commonly extended to a purchase-money mortgagor who borrowed funds in order to acquire the property.

b. Waiver Prohibitions

Another set of doctrines has been developed to prohibit the mortgagee from compelling the mortgagor to waive the protections which courts or statutes have given to him. These debtor rights arose independent of, and in spite of the mortgage contract to begin with, and it is assumed that any necessitous borrower would be automatically compelled to waive every form of protection were that permitted. Almost all of these rules are, therefore, held to be nonwaivable.

5. Nondiscrimination in Lending

Federal and state statutes generally prohibit lenders from discriminating against borrowers because of their race, color, national origin, religion, sex, age, handicap, or marital status. Lenders are also prohibited from "redlining", i.e., refusing to make loans within a demarcated neighborhood. They may be required to invest some of their loan funds in poorer neighborhoods where their branch offices receive savings deposits from the residents.

D. TITLE OR LIEN

The common law mortgage gave the mortgagee title; the mortgagee had, even prior to default, a fee simple subject to condition subsequent. Many jurisdictions now hold, however, that a mortgage gives only a lien upon the mortgaged property; i.e., a right to resort to the property upon default. Title remains in the mortgagor until divested by foreclosure sale.

II. MORTGAGE INSTRUMENTS

It is rare today to see a mortgage actually written as a fee simple subject to condition subsequent. Generally the instrument merely recites that the mortgagor "mortgages" the property to the mortgagee. In some jurisdictions a deed of trust is utilized instead, wherein the debtor (trustor) conveys the property to a third person (trustee) "in trust" for the benefit of the creditor (beneficiary), with instructions to reconvey on payment or sell on default.

In many cases it may not be clear whether the document is or is not a mortgage instrument. Courts generally hold that an instrument is a mortgage if it was intended to serve a mortgage function (i.e., secure an obligation) but this may not always be plain.

Illustration: Deed absolute: In return for $50,000, Mort gave Marie a deed to his property and received from her an option to repurchase the property one year later for $55,000. A court could decide that this was in fact a loan of $50,000 at 10% interest, even though no promissory note was ever executed. If the property was worth $100,000, such a result is especially likely. If it is determined to constitute a mortgage transaction, Mort may be able to recover the property even after the technical expiration of the option.

Illustration: Sale and Leaseback: In return for $50,000, Mort gave Marie a deed to his property, and received from her a 20 year lease to the property at a rent of $5,000 per year. This could be treated as a mortgage, with rent substituting for interest. If the arrangement included an option to repurchase 20 years later at an unrealistically low price, this is all the more likely. If the transaction is determined to constitute a mortgage transaction, Marie may be unable to evict Mort by the normal summary dispossession mechanisms available to a landlord if he fails to make a periodic payment.

III. POSSESSION AND RENTS

A common law fee simple subject to condition subsequent gave the mortgagee a present possessory estate; today, however, most mortgages permit the mortgagor to retain possession. The mortgagor's right to possession survives until a foreclosure sale has occurred, at which time the foreclosure purchaser may go into possession. It is possible for the mortgagor to put the mortgagee into possession immediately, in which case the mortgagee will be required to apply any profits from the land towards reduction of the mortgage debt. The mortgage may also contain a stipulation entitling the mortgagee to possession immediately upon default and before the foreclosure sale has occurred, but the mortgagee may nevertheless be required to perfect this right through court appointment of a receiver. In those states which give the mortgagor a right of post-sale redemption, possession after the foreclosure sale may be postponed until the redemption period has expired.

It is common for the mortgage to recite that the rents and profits from the mortgaged property are assigned to the mortgagee but that the mortgagor can collect them for his own account so long as he remains current on his obligation. A mortgagee may then, once there is a default, commence proceedings to have a receiver appointed to collect the rents and employ them to pay off senior liens, or to cover any deficiency judgment which may later be obtained.

IV. PRIORITIES

Mortgages are subject to the same principles of priority as apply to other interests in real property. They are recordable instruments and therefore are generally subject to the record system. A mortgage which is recorded prior to another mortgage is referred to as a senior or first mortgage. Sometimes a special priority status is given to a purchase money mortgage.

Priority controls the disposition of the foreclosure sale proceeds and also the title acquired by the foreclosure purchaser. When a senior mortgage is foreclosed, the property is sold free and clear of both the senior and junior mortgage, and the junior mortgagee receives only so much of the proceeds as are surplus after the senior is paid. However when a junior mortgage is foreclosed the property is sold subject to the senior mortgage, and none of the foreclosure sale proceeds go to the senior.

Illustration: Senior Foreclosure: Mort's property is subject to a bank's first mortgage of $50,000 and Marie's second mortgage of $10,000; his property has a fair market value of $55,000. If the bank forecloses, it will offer for sale a title free of both mortgages, and thus a bid $55,000 should be expected. In that case $50,000 will be given to the bank; the remaining $5,000 will be given to Marie (and she will have a right to collect her deficiency of $5,000 from Mort). If, on the other hand, the bid were $65,000, it would be allocated: 1) $50,000 to the bank; 2) $10,000 to Marie; 3) $5,000 to Mort (the surplus).

Illustration: Junior Foreclosure: The same facts as above, but Marie, instead of the bank, forecloses. Since she can only convey a title subject to the bank's mortgage, the bid may be only $5,000 if the property has a market value of $55,000 and is subject to a $50,000 debt. The $5,000 received from the sale will go to Marie and she may have a right to collect a deficiency from Mort ($5,000). The bank will receive none of the proceeds, since its mortgage is not affected by Marie's foreclosure. If, instead, the property were worth $65,000, there should be a bid of $15,000, of which $10,000 would go to Marie and $5,000 to Mort.

V. TRANSFERS BY THE PARTIES

A. TRANSFERS OF THE MORTGAGED PROPERTY

Regardless of whether a mortgage is viewed as a title or lien, the mortgagor may convey the mortgaged property. A complete prohibition on transfer is probably an invalid restraint upon alienation, although many mortgages contain provisions which make all future installment payments immediately due and payable in full upon a sale of the property unless the mortgagee consents to the transfer. Such "due on sale" clauses are made generally valid by the federal Garn–St. Germain Act which overrode all contrary state law in 1982.

A title subject to a mortgage remains so even when it is transferred, (so long as the mortgage has been properly recorded). If neither the original mortgagor nor the transferee pay the mortgage debt, there will be a foreclosure and the transferee will lose the land. A transferee is liable for a deficiency judgment after a foreclosure sale, however, only if the obligation has been *assumed;* i.e., if there has been a new promise that the note will be paid.

Illustration: Nonassuming transferee: Mort conveyed his house to Theresa, who did not assume the mortgage, and no one has paid Marie. Marie may foreclose and sell Theresa's house. A deficiency judgment may be obtained against Mort but not Theresa, since she never promised to pay the debt.

Illustration: Assuming transferee: The same facts as above except that Theresa did assume the debt when she took from Mort. Now Marie may sell the property and obtain a deficiency judgment against both Mort and Theresa. Mort remains liable because he signed the original note and has never been released from that obligation. Theresa is liable because of her promise to Mort to pay the debt. Marie may be regarded as being a third party beneficiary of Theresa's promise to Mort, or else as being equitably subrogated to the benefit Mort received from Theresa's promise to him to pay the debt to Marie.

B.   TRANSFERS OF THE MORTGAGE PAPER

As an obligee, the mortgagee may assign her rights to enforce the debtor/obligor's promises. Usually she does this by transferring the promissory note (which generally carries the mortgage along with it regardless of what actually happens mechanically). The transferee may take as a holder in due course, free from many contract defenses by the mortgagor, if the note was negotiable and the transfer was by way of negotiation (endorsement) rather than assignment. Problems arise in these cases when mortgagors are not notified of the transfers and thereafter make their payments to the wrong person, or when the original mortgagee sells participation interests in her loans to others and then goes bankrupt without properly completing (perfecting) her transfer of the documents to the investors. These matters are usually outside the scope of a normal Property course.

The federal government engages in "secondary market" activities, buying mortgages from banks, repackaging them into large pools of mortgaged backed securities (MBSs) and selling these collateralized mortgage obligations (CMOs) to Wall Street investors. This injects more funds into the real estate market.

PART THREE

MISCELLANEOUS PROPERTY DOCTRINES

This Part includes a variety of topics which are taught at scattered places in different Property courses (or not at all). Air, Water, and Support are sometimes covered collectively as Incidental Rights In Land or sometimes treated along with Easements. Agreed Boundaries may be covered as a part of Adverse Possession or under Deeds. Fixtures may be made a part of Landlord And Tenant or instead relegated to an advanced Mortgages or Commercial Code course. Trespass and Nuisance are often left for Torts or are treated as parts of Adverse Possession and Land Use respectively. Land Use may be a separate course and not covered at all in a basic Property course. These matters are presented here in a more or less sensible arrangement, but may readily be taken up in different order.

In this Part, except where the text indicates otherwise, the masculine pronoun refers to the owner of the property and the feminine pronoun refers to the other party encountered in the transaction.

375

CHAPTER THIRTEEN

AIRSPACE

Ownership of land generally includes ownership of the airspace above its surface. The advent of air travel has led to differences in treatment between air rights directly connected with surface uses and air rights in the upper atmosphere.

I. LOWER AIRSPACE

A landowner has the same rights and privileges regarding the lower reaches of the airspace directly over the surface of his land as he has with regard to the surface itself. Thus, he may, e.g., convey that space, lease it, permit limited uses to be made of it, and resist encroachments upon it.

Illustration: Len leases a second floor apartment in his building to Tina. Technically, this gives Tina a leasehold estate in some airspace located between ten and twenty feet over the surface of Len's land. If Tina enters any other second floor apartment without appropriate consent, she is trespassing into the airspace of those tenants.

Illustration: If Len converts his building into a condominium and conveys a second floor unit to Tina, she will have a fee simple estate in that airspace. If she mistakenly occupies the wrong unit for a long enough time, she may gain title by adverse possession to that different segment of airspace.

Illustration: Stan grants to Dita the right to string a powerline in a certain location across his property. She now has an easement in the airspace over his property. If Dita does this without Stan's consent and he fails to exercise his legal remedies within the appropriate time limits, Dita may acquire a prescriptive easement (or adverse possession) in the space occupied by the powerline. The same would also be true if Dita regularly drove golf balls over Stan's land or if the overhanging eaves on her roof intruded onto Stan's airspace for a long enough period of time.

II. UPPER AIRSPACE
A. TRESPASS

Congress has declared the upper airspace navigable and has given the public the freedom of transit there. Consequently, air flights at high altitudes over privately owned land are generally not trespassory and the rights of surface owners are subject to the public right of air travel. A surface owner retains conventional property rights in his air space only as high up as he reasonably needs. He may not be restrained from building a tall building even though it may interfere with air travel, but, on the other hand, he has no cause of action in trespass for flights above his land at heights beyond those he could ever reach through ground construction. A trespass occurs only when the flight is low enough to intrude upon actual or potential ground-based activity. Trespass is covered in chapter 18.

B. NUISANCE

A flight over land may be actionable as a nuisance if it disturbs the surface use of land by virtue of its noise, glare, danger, etc. If this theory is permitted, the flight need not be trespassory and may constitute a nuisance even if it emanates from a plane flying over adjacent land (or from a neighboring airport), rather than directly over the surface of the plaintiff's land. Nuisance is covered in Chapter 19. Damages, rather than injunctive relief, are usually awarded in such cases, except where the overflight is by a private party for cloud seeding or some other form of weather modification likely to affect the owner's land.

C. TAKING

Governmental overflights so frequent and disturbing as to render the surface valueless may amount to the taking of the owner's property, requiring that the government pay just compensation to the owner. Similarly, a governmentally operated airport (rather than the private airline companies) may also be liable for taking or damaging the property of its neighbors due to the noise of takeoffs and landings of its planes. Taking of property is covered in Chapter 20.

CHAPTER FOURTEEN

WATER

A person who owns land contiguous to a stream or lake is privileged to make certain uses, such as drinking, swimming, fishing of that water which passes over his land. But the landowner does not own the water itself; his rights and privileges are usufructuary rather than proprietary. Ownership of the water occurs only after it has been properly drawn off from the stream or lake, or if it is part of a lake or pond entirely surrounded by the land of one person. Rights of use in stream water are often referred to as *riparian* rights. Riparian rights on navigable or tidal bodies of water are subject to public and federal rights in those waterways. The public may be entitled to use such waters for swimming, fishing, boating and related recreational purposes under the public trust doctrine and may prohibit riparian activities which interfere with those uses. The federal government (under the Commerce Clause of the Constitution) has a navigational servitude in all navigable waterways of the United States and may interfere with riparian uses of water without liability in exercise of that power.

I. STREAM WATER

A parcel of land is deemed riparian when any part of it is contiguous to a stream and the balance of the parcel is owned by the same person, extends only a reasonable distance from the water, and is within the watershed. A portion of the land may thus lose its riparian character if its ownership is severed from that of the rest (and no part of the severed portion is itself contiguous to water). Conversely, in some jurisdictions, nonriparian land may become riparian when it is acquired by the adjacent riparian owner. Land adjacent to a lake is called littoral, and is subject to the same riparian rules.

A. PREFERRED PRIVILEGES OF USE

A riparian owner is privileged to use water from the stream for any purpose so long as this has no significant effect upon the quantity, quality, or velocity of the flow as it crosses lower riparian land. A riparian is also privileged to use water for domestic purposes even though this does affect downstream users.

Illustration: Ursula, an upstream landowner, draws off water from the stream to sell to others elsewhere. Her use of the water, however, has no effect on the stream as it then flows on over Don's land downstream. Even though this is a nonriparian use of the water, Don may not enjoin it.

Illustration: Ursula draws off water from the stream for drinking, bathing, irrigating her garden and watering her domestic livestock. During the dry season, these diversions mean that no water flows on down to Don's land. Nevertheless, Don cannot enjoin these domestic uses of water.

B. CORRELATIVE PRIVILEGES OF USE

Any nondomestic use of water by an upper riparian which does affect the quantity, quality, or flow of a stream is limited by the rights of the lower riparian. There are two rival doctrines regarding a lower riparian's rights:

Natural flow doctrine: A lower riparian is entitled to receive the natural flow of the stream without any significant alteration in quantity, quality or velocity. He need not show any special injury resulting from alteration of the flow.

Reasonable use doctrine: A lower riparian is entitled to receive such stream waters as he can put to beneficial use, with due regard for the correlative rights of the upstream user. He must show some injury as well as an alteration in the flow.

Illustration: Ursula diverts a significant portion of the stream for sale outside of her land. However, since Don makes no use of the stream water himself, this alteration of the flow affects none of his activities. In a natural flow jurisdiction he may enjoin Ursula's diversion. Such an injunction would not be granted to him in a reasonable use jurisdiction.

Illustration: Ursula diverts water for various commercial uses, e.g., for use in her mill or other manufacturing activity, or pollutes the stream with waste products from those uses. These activities affect the flow over Don's land and interfere with his own use of the water. If he has domestic needs for the water which are impaired, he may enjoin Ursula. If, however, he only needs the water for his commercial purposes, the ruling on an injunction may require some comparison of the social utility of the respective uses of the parties and the harm each would suffer from a deprivation of some or all of the water.

The older natural flow doctrine offers the advantages of certainty, since a lower riparian prevails merely by showing that the flow has been altered. On the other hand, it is nonutilitarian, often prohibits beneficial water uses and leads to waste of a valuable resource; it also compels a lower riparian to bring suit before he has suffered any injury in order to avoid the creation of prescriptive rights. The majority reasonable use doctrine permits litigation to be postponed until actual harm has occurred and leads to better utilization of scarce water, but it offers little certainty to the parties, and judicial decrees may require frequent modification as needs change.

C. APPROPRIATION SYSTEMS

Many western states have found the riparian system unsuited to their arid conditions and have developed a doctrine of appropriation rights as a substitute or complement to the riparian rules. In an appropriation system, the right to use water is acquired by obtaining a permit from a governmental agency, which is granted if the agency determines that the appropriator will make a beneficial use of the water sought. Priority of right to the water is controlled by the date of the permit or appropriation.

Illustration: April obtained a permit to appropriate a certain amount of water per day for her mining activities.

Subsequently, Jerry obtained a permit to use water from the same stream for his mines. If the stream level falls too low to allow both parties to take their full quotas, April will be preferred as the prior appropriator. Jerry may take his full allotment only if it does not interfere with April's rights, regardless of where their respective diversion points on the stream are located.

An appropriation permit may be granted to a non-riparian owner. Some states eliminate riparian rights entirely (the "Colorado Doctrine") so that even a riparian owner must apply for an appropriation permit in order to use the water crossing his land. Other states permit riparian and appropriation rights to coexist; (the "California Doctrine") here, a more complicated system of priority is necessary to reconcile the competing claims of various appropriators and riparians.

Illustration: Ursula acquired riparian land in 1850; April obtained a permit to appropriate water to her nonriparian land in 1860; Don acquired his riparian land in 1870 (when it came out of the public domain); Jerry obtained an appropriation permit in 1880. It is likely that Ursula's privilege to take water has the highest priority: she may divert water even though this injures all of the others, unless one of them can show that her activities are not reasonable or beneficial. April may divert water under her appropriation permit only if it does not interfere with Ursula's reasonable needs, but April may divert water even though this injures Don or Jerry. Don may divert water even though it injures Jerry but he may not do so if this would interfere with April's appropriation. (As a lower riparian, activity by Don would not affect Ursula, unless, by damming the stream, he caused the water to back up on her land). Jerry may appropriate water only if none of the other parties are injured thereby. (This assumes that the

California doctrine is in force, validating both riparian and appropriation rights. Under the Colorado doctrine, Ursula and Don would have no rights to water, having obtained no appropriation permits. The only parties entitled to water would be April and Jerry, with April, as the prior appropriator, having superior rights to Jerry.)

II. SURFACE WATER

Surface waters are those which tend to move from higher to lower ground (unlike still ponds or swamps or marshes) but which do not follow any clearly defined channel (unlike streams). These waters generally result from rain or snow; sometimes flood waters separated from the main body of the flood are similarly treated. Because such waters are generally unwanted, most litigation here concerns the right of a landowner to throw them off or to prevent them from crossing his land. In those rare situations where a landowner does seek to appropriate surface water, there is a general entitlement to do so.

There are three rival doctrines concerning disposal of surface waters:

Common enemy doctrine: A landowner may dam against surface waters, throw them back upon upper lands, or deflect them elsewhere. Only artificial discharge of large quantities of water onto the lands of others is prohibited.

Natural servitude doctrine: Lower land is servient to the natural drainage from above. Thus a lower landowner cannot obstruct or deflect such waters; nor, conversely, may the upper landowner cut channels so as to drain the water elsewhere. This rule, derived from the civil law, is often made subject to an urban exception to permit interference with the natural flow when it results from grading or construction.

Reasonable use doctrine: A landowner may drain off surface waters in connection with some reasonable use of the land as long as there is a reasonable necessity for the drainage, reasonable care has been taken to avoid unnecessary injury to others, and the benefit outweighs the harm. This more recent view claims to state directly the result that the many exceptions to the other two views have in fact produced.

Illustration: Surface waters tend naturally to flow down from Ursula's high land and over to Don's low land. Under the common enemy rule, Don would be entitled to erect a barrier to these waters so as to prevent them from leaving Ursula's land, or to cut a channel so as to have them pass onto Lowell's land below him. Under the natural servitude rule, neither activity would be so allowed. Under the reasonable use rule he may do either depending upon his need to drain his property, the care he takes to avoid unnecessary harm to Ursula or Lowell, and the benefits which accrue to him in keeping his land free of the waters versus the harm Ursula or Lowell would suffer.

III. UNDERGROUND WATER

A separate body of law regulates rights regarding diffused underground water which follows no ascertainable underground channel, and which either remains still or else percolates up to the surface. (Underground water which follows a defined channel follows the same rules as those for streams, but the presumption is that it is diffuse rather than channeled.) As with the rest of water law, there are rival views:

(a) **Absolute ownership doctrine:** A landowner has an unqualified right to pump out all of the water, even though this may deprive neighbors who overlie the same underground basin of water for their needs.

(b) **Reasonable use doctrine:** An overlying owner may pump out only so much water as may reasonably be applied to beneficial uses upon his overlying land. How much is reasonable may in part depend on whether the water used will seep back down to recharge the aquifer.

(c) **Correlative rights doctrine:** All overlying owners are to be treated as joint tenants of the underground basin, each limited to a reasonable proportion of the annual supply for beneficial use on the overlying land.

(d) **Appropriation:** The appropriation system may apply to underground water as well as stream water, permitting non-overlying owners to appropriate water from underground basins.

CHAPTER FIFTEEN

SUPPORT

An owner of land is entitled to have it remain naturally supported by the adjacent and underlying property of others. Consequently, activity by a neighbor or sub-surface owner which causes his land to subside may be actionable. Support received from neighboring land is referred to as lateral; support received from underlying land is referred to as subjacent. The rules relating to the two kinds of support are, for the most part, similar.

I. SUPPORT OF UNIMPROVED LAND

A. THE ABSOLUTE RIGHT TO SUPPORT

There is an absolute right to receive support for unimproved land, i.e., a neighbor whose activities cause an owner's unimproved land to subside will be liable even though her excavation was non-negligent and essential to the utilization of her own land. This absolute right applies only to land in its natural condition and does not exist when the land has already been weakened or improved. Liability under it arises only when there has been an actual subsidence because of removal of the surrounding land. Where subsidence is due to removal of water, the matter is treated as one of water law rather than support law.

Illustration: Nora excavated on her lot in order to build a house there. Despite her non-negligence, this caused Owen's unimproved land to subside. She is liable to him.

Illustration: The mining company has the right to remove minerals below the surface of Owen's land. Its underground tunnels have caused the surface of Owen's land to subside. The mining company is liable to Owen even though the tunnels were carefully cut.

Illustration: By virtue of excavations on Nora's land, the extent of lateral support which Owen's land receives from it has been reduced, but his surface has not subsided. Until there is some subsidence, Owen has no cause of action against Nora. Similarly, if Nora protects Owen's land from subsiding by installing artificial support as a replacement for the former natural support (e.g. a retaining wall), Owen has no cause of action against her unless she fails to maintain the retaining wall in an effective condition.

Illustration: Because Owen has discharged great amounts of water on his land, the natural cohesiveness of the soil there has been reduced. If Nora now carefully excavates on her own land, she will not be liable to Owen for any subsidence which occurs since his land is no longer in its natural condition.

B. PERSONS LIABLE

A landowner is liable only for her own acts, or the acts of her agents, which cause another's land to subside. She is not liable for acts of predecessors, successors, or strangers.

Illustration: Some years earlier, Nora's predecessor excavated on her land but Owen's land did not subside until

after Nora had acquired title. The predecessor may be
liable for damages (and Owen's cause of action did not
commence to run until the subsidence), but Nora herself is
not liable.

Illustration: Some years earlier, Nora excavated on her
land. Now, by virtue of further excavations conducted by
Nora's successor or by other neighbors, Owen's land sub-
sides. He has no cause of action against Nora since inter-
vening acts have caused the injury.

Illustration: An earthquake or flood so altered Nora's
land as to eliminate the natural support it previously
afforded to Owen's land, and his land subsided. He has no
cause of action against Nora.

II. SUPPORT OF IMPROVED LAND

A. EXTENT OF THE OBLIGATION

Land improved with buildings is subject to somewhat different rules concerning support. Many
courts hold that the absolute obligation of subjacent
support continues as before, and that a subsurface
excavator must furnish support to the surface owner's preexisting building as well as to his land. However, the removal of lateral support is actionable only
if the land would have subsided without the buildings
on it. Experts may be required to determine whether
the pressure of the improvements made the difference or whether their additional weight was offset by
the soil removed for their foundations when they
were built.

B. MEASURE OF DAMAGES

Courts are not in agreement as to the measure of damages where an actionable removal of lateral support of improved land occurs. In some jurisdictions, the owner may recover for the injuries to his land but not to his building, on the ground that a rule compelling the second improver to pay for damages to the first improver's building would give preferential treatment to the first, contrary to the policy that all owners should have equal rights to improve. In other jurisdictions, however, a removal of support makes the neighbor liable for injury to the buildings as well as to the land, on the ground that a tort has been committed and building damage is a foreseeable consequence. The measure of damages allowed in these cases may either be the cost of repairs (not exceeding the market value of the property) or the depreciation of market value, or the lesser of those two numbers.

A neighbor who excavates negligently (or maliciously) is liable for harm to land and buildings, regardless of the weight of the buildings. A court may find that an excavator acted negligently if she failed to warn the owner of her impending activities (so as to give him an opportunity to shore up his building first), or failed to shore up his building for him, or failed to make adequate preliminary soil studies. On the other hand, an owner may be guilty of contributory negligence if his building had an inadequate foundation or was built so close to the boundary as to inevitably subside when adjacent land was improved.

C. STATUTORY CHANGES

Some jurisdictions have statutory provisions which require the potential excavator to give notice to the owner of the nature of the excavation and, if she intends to excavate below a certain depth (often eight or twelve feet), shore up the owner's building, unless denied permission to do so.

III. AGREEMENTS REGARDING SUPPORT

A. RELEASE OF SUPPORT RIGHTS

An owner may release others from their duty to support his land. Such a release may be implied from the circumstances of a grant. A release of natural support rights does not include a release of liability for negligent or malicious removal of support.

B. ACQUISITION OF SUPPORT RIGHTS

An owner who realizes that his intended building will require additional support from adjoining land may obtain an easement of support from his neighbor. Such an easement may be implied when a building is sold and the supporting adjacent land is retained. No easement of support for a building arises by prescription, since the mere existence of a heavy building on a parcel of land generates no cause of action in the neighbor. See Chapter 5, p. 191.

CHAPTER SIXTEEN

AGREED BOUNDARIES

I. DIFFICULTIES IN ASCERTAINING BOUNDARIES

Although the boundary description contained in a deed may be easy to understand, it may nevertheless be difficult to convert the words of the description in the document into lines running through real space on the earth. Unless an owner employs a surveyor to mark out property lines, there may only be an approximate idea of where they are. Adjoining landowners frequently have difficulty in settling the precise location of their boundary lines.

Illustration: Owen's deed sets the northern boundary of his property as one mile north of the stream; the deed of his neighbor, Nora, describes her southern boundary as one mile north of the stream. Although on paper the two boundaries coincide, neither Owen nor Nora know precisely where one mile north of the stream is. It would require that they employ a surveyor to mark out this line with complete accuracy.

II. AGREEING ON A BOUNDARY

The doctrine of agreed or practically located boundaries permits neighbors, under certain circumstances, to fix a boundary which will thereafter operate as the legal line, even though a subsequent survey may reveal that the true line was originally somewhere else.

The doctrine will generally be held to operate only when the new boundary line results from a disagreement or uncertainty between the neighbors as to the true line. It does not apply if they were either certain or mistaken as to the old line when they established the new line.

Illustration: Certainty: Owen and Nora are both aware that the true boundary line runs ten feet north of the road between their properties. However, they find it more convenient to use the road as the boundary and they orally agree that the road will henceforth constitute their legal boundary. The agreement violates the Statute of Frauds and is therefore invalid. If they wish to change the boundary one must convey the ten foot strip to the other by a proper deed.

Illustration: Mistake: The true line between the properties runs 10 feet north of the road but both owners mistakenly believe that the road constitutes the true line. Any action they take based on this mistake will be invalid, and the parties will be relieved from the consequences of their mistake.

Illustration: Disagreement: Owen believes that the true line is ten feet north of the road and Nora believes that it is ten feet south of the road. In order to compromise their difference, they agree that the road will henceforth serve as their boundary. This agreement may be binding, even though oral, and will survive any later discovery that the true line was either north or south of the road.

Illustration: Uncertainty: Neither Owen nor Nora know where the true line is but, in order to settle the matter, they agree that the road will serve as their mutual boundary. This agreement may be binding even though oral, and will survive any later discovery that the true line was somewhere else. In some jurisdictions, the uncertainty must be justified, i.e. the parties cannot merely be too lazy to locate the real line.

III. ACQUIESCENCE

It is generally required that the parties acquiesce in the new boundary line. Frequently this is stated as the critical component of this doctrine, eliminating the need for proof of any actual prior agreement if acquiescence in the new line can be shown. Some courts require acquiescence equal to the Statute of Limitations for adverse possession, in which event this doctrine may function as an alternative theory of relief for the party possessing the disputed strip if one of the elements of adverse possession is missing from the case. Even without acquiescence or an explicit agreement, the owners may be bound by an "incorrect" line when both purchased from a common grantor who had marked it on the ground and written deeds which used lot numbers on a map rather than metes and bounds calls as descriptions.

IV. EFFECT

Once established, an agreed boundary binds not merely the parties but their successors as well, even though there may be nothing in the records to warn successors of such a change of boundary lines.

CHAPTER SEVENTEEN

FIXTURES

A fixture is some tangible object which was formerly treated as personal property but which has since become so connected with real property as to now be designated as real property even though it retains its original identity.

Illustration: A toilet seat, while sitting on the floor of a plumbing supply store, is personal property; once purchased and bolted down in a bathroom, it becomes a fixture, i.e., real property.

Illustration: Paint sitting in a can in a paint store is personal property. When opened and applied to a wall, it becomes real property. It is not a fixture, however, since it has lost the earlier separate identity it had when it was inside the can.

Illustration: A refrigerator in a kitchen is not a fixture, even though it is plugged into the wall. It remains personal property, although this could change if it were "built-in" to the kitchen.

I. FACTORS IN DETERMINING WHAT IS A FIXTURE

Courts consider a number of factors in determining whether or not to classify the item as a fixture:

1. *Method of annexation:* how firmly and securely the item is annexed to other real property.

2. *Appropriateness:* how well the item has been adapted to the adjacent real property and how appropriately it fits with that real property.

3. *Removability:* how much harm to the realty will result from removal.

4. *Intent:* what is the annexor's objective intent, as inferred from the above considerations as well as from his relationship to the real property, in particular, whether or not he owns the real property.

II. WHERE THE ANNEXOR ALSO OWNS THE REAL PROPERTY

In many situations, the person affixing personal property to real property owns both of the assets. Nevertheless, it may be important to determine whether the affixed item is real or personal property.

1. Property taxation. Since real and personal property are frequently taxed at different rates, characterization may be necessary in order to calculate the tax.

2. Eminent domain. When land is taken by eminent domain, the condemning authority may be liable to pay for real property, but not for personal property.

3. Mortgages. A real estate mortgage generally covers all of the mortgagor's originally owned or "after acquired" real property, but not personal property. On foreclosure, however, personal property assets which have become fixtures are subject to sale.

4. Conveyances. A contract for the sale of real estate obligates the vendor to convey all real property but not personal property to the purchaser. Whether this includes, e.g., the wall-to-wall carpeting or venetian blinds may depend on whether they are treated as fixtures (unless the contract explicitly covers these items).

5. Death. At common law, real property went to the heirs of an intestate while personal property went to the personal representative for his next of kin. That distinction rarely exists today, although a similar issue could arise if the decedent left a will devising his real and personal assets separately.

III. WHERE THE ANNEXOR DOES NOT OWN THE REAL PROPERTY

The person owning and annexing the personal property may not own the real property to which it is annexed. If the item is determined to have become a fixture, then title will pass from the annexor to the owner of the real property despite any actual subjective intent to the contrary.

1. Tenants. If a tenant annexes an item so as to make it a fixture, it may become the property of the landlord, and removal thereafter by the tenant would constitute waste. Nevertheless, many states permit a tenant to remove trade fixtures or expand this category to include ornamental and domestic fixtures as well. Removal, however, may be limited to cases where not too much injury to the premises will result.

2. Strangers. One who enters onto the property of another and affixes chattels there will generally lose the right to remove them, unless a betterment or innocent improver statute gives the right to remove them or to recover their reasonable value from the owner.

3. Chattel sellers. Personal property is often sold on credit under an agreement reserving title or a security interest to the seller until the price is fully paid. The agreement may be enforceable as between the parties, but if the item becomes a fixture, the rights of other parties, (e.g., the landlord where the purchaser was a tenant, or the real estate mortgagee where the purchaser was a mortgagor) may make the resolution of the issue more difficult. Section 9–313 of the Uniform Commercial Code, now widely adopted, establishes a set of priorities for many of these situations, and involves such considerations as whether any document creating the personal property security interest was filed in the real estate records, whether a construction loan was involved, and whether the goods are readily removable.

CHAPTER EIGHTEEN

TRESPASS

I. THE PROTECTION OF POSSESSION

As indicated in the chapter on Adverse Possession, a possessor of land, whether or not its owner, has certain rights by virtue of that possession. He may, subject to certain principles of reasonableness, protect his possession from intruders by erecting barriers to their entry or by physically expelling them. He also has certain judicial remedies against those who intrude. When the intrusion amounts to a dispossession, he may bring an action in ejectment (or risk becoming subject to a claim of adverse possession). When the intrusion does not amount to a dispossession, the appropriate relief is usually damages for trespass. This chapter does not attempt a complete review of the law of trespass, which is generally covered in textbooks on Torts. The emphasis here is on those features of trespass law most relevant to a Property course.

II. WHAT IS A TRESPASS

Any intentional intrusion made on property possessed by another is a trespass. Liability is absolute and independent of motive, extent, duration or harm, although these factors may affect the amount of damages. A negligent intrusion may also constitute a trespass, but only if some harm results from it. A truly nonvolitional intrusion is not a trespass at all, but mistake as to location does not make the entry nonvolitional.

Illustration: Trish is carried across Paul's land by kidnappers. Although they may be guilty of trespass, she is not, since her entry was not intentional.

Illustration: Trish, Paul's neighbor, walks on his property, believing she is still on her own land. She is a trespasser (since she intended to be where she is), even though she was mistaken as to the ownership of the property.

Illustration: Trish negligently runs her car off the road and onto Paul's land. If this does any harm to the land, she is liable for it in trespass.

A. INTRUSIONS NOT BY THE TRESPASSER

A trespass occurs when there is physical intrusion on land; it is not required that the trespasser personally be the intruder. There may be intrusion by agents of the trespasser, or by physical objects set in motion by her (such as rolling a car or firing a bullet across land).

Illustration: Trish's animals wander over Paul's land. At common law, she would be liable for their trespasses. Many states, however, have altered these rules with fencing statutes. There is also, generally, no liability for the intrusion of dogs, cats, or other such animals whose movements are difficult to control.

B. TOUCHING THE BOUNDARY

A trespass also occurs when the trespasser comes in contact with the vertical boundary lines of the possessor's property, even though that line is not crossed.

Illustration: Trish piles dirt up against the wall of Paul's house which is on his lot line, or fastens a clothes line to his wall. In either case she is trespassing.

C. ABOVE AND BELOW THE SURFACE

A trespass may occur above or below the surface since the possessory right is deemed to extend vertically in those directions from the boundary line on the surface. An underground intrusion such as a slant well is a trespass (although the depletion of migrant minerals such as water, oil, or gas from a common basin by a perpendicular well dug on neighboring land is not). An intrusion into air space, such as made by a building or wire or other permanent object is also a trespass and may lead to the acquisition of prescriptive rights of possession or use. An isolated non-permanent intrusion, such as firing a gun over land, is also a trespass, although there are special rules dealing with airplanes' overflights. On airspace, see Chapter 13.

III. PRIVILEGED ENTRIES

A. CONSENT

One who enters land with the consent of its possessor is not trespassing. The invitation makes her a licensee or invitee. The license may be oral or implied. Once it expires or is revoked, failure to leave within a reasonable time, however, will constitute a trespass.

Illustration: Trish enters a restaurant in order to dine. Her entry is not trespassory because it may be implied from the circumstances that the public is invited to enter. However, if she refuses to leave after closing time, she is guilty of trespass.

B. SOCIAL NEED

In certain situations, public policy requires a possessor to tolerate the entry of others onto his land. His right of undisturbed possession is subject to the general public interest.

Illustration: Trish (or the police) enter onto Paul's property to break up a fight or to stop a crime from being committed there. The entry is privileged.

Illustration: A building inspector or other public official enters onto the property in pursuit of an official duty. The entry is privileged (although a warrant may be required if the entry would amount to a search or seizure within the meaning of the Fourth Amendment).

Illustration: Paul's house is on fire and Trish enters in order to extinguish it before it spreads to her own property. She is privileged to do so.

C. PROPERTY RIGHTS

In certain cases a person may be entitled to enter on land of another in order to protect certain property interests. This is not a general license to wander freely but is limited to what is necessary to protect the property interest.

Illustration: Paul holds an estate subject to condition subsequent and Trish holds the power of termination over that estate. One way for Trish to exercise the power after the condition has occurred is by making the entry onto Paul's land. A peaceable entry by her in order to perfect the power is not a trespass. See Chapter 2, p. 39.

Illustration: As Paul's landlord, Trish may be permitted to enter in order to "view waste," i.e. to make sure that he is not committing waste. Such a limited entry is not trespassory. See Chapter 4, p. 135.

Title to the real property does not constitute an absolute privilege to enter on it. An owner is privileged to make a peaceable entry onto property in the possession of another but may not use force to do so. In most jurisdictions, civil as well as criminal liability attaches to any forcible entry.

Illustration: Because Paul was in arrears on his rent, his landlord Trish broke open the door to his apartment while he was away and removed his belongings. Although she is entitled to have him evicted, she may not commit this forcible entry and trespass.

Illustration: In a dispute between Trish and Paul over the location of their boundary line, Trish demolished the fence which Paul has erected and stepped over it. Trish is guilty of trespass (and forcible entry), even though a survey may ultimately determine that Paul's fence was encroaching onto her property and that she owned the disputed strip.

IV. REMEDIES
A. NOMINAL DAMAGES

A possessor may always recover at least nominal damages for any trespass, and need not show that he has suffered any harm from the trespass. An action for nominal damages is sometimes brought in order to establish a property right, to settle a boundary dispute, or to protect against the running of the Statute of Limitations.

B. COMPENSATORY DAMAGES

A possessor may recover compensatory damages for actual harm suffered from a trespass. If permanent injury has occurred, the measure of damages is either the diminution of value of the property or the cost of restoration. Consequential damages, such as personal injuries, mental anguish or lost profits may also be recovered, subject to general tort principles of foreseeability and mitigation of damages. In certain cases, the possessor may recover based on the benefit received by the trespasser. Where the trespasser removes assets from the property, she may be liable for their value or she may be required to return the goods or pay a royalty for them. A trespasser who improves the property is sometimes allowed to offset the value of her improvements against her trespass liability. Where the trespass is continuing but the injury is not permanent, damages will be awarded only for injuries caused prior to the date of judgment. The possessor may file subsequent actions against the trespasser for harm caused since the prior judgment.

C. PUNITIVE DAMAGES

Where the trespass is malicious or wanton, courts may impose exemplary or punitive damages upon the trespasser. In some jurisdictions the wrongful cutting of timber subjects a trespasser to double or triple damages.

D. EQUITABLE RELIEF

An injunction may be granted where damages will be difficult to calculate or where the harm will be irreparable. In order to eliminate multiple lawsuits an injunction may also be granted against trespasses which will probably continue in the future. Occasionally a court will order the removal of an encroaching building, but usually only after balancing the hardship which such an injunction would cause to the defendant against the hardship the plaintiff will suffer if it is not granted. (The denial of an injunction in such a case amounts to the exercise of a right of private eminent domain by the defendant). Injunctive relief may also be granted to the holder of a future interest who lacks standing to bring a damage action at the present time.

E.   RELIEF ACCORDING TO THE STATUS OF THE PLAINTIFF

The plaintiff in an action for damages for trespass must either possess the property or else hold a present possessory interest in it. It is the possessory right, not ownership, which is protected. Thus trespass may be brought by a tenant under a lease, a purchaser in possession under a land contract, a co-tenant in possession (whether alone or with others), an adverse possessor, or a mere peaceful possessor of another's property (although owners of shopping centers, notwithstanding their ownership of the sidewalks and parking lots, are often prohibited from excluding political and religious pamphleteers from those areas because they are treated as public rather than private places). A holder of a nonpossessory interest may recover only when he can show some injury to his interest; harm is a prerequisite to any such action which technically, does not sound in trespass.

Illustration: Trish intruded upon the apartment which Paul rents from his landlord Laura. Paul may recover at least nominal damages from Trish, but Laura may recover only for any permanent harm to the apartment caused by Trish. Laura's mortgagee may recover only if the security has been impaired by Trish.

Illustration: Trish trespassed over a road on Paul's property. Dita, who has an easement of right of way over the road, has a cause of action against Trish only if the intrusion unreasonably interfered with her use of the road.

CHAPTER NINETEEN

NUISANCE

I. NUISANCE VERSUS TRESPASS

A property owner who suffers an unreasonable interference with the use and enjoyment of his property is entitled to relief against the person who has caused the discomfort. Trespass is the appropriate remedy if the interference arises from a physical invasion, but where the invasion is nonphysical, the correct form of action is nuisance. Nuisance differs from trespass in that harm is an essential element of this cause of action (whereas trespass lies for any physical intrusion regardless of harm). Furthermore, trespass is available only to those holding possessory interests, while nuisance is available for the protection of any interest in property. Prescription is available as a defense for both physical and nonphysical interferences permitted to continue too long.

Illustration: Nora, a neighbor, works on cars on her property. If she drives the cars onto Owen's property, she is guilty of trespass and liable at least for nominal damages regardless of harm. On the other hand, if the cars make a great deal of noise in Nora's garage, Owen may recover in nuisance if he can show that the noise unreasonably interferes with activities on his land. (If his land is vacant, or if his house is situated far from the noise, he cannot sue for nuisance.)

Illustration: If Nora parks her cars on Owen's driveway, she has committed a trespass as to him, but with regard to Dita—who has an easement to drive across the driveway—Nora is not liable in trespass, since Dita's property interest is nonpossessory. Dita may recover only if she can show that Nora's parking unreasonably interferes with her use of the driveway.

There is also a doctrine of public nuisance, not covered here, which involves conduct harmful to the health, safety, or morals of the entire community. A property owner may sue in such a case only if he suffers some special harm or if the activity also constitutes a private nuisance as to him. This chapter deals with the law of private nuisance insofar as it is relevant to a Property course. Many of the more technical features of nuisance law, which are usually covered in a Torts course are omitted here. In this chapter, nuisance is regarded as a problem of neighbors, where activity of one landowner interferes with the activities of an adjacent landowner.

II. DETERMINING WHETHER THERE IS A NUISANCE

The activities of neighbors which are held to constitute nuisances generally involve some interference with the physical senses caused by e.g., smoke, dust, odor, noise, light or heat, which would bother a normal person making a normal use of his own property. An activity which is merely visually offensive is generally not regarded as a nuisance, although those which cause fright (such as funeral parlors) or moral outrage (such as brothels or gambling halls) may be.

A nuisance usually involves intentional conduct by the defendant, and negligence is irrelevant, although the existence of malice may convert an otherwise legitimate activity into a nuisance.

In order to determine whether to treat the challenged activity as a nuisance causing unreasonable harm to another, courts generally engage in a balancing of the respective interests of the parties (often referred to as comparing the gravity of the plaintiff's harm with the utility of the defendant's conduct). The Restatement of Torts §§ 827, 828, include as components of the gravity of harm: its extent and character, the social value of the activity harmed and its suitability to the locale, and the difficulty for the plaintiff to avoid harm. Factors in determining the utility of the defendant's conduct are: its social value and suitability to the locale, and the impracticality of preventing harm to plaintiff. Priority of use is not a complete defense but may be treated as a factor; thus it might be relevant that the plaintiff has "come to the nuisance".

III. RELIEF

Damages are the appropriate remedy for a nuisance which has ceased to exist. The plaintiff is entitled to recover for harm to property and person. In the case of a permanent nuisance, i.e., one that threatens to continue on indefinitely, an award of damages constitutes a form of private eminent domain, with the defendant paying for the plaintiff's property interests it has appropriated.

If an injunction against the nuisance is sought, courts generally balance the harm which the granting of the injunction would cause to the defendant against the benefit which the plaintiff would thereby receive; the factors employed here are basically the same as are used to determine whether the defendant's activity constituted a nuisance in the first place but the weight to be given them is changed because of the context. Some economists argue that the injunction should be granted only if it is determined that the defendant can avoid the harm at a lower cost than the plaintiff; the equities of the situation are relevant only to the question of damages (which could be awarded either to the plaintiff who is denied an injunction or instead to the defendant who is made subject to an injunction).

Illustration: Nora's race track emits such bright light when she has night racing there as to impair Owen's drive-in movie business next door. In deciding whether to enjoin Nora from night racing, a court might compare the relative avoidance costs and grant the injunction if it determines that is cheaper for Nora to shield her lights or give up night racing than it is for Owen to build a high wall. It would also be possible to condition the injunction on Owen's compensating Nora if the court decides that equitable principles require this. (In such a case the court has effectively held that Nora does have an entitlement to emit light but that it is one which Owen can compel her to sell to him, whether she wants to or not, and for a price set by the court rather than the parties. This is a "liability entitlement" rather than a "property entitlement" because of its similarity to a personal injury award where a judge or jury rather than the parties sets the price of a broken limb.) Alternately, if the court determined that corrections by Owen would be cheaper, it could deny an injunction to him if

Nora agreed to reimburse him for his avoidance costs. It would also be possible to grant or deny the injunction without reallocating costs. If this is not a situation where the problem can be eliminated through corrective measures, the same analysis might be used to consider the relative costs of either party's relocating away from the other.

A nuisance imposes an external cost upon another's land. The granting of an injunction may be regarded as compelling the defendant to internalize that cost or else as reversing the externality. When neighboring activities are incompatible, a court is almost inevitably drawn into judicial zoning.

Illustration: Nora's foundry is next to Owen's laboratory; noise or vibrations from the foundry make laboratory work impossible. At present, therefore, Nora is imposing an external cost on Owen's land. However, if Owen obtains an injunction, then his entitlement to a zone of silence around his laboratory will prohibit her foundry activity and he will then have imposed an external cost on her land. Either her work makes his work impossible (if she is not enjoined) or else his work makes hers impossible (if she is enjoined). Either activity is compatible with many other kinds of activities, but not with each other. It may be hard to find a neutral principle to resolve the conflict.

IV. PUBLIC NUISANCE

A nuisance is public when it affects the entire community rather than just a few neighbors. It is remedied by an action brought by public officials, although an individual may sue for damages or an injunction if he can show special harm to himself or his property over and above what everyone else is suffering.

CHAPTER TWENTY
LAND USE REGULATION

This chapter deals with the relationship between the owner of land and the general public concerning the kinds of activities which occur upon his land. The public interest is manifested by way of: 1) legislative action regulating land use activities; 2) administrative agency action determining whether permits for the activities should be granted, denied or modified; and 3) judicial action between government and owner, or government and neighbors over the validity of the land use regulation or its application to a parcel of land. (Because of these special characteristics, the illustrations in this chapter take a different form: the owner and neighbor remain as Owen and Nora, but the governmental agency involved is given various designations, according to its real title. All of the illustrations are based on actual cases or statutes; case, but not statutory citations, have been included.)

I. TYPES OF LAND USE REGULATION
A. ZONING

1. Typical Zoning Devices

The most common form of local land use control is zoning. All or part of the city or county (referred to as the community in this chapter) is divided geographically into zones (districts), and different regulations are written to apply in each zone. The regulations are set forth in a *zoning ordinance;* the geographical depiction of each zone is set forth in a *zoning map.* The regulations differ from zone to zone but they apply uniformly to all parcels of land located within a zone.

a. Lot, Building and Use Regulations

Zoning ordinances generally regulate the size and shape of the land, the size and shape of the structures on the land, and the nature of the activity which occurs on the land or in the structures.

(1) Lot Regulations

(a) Minimum Lot Size

Many zoning ordinances establish a minimum size before a lot will be permitted to accommodate any building or activity. This is done to reduce density so as to eliminate overcrowding, increase light and air, improve police and fire services, and reduce demands on natural resources. Lot size minimums run from lows of 2,000 square feet in dense urban areas, to 4 and 5 acres in suburban and rural areas, and up to 20 or more acres in farm communities.

(b) Minimum Frontage

A related form of regulation is lot frontage, setting a minimum requirement as to how much width there must be where a parcel fronts upon a public street. In urban areas this may be as low as 20 feet, whereas in the suburbs it may run to 100 or 200 feet. The requirement may be tied to some other variable, such as the depth of the lot, or the width of the surrounding lots.

(2) Building Regulations

(a) Height

Building heights are usually regulated in absolute terms, by feet or stories, independently of the lot area, although the height limit may vary according to the topography (e.g. 30 feet along the coast, or at the top of hills) or according to use (buildings in commercial zones may be allowed greater height than those in residential zones). Height may also be related to bulk, so that a building may be taller if it is made narrower, or if it is stepped back as it rises so as to increase light and view at ground level. The limit may also be dependent upon the heights of the adjacent buildings or the average height of buildings on the block. Special adjustments may be established for buildings erected on sharply sloping ground.

(b) Bulk

(1) Yards. Building bulk is generally regulated as a function of lot size. Front, back and/or side yard requirements prohibit the building from occupying the entire parcel by mandating open space along all or part of its perimeter. A front yard requirement

(that the building must be a certain distance from the front lot line) is usually referred to as a setback regulation. A side yard requirement means that the buildings will be detached from one another. Rear yard requirements are common in residential districts. The requirements may be expressed in absolute numbers or averaging principles may be employed, requiring front or rear setbacks consistent with the buildings on the adjacent parcels or with the average setback on the block. Many communities have no front or side setback requirements, thus permitting contiguous buildings to extend all the way up to the lot lines, especially in commercial areas. In dense residential neighborhoods there may be a small front or side yard requirement of 5 to 10 feet; in more spacious suburbs the requirements may be as high as 50 feet in front and 40 feet along the side. All of these requirements generally vary from zone to zone.

(2) Open Space. Building bulk is also regulated by a direct open space requirement, prohibiting the building from occupying more than a certain percentage of the lot (sometimes as low as 20% in the suburbs). Such an open space requirement will generally coexist with the yard requirements described above, so as to control the placement of the building on the lot.

(c) FAR

A floor-area ratio requirement may regulate the overall bulk of a building according to the size of the lot, without determining its precise shape. A ratio of

2:1 for instance, permits the lot owner to erect a building containing two square feet of floor space for every one square foot of lot area, which can be accomplished by erecting a two-story building covering the entire lot, a four-story building covering 50% of the lot, an eight story building covering 25% of the lot, etc. (Height limits, open space and yard requirements may limit the owner's options, however.) Residential FAR's often range from 2:1 to 5:1; in downtown areas they may vary from 15:1 to 20:1. (The FAR of the Empire State Building is 25:1). Some ordinances permit the FAR to be increased if the owner provides certain amenities, such as plazas, public parking or rapid transit access.

(d) Minimum Floor Space

Suburban zoning ordinances often reflect a policy of prohibiting residential structures from being too small, rather than too large, and require that residential structures be of a certain minimum size, e.g. 1,000 square feet of floor space. If the requirement is judicially perceived as designed to exclude the poor rather than to prevent overcrowding, it may be held invalid, especially if it is combined with an unjustifiably large minimum lot size requirement. Exclusionary zoning is covered at page 469.

Illustration: The zoning ordinance of Berlin Township, New Jersey, which required a minimum floor space of 1,600 square feet, a minimum lot size of one acre, and a minimum frontage of 200 feet in single family residential zones was held invalid by the New Jersey Supreme Court. Home Builders League of South Jersey, Inc. v. Township of Berlin (1979).

(e) Architectural and Site Plan Review

A community may provide for design control of new structures by requiring all building plans to be submitted to a local review board (usually composed of architects) for approval prior to the issuance of a building permit. Since aesthetic considerations are not always regarded as legitimate factors in land use regulations, many design review ordinances recite a concern with the preservation of property values as a prime consideration. Also, in order to withstand challenges based on vagueness and improper delegation of legislative power to a nonelected review board, such ordinances often attempt to prescribe aesthetic standards in considerable detail.

Illustration: The Architectural Board of Review of Cleveland Heights, Ohio, is charged with "regulating according to proper architectural principles the design, use of materials, finished grade lines and orientation of all new buildings." Reid v. Architectural Bd. of Review of Cleveland Heights (1963).

Illustration: The Architectural Board of Ladue, Missouri, is given power to approve building plans to see that they "conform to certain minimum architectural standards of appearance and conformity with surrounding structures, and that unsightly, grotesque and unsuitable structures, detrimental to the stability of value and welfare of surrounding property structures and residents, and to the general welfare and happiness of the community be avoided, and that appropriate standards of beauty and conformity be fostered and encouraged." State ex rel. Stoyanoff v. Berkeley (1970).

Illustration: The Board of Architectural Review of Westchester County, New York, may disapprove any application if it finds that the structure would provoke any of the following "harmful effects" by reason of (a) "monotonous similarity" (b) "striking dissimilarity or visual discord or inappropriateness" to nearby buildings or (c) "visual offensiveness or other poor qualities of exterior design."

Site plan review is less predictable. A community board may have power to review all aspects of a project and may demand changes in the project as a condition for final approval, notwithstanding that it is in complete compliance with all existing zoning and other standards. Such standardless review gives planners powerful discretionary control over proposals. It also significantly moves the nature of land use regulation from its original concept as one containing preset standards applicable to all property owners in the district. (Landowners "as of right" had the power to complete projects which were designed in conformity with the standards).

(3) Regulations on Activities

Zoning is best known for its creation of use districts, zones where certain activities are prohibited, although identical activities are permitted in other zones elsewhere in the community. An original premise behind zoning was that some uses of land are incompatible and must be kept separated for the protection of one (or both) of them. In particular, residential areas were deemed to need protection from commercial and industrial intrusion.

Zoning was originally "cumulative", meaning that lower uses (commercial and industrial) were excluded from higher use (residential) zones, whereas higher uses were permitted in lower use zones. Today commercial and industrial areas are often given similar protection against residential intrusion of residencies. This is noncumulative zoning where, within each district the enumerated uses are exclusive.

Zoning ordinances exclude activities either by explicitly enumerating the uses which are prohibited in a zone, or by virtue of listing only those uses which are permitted there, thereby excluding all others not enumerated. Serious questions of validity are raised when a zoning ordinance excludes a lawful use from everywhere within the community.

Illustration: In Weston, Connecticut, a zoning ordinance classified the entire town as residential and farming, thereby excluding all commercial activities. It was upheld on the ground that "the business and industrial needs of its inhabitants are supplied by other accessible areas in the community at large." Cadoux v. Planning & Zoning Comm'n of Town of Weston (1972).

Illustration: West Whiteland Township, Pennsylvania, by its zoning ordinance, entirely excluded rock quarries. It was held invalid by the Pennsylvania Supreme Court under a standard that "a zoning ordinance which totally excludes a particular business from an entire municipality must bear a more substantial relationship to the public health, safety, morals and general welfare than an ordinance which merely confines that business to a certain area in the community." Exton Quarries, Inc. v. Zoning Bd. of Adjustment of West Whiteland Township (1967).

(a) Residential

Residential uses are commonly subdivided according to intensity. Categories may include single family, two family (flats), and multiple family residences (apartments). Other categories may include or exclude different kinds of residential use: hotels, motels, apartment complexes, garden apartments, mobile home parks, boarding houses, fraternity and sorority houses, dormitories and various forms of institutional housing (asylums, orphanages, halfway houses).

The exclusion of apartment buildings in single family residential zones has been upheld ever since the United States Supreme Court first validated zoning in Village of Euclid v. Ambler Realty Co. (1926). However, the exclusion of housing which best accommodates low-income persons may be held invalid as exclusionary. Exclusionary zoning is covered at p. 469. Constitutional issues involved in "single family" zoning are covered at p. 463.

(b) Commercial

Most communities have some commercial zones as well as residential. There may be only one commercial category, covering all permitted commercial uses, or there may be a division, e.g., central district commercial (large department stores), neighborhood commercial, retail, office. Garages and gas stations may be treated specially, as is also often done with regard to liquor stores, bars, drive-ins, theaters and restaurants.

Illustration: The Borough of Fair Lawn, New Jersey, zoning ordinance prohibits, in certain business zones "drive-in restaurants or refreshment stands, commonly called snack bars, dairy bars, hamburger stands or hot dog stands where customers and patrons are served food, soft drinks, ice cream * * * for their immediate consumption * * * outside the confines of the building or structures in which the business is conducted. * * *" Morris v. Postma (1964).

Some ordinances attempt to bring all such activities together, whereas others seek to disperse them.

Illustration: The Detroit, Michigan, zoning ordinance prohibits any "adult theater" from being located within 1000 feet of any other "regulated use" (or within 500 feet of a residential area). Regulated uses include: adult theater or bookstore, topless cabaret, bar, hotel or motel, pawnshop, pool hall, second hand store, shoe-shine parlor or dance hall. Young v. American Mini Theatres (1976).

Illustration: The Boston, Massachusetts, zoning ordinance creates an Adult Entertainment District in which adult book stores and adult entertainment are allowed (and in which the general prohibition of moving or flashing signs does not apply). Since such uses are forbidden in all other districts the area has become known as the "Combat Zone".

(c) Industrial; Performance Standards

It is possible to classify various types of industry and to create different zones for each. Today, many communities have set aside areas as exclusive industrial parks, prohibiting residential and commercial activities there to keep them from interfering with the industrial activities. Industrial regulations often are directed not at the specific activity being conducted but at the external effects created by the activity. Thus "performance standard zoning" regulates the smell, noise, smoke, vibrations, etc. from the activity, rather than the activity itself.

Illustration: The Village of Lake Success, New York, zoning ordinance provides that in a district which permits "offices, scientific and research laboratories, assembly, fabrication and finishing of articles of small compass and high value (cameras, watches, electronic instruments), (inside) storage facilities," etc., there is prohibited "any use which will cause smoke, gas, dust, odor or other pollutant, noise perceptible beyond the boundaries of the site of the use, discharge of waste into any watercourse, dissemination of glare, vibration, heat or electromagnetic interference beyond the immediate site, or physical hazard by reason of fire, explosion or radiation * * *." Brechner v. Incorporated Village of Lake Success (1960).

2. Mapping

In addition to the text of a zoning ordinance, which describes the bulk, area and use restrictions, there will also exist a zoning map showing the location of each of the zones where such restrictions apply. The boundaries of the different types of districts may overlap (as where there is one height limit for all residential districts and another for all commercial districts), or there may be different mapped areas for different purposes (as where height limits are imposed on all coastal areas, although some parts of the coast are zoned residential and other parts commercial). There may be but one map, with all bulk and area standards dependent upon the use district (e.g., the height limit in all residential zones is 40 feet), or there may be separate (overlay) use and bulk maps.

a. Size of the Zone; Spot Zoning

If a very small area is mapped for a use significantly different from that permitted in the surrounding area, it may be labeled as spot zoning, and held invalid as such. This is especially likely if the classification results from a rezoning rather than an original zoning of the parcel. Rezoning is covered at page 430.

Illustration: In 1951 the Board of Public Works of the City of Paterson, New Jersey, amended its zoning ordinance to reclassify a single lot, 120 × 141 feet, from residence to business, so as to permit the lot owner to erect a bank there. The area was regarded as the finest residential neighborhood in the city, and the lot had been vacant for 40 years. The action was held invalid. Conlon v. Board of Public Works of City of Paterson (1953).

b. Zoning Boundaries

If the zoning boundaries do not coincide with the lot lines, this may put a single parcel of land within two different zoning districts. Some ordinances provide that in such a case the entire lot is subject to whichever classification is more (or less) severe or to whichever covers the greater geographic part of the lot. In small communities, mapping can be done so as to precisely coincide with all existing lot lines. The problem can also be avoided by making all zoning lines run down the center of public streets, but that would put opposite sides of the same street into different districts, which is generally undesirable. If no corrective action is taken as to a split lot, it will remain subject to two different classifications unless a court holds the mapping invalid.

Illustration: The zoning map of Cambridge, Massachusetts, classified a 100 foot strip of plaintiff's parcel (along the street) as residential, while leaving the rest unrestricted. Even though the actual use of the other side of the street was residential, it was held that the city had acted arbitrarily in not running the zoning line along the street frontage of the property.   Nectow v. City of Cambridge (1928).

3. Special Zoning Tools

a. *Special Exceptions (Conditional Uses)*

Under the zoning system previously described, a use is either permitted as of right, if the ordinance includes it as an allowable activity, or else is absolutely barred.   However, not all activities are so readily subject to a simple yes/no classification.   If the community believes that some activities might be appropriate within a certain zone, depending upon the existence of other factors, it may create a category of conditionally (rather than absolutely) permitted uses to cover them.   These uses are permitted only after a discretionary decision has been made by the appropriate zoning agency; they are usually called special exceptions.   Since it is possible for the zoning agency to permit the activity to occur only under certain conditions (such as the landscaping of the premises so as to prevent bother to the neighbors), they are also known as conditional uses.   While the agency may have discretion to grant, deny or condition a permit, it may only do so if the zoning ordinance includes the activity as one which may be permitted as a special exception or conditional use.

Illustration: The zoning ordinance of Owatonna, Minnesota, permits drive-in businesses, which require the cutting of the curb or driving over the sidewalk, such as gasoline stations or car lots, as special uses in commercial districts only after a public hearing and $2/3$ vote of the city council. Alexander Co. v. Owatonna (1946).

Illustration: The zoning ordinance of Millburn, New Jersey, states that schools, hospitals, clubs and cemeteries may be located within the community only if the Board of Adjustment finds, in its judgment, that "as it is proposed to be located it will not be detrimental to the health, safety and general welfare of the community and is reasonably necessary for the convenience of the community" and the permit for such structure or use shall be "subject to such requirements as to front, side & rear yards, and other reasonable conditions as to structure or use as the governing body may see fit to impose". Tullo v. Millburn Township, Essex County (1959).

A city may create a zoning classification, but not actually map any particular district for it at that time, instead declaring the standards which must be met for any parcel of land or project to qualify for such a designation. Thereafter an interested owner must apply to have his land so reclassified and the appropriate administrative body determines whether this is appropriate under the legislative guidelines. Until it is so mapped, such a zone "floats".

b. Floating Zones

It is possible for a city to create a zoning district without locating it on the zoning map at that time. The city council may prescribe the standards applicable to that district, but leave it to an administrative body or application of a property owner before any particular piece of land is given that zoning designation. This has been done with regard to industrial parks, mixed apartment-commercial zones, and mobile home parks.

Illustration: The zoning regulations of Farmington, Connecticut, provide, "Restricted Apartment zones may be des-

ignated on the zoning map and may also be established in
any other zone by petition in accordance with the following
procedure * * *." The regulations then provide that the
zoning cannot be approved if it is "inconsistent with the
public welfare or * * * does not fully safeguard the appropriate use of the land in the immediate neighborhood [or]
unless there is clear evidence of safe and satisfactory means
of providing water supply and sewage disposal." There are
also "limitations and requirements as to use, area, yards
and courts, spaces between structures, building coverage,
and building and dwelling size, as well as special requirements for parking areas, access ways and sidewalks, and
recreation and open space." Miss Porter's Sch., Inc. v.
Town Plan and Zoning Comm'n of the Town of Farmington
(1964).

Illustration: The 1947 zoning ordinance of Tarrytown,
New York, provided that the boundaries of its apartment
zone would be "fixed by amendment of the official village
building zone map at such times in the future as such
district or class of zone is applied to properties in this
village." Rodgers v. Village of Tarrytown (1951).

c. Cluster Zoning

To avoid monotonous development, with each house
having the same front and side yard and general
layout, a community may enact cluster zoning, which
permits developers to depart from the standards as to
individual parcels so long as those standards are
maintained with regard to the overall project. If, for
instance, the ordinance requires 50% open space for
each lot, a developer of two lots might have the
option of clustering 2 houses on one lot and leaving
the other lot entirely as open space.

Illustration: The zoning ordinance of South Brunswick
Township, New Jersey, provides that a subdivider may be

allowed to reduce minimum lot size and frontage requirements for individual lots with the subdivision by up to 30%.
If:

(1) the resulting "net lot density" of the area is no
greater than would otherwise be allowed

(2) there is compliance "with all other provisions of the
zoning ordinance, such as front, rear and side setbacks,
size of buildings, etc."

(3) the subdivider donates to the city a "usable" five
acre tract for public purposes and

(4) "if the tract to be subdivided is located in a zone
which requires a minimum lot size of 20,000 square feet
or less, the developer must donate, exclusive of open
drainage water courses, twenty percent of the tract to the
township; if the tract to be subdivided is located in a zone
which requires a minimum lot size in excess of 20,000
square feet, the developer must donate, exclusive of open
drainage water courses, thirty percent of the tract to the
township." Chrinko v. South Brunswick Township Planning Bd. (1963).

d. Planned Unit Development

The same clustering principle may be applied to
uses, as well as to bulk and area. If the subdivider is
permitted to determine the allocation of space for
commercial and residential activities, within overall
limitations, the project may be referred to as a
Planned Unit Development. Instead of local officials
mapping out residential and commercial, or apartment and house districts ahead of time, the subdivider prepares the map of those activities, subject to
the percentages established by the community.
There may also be a zoning reclassification (to PUD)
and site plan review at the same time and perhaps all

under the aegis of one agency, in order to reduce the costs of delay and the dangers of inconsistent demands from different reviewing boards.

Illustration: The zoning ordinance of New Hope, Pennsylvania, includes a PUD district within which there can be "single family attached or detached dwellings, apartments, accessory private garages, public or private parks and recreation areas including golf courses, swimming pools, ski slopes, etc. (so long as these facilities do not produce noise, glare, odor, air pollution, etc., detrimental to existing or prospective adjacent structures); a municipal building; a school; churches; art galleries; professional offices; certain types of signs; a theater (but not a drive-in); motels and hotels; and a restaurant. The ordinance then sets overall density requirements. The PUD district may have a maximum of eighty percent of the land devoted to residential uses, a maximum of twenty percent for the permitted commercial uses and closed recreational facilities, and must have a minimum of twenty percent for open spaces. The residential density shall not exceed ten units per acre, nor shall any such unit contain more than two bedrooms. All structures within the district must not exceed minimum height standards set up in the ordinance. Finally, although there are no traditional 'setback' and 'side yard' requirements, ordinance 160 does require that there be 24 feet between structures, and that no townhouse structure contain more than twelve dwelling units." Cheney v. Village 2 at New Hope, Inc. (1968).

e. *Holding Zones*

A holding zone is a classification imposing such restrictive use on land as to render it undevelopable for the time being. When a community is not yet ready to classify all of the land within its borders, it may zone some areas, e.g., single family residence on minimum lot sizes of 10 acres, not because it really believes that this is appropriate but because it will prohibit development there until the comprehensive plan is finished. This purpose may also be accomplished by interim zoning. Overrestrictive zoning also forces owners to always apply for rezoning in order to accomplish any development and is thus often referred to as "wait and see" zoning.

4. Zoning Relief

a. *Variances*

A zoning ordinance will usually provide that a property owner who would suffer unnecessary hardship if the zoning ordinance were strictly enforced as to his property may be entitled to a variance permitting him to deviate from the ordinance in respect to some aspect of lot, building or activity regulation. This relief is usually granted by a special agency, often called a board of adjustment. It is usually required that there be special circumstances unique to the parcel, that the hardship not be self-inflicted, that suitable conditions be imposed so as to minimize adverse effects on the neighborhood, and that the intent of the comprehensive plan be preserved.

Illustration: The Standard State Zoning Enabling Act authorizes the board of adjustment to grant a "variance from the terms of the ordinance as will not be contrary to the public interest, where, owing to special conditions, a literal enforcement of the provisions of the ordinance will result in unnecessary hardship, and so that the spirit of the ordinance shall be observed and substantial justice done."

Illustration: California's enabling legislation provides: "Variances from the terms of the zoning ordinances shall be granted only when, because of special circumstances applicable to the property, including size, shape, topography, location or surroundings, the strict application of the zoning ordinance deprives such property of privileges enjoyed by other property in the vicinity and under identical zoning classification. Any variance granted shall be subject to such conditions as will assure that the adjustment thereby authorized shall not constitute a grant of special privileges inconsistent with the limitations upon other properties in the vicinity and zone in which such property is situated. A variance shall not be granted for a parcel of property which authorizes a use or activity which is not otherwise expressly authorized by the zone regulation governing the parcel of property."

Illustration: The zoning ordinance of the District of Columbia provides that its Board of Adjustment may grant a variance "where, by reason of exceptional narrowness, shallowness, or shape of a specific piece of property at the time of the original adoption of the regulations or by reason of exceptional topographical conditions or other extraordinary or exceptional situation or condition of a specific piece of property, the strict application of any regulation would result in peculiar and exceptional practical difficulties to or exceptional and undue hardship upon the owner of such property * * * so as to relieve such difficulties or hardship, provided such relief can be granted without substantial detriment to the public good and without substantially impairing the intent, purpose and integrity of the zone plan as embodied in the zoning regulations and map."

b. *Rezoning (Amendments)*

A property owner may seek relief from the existing ordinance by attempting to have it amended. This may occur by revision of the text of the zoning ordinance (e.g. lowering the height limit or changing the list of activities permitted in a given zone), or by amendment to the zoning map (reclassifying the parcel from one zone to another). Rezoning of property is in form a legislative act, done by the city council (as opposed to the administrative act by the board of adjustment in granting a variance). The distinction may be significant for purposes of judicial review, since legislative acts are generally subject to a more deferential analysis than are administrative acts. On judicial review, see page 457. However, some courts do not confer the same presumption of validity upon rezoning as is given to original zoning. When a small parcel is granted a rezoning for the benefit of its owner rather than for the general welfare, it may be characterized as spot zoning, and held invalid by the courts. Many statutes require a supermajority vote by the legislative body (e.g., 67% rather than 51%) to rezone property where some percentage of the neighbors have filed a protest against the proposal.

Illustration: Fawn Township, Pennsylvania, rezoned an 80 acre doughnut shaped parcel from residential so that its owner could operate a motorcycle racecourse there (while all of the neighboring land, including the parcel surrounded by the doughnut, was left with the residential classification). The action was judicially invalidated as illegal spot zoning on the ground that there were no relevant differences between that parcel and its surroundings. Appeal of Benech (1977).

Illustration: The rezoning by Prince George's County, Maryland, of a parcel from low density residential to mixed commercial and residential by the county was held invalid on the ground that there was no showing of any mistake in the original zoning classification or of any change in condition in the area since the original classification, as is required in Maryland. MacDonald v. Board of County Commissioners for Prince George's County (1965).

Illustration: The rezoning of a parcel of land in Washington County, Oregon, from single family residential to "planned residential", so as to permit a mobile home park to be constructed there, was held invalid on the ground that the party proposing the change in zoning had failed to establish a public need for change of the kind in question or that such need is best served by changing the classification of that particular parcel compared with other available property, as is required in Oregon. Fasano v. Board of County Commissioners of Washington County (1973).

c. Contract Zoning

Local government may be willing to grant an owner's request to upzone his parcel so long as certain restrictions are imposed on his intended use so as to reduce its adverse effects on other land, or because certain inducements are offered by him which are sufficiently valuable to the community to warrant the zone change. If both sides make such an arrangement, the rezoning which results may be referred to as contract zoning (or conditional zoning). The restrictions specially imposed upon the parcel so rezoned may relate to physical conditions (such as reducing lot coverage below what is generally required in the new zone) or to the use involved (such as limiting the owner to the particular use intended, even though numerous other uses would be allowed under the new zoning classification); inducements offered by an owner might consist of a dedication of land to the city or special beautification of the property involved (e.g., landscaping along the front lot line). The arrangement may be executed either by recordation of a deed or set of covenants made by the owner in favor of the community, or by provision in the zoning amendment making it conditional upon the owner's fulfillment of those promises. This is generally done on an individual basis, although the general zoning ordinance may explicitly provide for such situations.

Some courts do not permit these arrangements, holding that they violate the principle of zoning uniformity (since restrictions are applied to one parcel in a zoning class which are not applicable elsewhere), or because they amount to a bargaining away of the local police power, or are not authorized by statute. Where upheld, courts usually observe that the property could have been rezoned without the additional restrictions, and that these restrictions cannot be complained of by the neighbors (who are benefitted by them) or by the property owner (who has consented to them).

Illustration: The county of Peoria, Illinois, rezoned a five acre tract from agricultural to commercial in order to permit the owner to construct a dance hall there, after obtaining the owner's agreement to restrict the premises to such a use and to waive the right to engage in any other use permitted under the commercial zoning classification, and also to dedicate to the county land to provide access to the highway, which he did by way of recorded restrictive covenant. Ziemer v. County of Peoria (1975). (Held invalid).

B.   SUBDIVISION REGULATION

A local government may impose additional regulations over and above zoning restrictions when land is subdivided into individually saleable or buildable lots.

The community has an obvious interest, when a large parcel of farm land is converted into individual home-sites, to see that the new streets tie into existing city streets and are not too narrow for local fire trucks. The same concern exists with regard to linkage with all other municipal services, including water and sewage, as well as parks, playgrounds and schools. Local government may control these features by requiring that no newly subdivided lots be sold except by reference to a recorded subdivision map and also prohibiting any subdivision map from being so recorded except with local approval.

Illustration: The Standard City Planning Enabling Act provides that the local "planning commission shall adopt regulations governing the subdivision of land within its jurisdiction. Such regulations may provide for the proper arrangement of streets in relation to other existing or planned streets and to the master plan, for adequate and convenient open space, for traffic, utilities, access of fire-fighting apparatus, recreation, light and air, and for the avoidance of congestion of population, including minimum width and area of lots. Such regulations may include provisions as to the extent to which streets and other ways shall be graded and improved and to which water and sewer and other utility mains, piping, or other facilities shall be installed as a condition precedent to the approval of the plan." These provisions today are often to be found in a state's Subdivision Map Act.

1. What Is a Subdivision

The state subdivision enabling act usually declares what sort of land division is to be treated as a subdivision subject to local regulation. Many divisions of title may be treated as subdivisions for cer-

tain purposes and not for others. It is common for
subdivisions of fewer than 5 parcels to be exempt
from regulations imposed on larger subdivisions, although special provisions may apply to attempts by
subdividers to evade the regulations by periodic
"quartering" of land. Subdivisions of very large individual parcels (1, 2 or 40 acres) are also often exempted from regulation. An apartment building is generally not treated as a subdivision, even though "the
division of the property for lease, sale or financing" is
a common definition of subdivision. However, condominium projects are often treated as "vertical subdivisions," and the conversion of an existing apartment
building into a condominium may require local subdivision approval.

2. The Subdivision Process

A subdivision is created when an owner of unsubdi-
vided acreage (e.g., 40 acres of farmland without
roads) submits a tentative or preliminary map of a
proposed subdivision to the local government which
shows where individual lots, roads, public utilities,
etc. will exist. It is then reviewed by all interested
agencies, e.g., the fire department (to make sure
roads are wide enough for their trucks and buildings
are spaced far enough apart to avoid a conflagration),
the police department, the planning department, the
parks department and the streets department, all of
whom may demand changes in the plan to satisfy
their own standards. If the applicant successfully
revises the plan to accommodate these official demands the proposed map is approved. The applicant

then constructs the public improvements shown in the map (e.g., builds the roads, and perhaps dedicates them to the government). A final subdivision map is then approved by the government and recorded in the public records. Thereafter the subdivider is permitted to sell lots in the subdivision to members of the public (through deeds which refer to the recorded final subdivision map for boundary locations). Building permits may also then be issued (to the subdivider or to individual lot buyers), if the building plans conform to the applicable zoning and other land use regulations. Sometimes, in order to assure the developer that the rules will not be changed during this lengthy process (perhaps because of an election), a development agreement will be executed between the developer and the government.

3. Subdivision Exactions

A community may also require the subdivider to make certain donations to it as a condition for approving the subdivision map. The subdivider may be required to dedicate the streets to the city or to pay for the installation of the utility lines. Recently, communities have increased their demands upon subdividers to include a broader range of municipal services and many now require the dedication of land for parks, schools or public buildings, or the payment of certain fees in lieu of these dedications.

Illustration: The Minnesota Subdivision Act provides that municipal subdivision regulations "may require that a reasonable portion of each proposed subdivision be dedicated to the public for public use as parks and playgrounds." In residential subdivisions of less than 30 acres, there may be provisions for the subdivider to elect to contribute an equivalent amount in cash. In determining the extent of the dedication, the regulations "may take into consideration the open space, park, recreational or common areas and facilities which the subdivider has provided for the exclusive use of the residents of the subdivision." Pursuant to this, the City of Bloomington imposed a requirement of 10% of the value of the undeveloped land proposed to be subdivided. Collis v. City of Bloomington (1976).

Illustration: The California Subdivision Map Act provides: "There may be imposed by local ordinance a requirement that areas of real property be reserved for parks, recreational facilities, fire stations, libraries or other public uses." Another section authorizes requiring the dedication of land or payment of fees in lieu "for classroom and related facilities for elementary or high schools" where existing schools are overcrowded. Under a related provision, the City of Walnut Creek imposed a dedication requirement of 2½ acres of park or recreation land for every 1,000 new residents, or an equivalent fee if no park was designated on the master plan and the subdivision was within ¾ of a mile of a park or proposed park. Associated Home Builders of Greater East Bay, Inc. v. City of Walnut Creek (1971).

State courts have not adopted a uniform standard for determining the validity of such local demands. The most strict view holds that the charge be specifically and uniquely attributable to the subdivision activity; at the other extreme is a standard which only requires that there be a reasonable relationship between the charge for facilities and the use of the facilities made by the future inhabitants of the subdivision. The United States Supreme Court held that the demand of the California Coastal Commission for an easement of access over beachfront owners' property as a condition for permitting the owners to rebuild their house constituted an impermissible "taking" of their property because there was no "nexus" between the demand (for parallel access from one coastal lot to the next) and the harm the Commission claimed it was attempting to alleviate (loss of coastal views from the highway inland from the coast). Nollan v. California Coastal Commission (1987). Subdivision exactions are covered further under "Taking," at p. 464.

C. GROWTH MANAGEMENT

A community may seek to regulate its rate of residential growth in order to reduce the strain which new population imposes upon municipal services and budgets. Zoning and subdivision regulations often have indirect growth inhibiting effects by reducing the supply of available land for development (e.g. open space zoning, large minimum lot sizes), by pricing out much lower-cost housing (e.g. exclusion of apartment and/or trailer parks), or by restricting entry to certain classes of persons (e.g. single family districts involving a consanguinity standard). Growth management regulations, on the other hand, deal with this issue directly by restricting the number of residential building permits which may be issued by the community. Some of the numerous techniques for restricting growth are indicated in the illustrations.

Illustration: Moratorium: An initiative ordinance enacted in Livermore, California, provides that no further or additional building permits may be issued until classrooms are not overcrowded, schools are not on double session, sewage treatment facilities meet regional quality standards and water supplies are adequate. Associated Home Builders of Greater Eastbay, Inc. v. City of Livermore (1976).

Illustration: Cap: An initiative ordinance in Boca Raton, Florida, provided that no residential building permit would be issued after there were 40,000 dwelling units within the city. Boca Raton v. Boca Villas Corp. (Fla.1979). (Held invalid).

Illustration: Points: In Ramapo, New York, a building may not be erected until the property owner has acquired the requisite number of points, which are based upon the availability of sewage, drainage, parks and recreation, roads, and firehouses. The developer may increase the point count by providing these services personally rather than waiting for the town to supply them. Golden v. Planning Bd. of Ramapo (1972).

Illustration: Quota: Petaluma, California, issues 500 permits per year for residential projects of over 4 units. These are awarded to applicants according to a point system similar to Ramapo's, except that design and environmental amenities, provision for low and moderate income persons, and geographical balancing in town are additional pointworthy considerations. Construction Industry Ass'n of Sonoma County v. City of Petaluma (1975).

Illustration: Percentage: Raymond, New Hampshire, limits the number of building permits a person may receive to one a year for every 10 acres of land owned; thus the owner of 40 acres can obtain 4 building permits a year. Beck v. Town of Raymond (1978).

D. LANDMARKS AND HISTORIC DISTRICTS

Many communities seek to protect their historic buildings and neighborhoods by specially designating them and subjecting them to stringent design control. The owner of a property designated as a landmark or located within an historic district is then prohibited from altering its external appearance without first obtaining a permit from the appropriate regulatory agency. In return, the owner may be given a property tax reduction, or may be permitted to put the building to an otherwise unpermitted use in order to generate an economic return. In some situations the community may purchase a preservation easement in the facade or structure, thereby eliminating the owner's right to destroy the historic features of the building.

Illustration: Historic architecture in the French Quarter of New Orleans is regulated by the Vieux Carre Commission (created in the Louisiana Constitution). No building may be altered or sign displayed without a permit from the Commission, which is also authorized to grant property tax exemptions to such buildings.

Illustration: By statute, cities in New York are "empowered to provide by regulations, special conditions and restrictions for the protection, enhancement, perpetuation and use of places, districts, sites, buildings, structures, works of art, and other objects having a special character or special historical or aesthetic interest or value. Such regulations * * * may include appropriate and reasonable control of the use or appearance of neighboring private property within public view, or both." If the measure constitutes "a taking of private property it shall provide for due compensation, which may include the limitation or remission of taxes."

Illustration: Based upon the above statute, New York City permits an area to be designated as an historic district, subject therefore to special regulation if it contains improvements which "(a) have a special character or special historical or aesthetic interest or value; and (b) represent one or more periods or styles of architecture typical of one or more eras in the history of the city; and (c) cause such area, by reason of such factors, to constitute a distinct section of the city." A landmark is "any improvement, any part of which is thirty years old or older, which has a special character or special historical or aesthetic interest or value as part of the development, heritage or cultural characteristics of the city, state or nation and which has been designated as a landmark * * *." Pursuant to the ordinance, the city refused to permit the owner of the Grand Central Terminal from erecting a 53 story office building above the structure. Penn Central Transp. Co. v. New York City (1978).

E. ENVIRONMENTAL PROTECTION

State law may require local government to study the environmental effect of any action it considers taking, including the granting of approval for private land development. Thus the appropriate agency may be required to prepare an environmental impact statement or report prior to approving a subdivision, re-zoning land, or granting any other form of development permit. The requirement may be entirely procedural, requiring a study but not dictating how the agency must respond to unfavorable data, or there may also be a substantive requirement compelling it to avoid adverse environmental effects.

Illustration: The California Environmental Quality Act requires that all agencies which regulate activities of private individuals (which includes those "involving the issuance to a person of a lease, permit, license, certificate or other entitlement for use") give major consideration to preventing environmental damage. An environmental impact report is to be prepared which identifies significant effects of a project on the environment, identifies alternatives to it, and indicates how these significant effects can be mitigated or avoided. An agency should not approve such a project if there are feasible alternatives or mitigation measures which would substantially lessen the environmental effect, unless economic, social or other conditions make the alternatives or mitigation measures infeasible.

The federal Comprehensive Environmental Response, Compensation and Liability Act (CERCLA, commonly referred to as Superfund) and comparable state laws impose a duty to clean up contaminated properties. Absolute liability is imposed upon the present owner, whether or not he was the polluter, unless he can come within the "innocent landowner" defense by showing that the contamination was caused by a third party who was not an agent of the owner or within a "contractual relationship" with him. A deed creates a contractual relationship between buyer and seller (thus making the current owner responsible for previous owners' contaminations). There is an exception if the owner acquired the property after it was already contaminated but "had no reason to know" of it, despite making "all appropriate inquiry into the previous ownership and uses of the property", exercising due care, and taking appropriate precautions against "foreseeable acts or omissions" of third parties. This effectively requires every purchaser to make a *due diligence* investigation (or *environmental audit*) of the condition of the property and to negotiate with the vendor for appropriate contractual provisions relating to known or later discovered contamination.

Most litigation over clean up (*response*) costs occurs between private parties rather than between owner and government. Owners who are compelled to clean up attempt to recover over against their sellers (who may attempt to rely upon "as is" clauses for their defense). They may try to compel their property insurance carriers to pay for their clean up or defense costs, which requires a modern interpretation of policies written many years ago when toxic wastes were not of concern to the parties. Mortgagees are concerned whether they should attempt to foreclose on loans secured by contaminated properties when outside bidders will subtract the costs of cleanup from their potential bids (thereby giving such costs priority over the mortgage) or whether they can merely walk away from such loans without being held liable themselves to clean up the property. Most of these questions are far from being answered.

F. EMINENT DOMAIN

Government can control the use of land directly by acquiring property itself and then exercising the prerogatives of an owner towards it. This is usually how communities manage parks, civil buildings, airports, etc.

If the current owner of the desired parcel is not willing to sell, the government, unlike private individuals, can judicially compel its transfer through an eminent domain (or condemnation) action. In such a proceeding, the government must prove that there is a "public use" involved, but this requirement is significantly softened by judicial deference to legislative determination as to what best serves the public.

Illustration: A land reform statute in Hawaii, requiring large landowners to sell parcels to their tenant occupants at governmentally set prices in certain cases was upheld by the United States Supreme Court as involving a public use, even though lower courts had viewed this mandatory transfer of property from one private party to another to the contrary. Hawaii Housing Authority v. Midkiff (1983).

Illustration: Urban renewal ("slum clearance") projects are upheld as involving a public use of property notwithstanding that the buildings taken from their present owners may be then transferred to new private owners. See Berman v. Parker (1954).

The government is required to pay "just compensation" for property so taken. The amount to be paid is set by a jury after hearing evidence of fair market value presented by both sides. In certain cases government is permitted to take the land immediately and pay the owner later after fair market value has been determined.

II. THE LAND USE REGULATION PROCESS

A. WHO MAY REGULATE LAND

1. Federal Regulation

The federal government has never exercised direct land use control over privately owned land. It does regulate all land which it either owns or administers (e.g. national forest land, Indian trust land) and, by virtue of its supremacy, is not subject to state or local control where it does so regulate. Furthermore, although there is no federal zoning or national land use plan operative in the United States, the federal government through its commerce and budgetary powers plays a significant indirect role in the regulation of land uses.

Illustration: Under the Federal Water Pollution Control Act, all dredging and filling in most of the nation's waters is subject to approval by the Army Corps of Engineers.

Illustration: Under the 1970 Clean Air Amendments to the Clean Air Act, state and local governments are required to submit plans for improving air quality standards to the federal Environmental Protection Agency. These plans include matters of location of shopping centers, sports complexes, sewer lines and industrial developments.

2. State Regulation

Some land is regulated directly at the state level. Certain areas of a state (e.g. those of critical environmental concern), may be subject to a direct state permitting process over and above or in lieu of the local procedure. Alternatively, the state may make threshold classifications of land, confining local regulation to control within those classifications.

Bernhardt, Real Prop. 3rd NS—17

Illustration: In Hawaii, all land has been classified as urban, rural, agricultural or conservation by the State Land Use Commission and the state has restricted the permissible activities within those classifications. Counties may adopt more strict regulations within each of these districts but the state alone controls land use decisions within the conservation districts. Enforcement, however, is a county rather than state responsibility.

Illustration: In Vermont, a building or development permit must be obtained not only from the local agency, but also from a state agency, thus giving the state a veto over local development.

3. Regional Regulation

Certain lands may be subject to control by a regional agency, operating below the state level but above the local level. The region may come into existence because the communities there decide to form a regional association, or it may be created by the state directly because of a statewide interest in the area.

Illustration: The Regional Planning Act in Minnesota provides that any two or more counties, cities or towns may enter into an agreement for the conduct of regional planning activities, which shall provide for a regional planning board to prepare a regional development plan for review by the participants.

Illustration: A California statute provides that no one may do any significant development work along the coastline of the San Francisco Bay without obtaining a permit from the Bay Conservation Development Commission over and above all local permits which must be obtained from the local government involved.

Illustration: The Tahoe Regional Planning Agency, created by statutes of the states of California and Nevada and ratified by an act of Congress, must ensure that all projects in the area comply with the agency's own regional general plan, ordinances, rules, regulations and policies. While local municipalities may enact their own land use ordinances, these may not be less stringent than those promulgated by TRPA. The agency, consisting of two separate state groups, the CTRPA and NTRPA, cannot approve a project unless a majority of both the CTRPA and NTRPA members of each state's delegation to the agency vote favorably.

Illustration: Under Circular A–95 of the Office of Management and Budget, any local agency seeking federal assistance for a variety of enumerated programs (including land use activities) must first submit it to the regional clearinghouse, as designated by the governor of the state, for evaluation and comment. These regional clearinghouses are often the local council of governments in the region.

4. Local Regulation

Power to regulate land derives from the police power and is therefore vested within the state. However, state legislatures have generally delegated the regulation of land to their cities and counties. Delegation occurs through the enactment of a zoning enabling act, a subdivision enabling act, or similar form of statutory authorization. These statutes both enable and set the limits of local regulation of land. A land use regulation not authorized by the enabling act may be set aside as ultra vires.

Illustration: The Standard State Zoning Enabling Act, (prepared by the United States Chamber of Commerce in 1928) provides that cities are empowered, " * * * to regulate and restrict the height, number of stories, and size of buildings and other structures, the percentage of lot that may be occupied, the size of yard, courts, and other open spaces, the density of population, and the location and use of buildings, structures, and land for trade, industry, residence, or other purposes".

Illustration: The American Law Institute Model Land Development Code (1976), provides that each local government is, " * * * authorized to plan or otherwise encourage, regulate, or undertake the development of land in accordance with this code".

Illustration: The California Government Code provides that the legislative body of any county or city may: "Regulate the use of buildings, structures and land as between industry, business, residents, open space, including agriculture, recreation, enjoyment of scenic beauty and use of natural resources, and other purposes. Regulate signs and billboards. Regulate location, height, bulk, number of stories and size of buildings and structures; the size and use of lots, yards, courts and other open spaces; the percentage of a lot which may be occupied by a building or structure; the intensity of land use. Establish requirements for off-street parking and loading. Establish and maintain setback lines."

Since most local land use regulation requires state authorization, any novel regulation may be challenged on the ground that it is not so authorized. Issues such as whether delegated local power to regulate land subdivision and building construction includes the power to control or slow down growth, whether the power to regulate the bulk of buildings includes design or architectural review; whether the power to regulate subdivisions includes the power to compel subdivision exactions; whether the zoning enabling act permits use of the initiative and referendum process; whether the requirement of mapping and uniform regulations in a zone prohibits such devices as floating zones and planned unit developments are all questions of enabling authorization. These matters are resolved according to the language of the state enabling acts and the attitude of the state judiciary towards local innovation.

5. Citizen Regulation

When the citizens are discontent with the way their officials regulate the land in the community, they may take matters into their own hands. The voters may seek to nullify the acts officials have already taken by the power of referendum, or they may undertake to enact laws by the power of initiative. Many significant land use decisions come into being from the initiative process or are repudiated by referenda. Height limits and growth restrictions are often created by the initiative process; the referendum is often employed to reject the approval of some large scale commercial or residential project.

Illustration: The voters of Eastlake, Ohio, amended their city charter to require that, for any change in any zoning classification made by the city council "it shall be mandatory that the same be approved by a 55% favorable vote of all votes cast of the qualified electors of the City of Eastlake at the next regular election, if one shall occur not less than 60 or more than 120 days after its passage, otherwise at a special election. * * * " City of Eastlake v. Forest City Enterprises (1976).

Illustration: Article XXXIV of the California Constitution provides: "No low rent housing project shall hereafter be developed, constructed or acquired in any manner by any state public body until, a majority of the qualified electors of the city, town or county, as the case may be, in which it is proposed to develop, construct, or acquire the same, voting upon such issue, approve such project by voting in favor thereof at an election to be held for that purpose, or at any general or special election." James v. Valtierra (1971).

Not all states permit local governments to regulate land use through the ballot box. The procedural requirements of the state's enabling act, as to planning department studies, consistency with the comprehensive plan, and notice and hearing rights of affected property owners, may be taken as dictating nonapplicability of an electoral process which affords no room for such safeguards. Some courts permit the referendum but not the initiative on the ground that the required preliminary and procedural steps are preserved in a referendum, which only adds the additional step of voter ratification to the process. Others permit both referendum and initiative, but limit application to matters of general land use regulation, denying their propriety in e.g., cases of small parcel rezonings, where the action is more properly characterized as administrative rather than legislative.

B.   THE PLANNING PROCESS

1. The Comprehensive Plan

State enabling acts generally require that local land use regulation be done in conjunction with planning. This may be held to require no more than some forethought and generalized consideration of the community's needs (as opposed to an impulsive response to an isolated development). Or, at the other extreme, it may require the drafting, beforehand, of a separate document (a master plan, general plan, or comprehensive plan) which sets forth goals and policies with regard to some physical aspect of the community. The requirement may further mandate that all subsequently enacted land use regulation be consistent with the plan (or risk being held invalid by the courts for inconsistency).

Illustration: The Standard City Planning Enabling Act, prepared by the U.S. Department of Commerce in 1928, provides that the local planning commission shall prepare "a master plan for the physical development of the municipality, * * * including, among other things, the general location, character, and extent of streets, viaducts, subways, bridges, waterways, water fronts, boulevards, parkways, playgrounds, squares, parks, aviation fields, and other public ways, grounds and open spaces, the general location of public buildings and other public property, and the general location and extent of public utilities and terminals, whether publicly or privately owned or operated, for water, light, sanitation, transportation, communication, power, and other purposes; also the removal, relocation, widening, narrowing, vacating, abandonment, change of use or extension of any of the foregoing ways, grounds, open spaces, buildings, property, utilities, or terminals; as well as a zoning plan for the control of the height, area, bulk, location, and use of buildings and premises. * * * The plan shall be made with the general purpose of guiding and accomplishing a coordinated, adjusted, and harmonious development of the municipality and its environs which will, in accordance with present and future needs, best promote health, safety, morals, order, convenience, prosperity, and general welfare, as well as efficiency and economy in the process of development; including, among other things, adequate provision for traffic, the promotion of safety from fire and other dangers, adequate provision for light and air, the promotion of the healthful and convenient distribution of population, the promotion of good civic design and arrangement, wise and efficient expenditure of public funds, and the adequate provision of public utilities and other public requirements".

Illustration: The Model Land Development Code (1976), provides that: "a local government may adopt a Local Land Development Plan (in words, maps, illustrations or other media of communication) setting forth objectives, policies and standards to guide public and private development of land within its planning jurisdiction and including a short-term program of public actions."

2. The Planning Commission

Many communities have, or are required by the enabling act to have, a planning commission, assisted by a planning department, to handle its planning functions. The planning department consists of paid professional city planners; the planning commission is composed of members of the community who are appointed by the local legislative body. The planning commission is charged with various tasks regarding the master plan and land use ordinances.

Illustration: The Florida enabling act provides that a local planning commission shall:

"(1) Acquire and maintain such information and materials as are necessary to an understanding of past trends, present conditions, and forces at work to cause changes in these conditions. Such information and material may include maps and photographs of manmade and natural physical features of the area concerned, statistics on past trends and present conditions with respect to population, property values, economic base, land use, and such other information as is important or likely to be important in determining the amount, direction, and kind of development to be expected in the area and its various parts.

(2) Prepare, adopt, and from time to time amend and revise a comprehensive and coordinated general plan for meeting present requirements and such future requirements as may be foreseen.

(3) Establish principles and policies for guiding action in the development of the area.

(4) Conduct such public hearings as may be required to gather information necessary for the drafting, establishment and maintenance of the comprehensive plan and such additional public hearings as are specified under the provisions of this part.

(5) Make or cause to be made any necessary special studies on the location, condition, and adequacy of specific facilities in the area. These may include, but are not limited to, studies on housing, commercial and industrial conditions and facilities, public and private utilities, and traffic, transportation and parking."

3. Land Use Ordinances

Enactment of the land use plan and ordinances is usually done by the local legislative body following recommendation by the planning commission and appropriate public hearings. The legislative body also establishes the official zoning map, and approves all proposed amendments to the map or zoning ordinance or master plan. It is usually not involved in the approval of subdivision maps or the granting of special exceptions (usually done by the planning commission), or in the granting of variances (usually done by the board of adjustment), although it may review such actions.

4. Interim Ordinances

The state enabling act may permit a community to enact a land use regulation without having first drafted a comprehensive plan or without first holding public hearings on the proposed measure in order for it to preserve the integrity of the regulation from destruction by premature land development (which is all the more likely to occur when property owners know that regulations are contemplated). This emergency or interim power may be limited to certain periods of time (e.g., 18 months), or to certain forms of governmental action (prohibitions rather than permissions), and may require the approval of a special supermajority of the local legislative body.

C. ENFORCEMENT

An owner who seeks to subdivide land not in compliance with the subdivision ordinance will not be permitted to file the appropriate subdivision map. An owner who seeks to construct a building not in accordance with the appropriate zoning and building regulations will be denied a building permit. An owner who seeks to engage in an activity not permitted by local zoning and licensing regulations will be denied a permit to do so in such cases where a permit is necessary. The community may sue to enjoin an improper activity or demolish an illegal structure, may seek criminal sanctions, or may employ self-help. An owner of property may be required to certify its compliance to any purchaser or tenant prior to sale or lease, or the transfer of a noncomplying property may be made unlawful or subject to a right of rescission by the transferee. There may be a requirement of a pre-transfer code inspection, or the community may have the power to record a notice of violation of an ordinance so as to cloud the owner's title.

Enforcement of land use regulations is usually vested exclusively in local officials, although occasionally neighbors may be able to sue to enjoin or recover damages for a violation.

1. Nonconforming Uses

Land use regulations generally apply only prospectively, and are not imposed upon those buildings or activities which were already existing before enactment of the regulation. It was originally assumed that nonconforming uses would naturally disappear, but such structures and activities instead tend to endure by virtue of their monopolistic advantages. Consequently, many communities now attempt to apply their zoning regulations to them directly. The courts generally do not permit the immediate abatement of nonconforming structures or uses, but a community may be allowed to "amortize" the activities by giving them a limited amount of time to wind up their nonconforming features. The community may also prohibit a nonconforming structure from being enlarged or altered or put to any other nonconforming use and may prohibit the resumption of any nonconforming use after it has been abandoned or the structure has been destroyed.

Illustration: A New Orleans, Louisiana, zoning ordinance provides "No building or portion thereof or land used in whole or in part for nonconforming purposes according to the provisions of the Ordinance, which hereafter becomes and remains vacant for a continuous period of 6 calendar months shall again be used except in conformity with the regulations of the district in which such building or land is situated. Neither the intention of the owner nor that of anybody else to use a building or lot or part of either for any nonconforming use, nor the fact that said building or lot or part of either may have been used by a makeshift or pretended nonconforming use shall be taken into consideration in interpreting and construing the word 'vacant' as used in this section; * * *." Fuller v. City of New Orleans, Dept. of Safety & Permits, Bldg. Inspection & Permits (1975).

Illustration: A Los Angeles, California, ordinance provides, "The nonconforming use of a conforming building or structure may be continued, except that in the residential zones any nonconforming commercial or industrial use of a residential building or residential accessory building shall be discontinued within five (5) years from June 1, 1946, or five (5) years from the date the use becomes nonconforming, whichever date is later. * * * The nonconforming use of land shall be discontinued within five (5) years from June 1, 1946, or within five (5) years from the date the use became nonconforming, in each of the following cases: (1) where no buildings are employed in connection with such use; (2) where the only buildings employed are accessory or incidental to such use; (3) where such use is maintained in connection with a conforming building." City of Los Angeles v. Gage (1954).

Illustration: An ordinance of Santa Cruz County, California, provides "a nonconforming use may be ordered to be terminated by order of the board of supervisors upon recommendation of the planning commission within a period to be specified in such order * * * If the nonconforming user has not made a substantial investment, or the investment can be substantially utilized or recovered through a then permitted use, such order may require complete termination of the nonconforming use within a one year minimum after the date of the order. In making such recommendation, the planning commission shall consider the total cost of property and improvements, the length of time, the adaptability of the land and improvements to a then permitted use, the cost of moving and re-establishing the use elsewhere and other related factors. Where the nonconforming use involved the removal of natural products, the amount or percentage of depletion shall be deducted from the cost of investment, and the current need for the product and its availability elsewhere shall be considered." People v. Gates (1974).

III. JUDICIAL REVIEW

A. THE ROLE OF THE JUDICIARY

Courts are required to consider the validity of local regulatory action in a variety of contexts. Government may be suing the owner to compel him to comply with its regulations; the owner (or parties supporting him, such as brokers and contractors) may be suing to invalidate the regulations; a neighbor (or neighborhood organization) may be seeking to force government to reject the owner's proposal or to enforce some restriction against the owner; or interested outsiders, such as housing and welfare organizations, may be attempting to invalidate neighborhood "exclusionary" activities (discussed below).

Where legislative action is involved, the courts generally employ an "arbitrary and capricious" standard, invalidating the action only if it fails to constitute a rational means towards reaching a legitimate end. If, however, the action infringes upon a constitutionally protected interest, then a "strict scrutiny" test

may be utilized, requiring the showing of a compelling state interest to support the action. If the action
is deemed to be adjudicatory (or quasi-judicial or
administrative), rather than legislative, then the
standard of judicial review is generally that of "abuse
of discretion," with the court asking whether there is
"substantial evidence" in the record to support the
action. If a fundamental or vested right is involved,
the court may make an independent judgment in the
matter rather than merely reviewing the agency action.

For many courts, an action is deemed legislative if
it has been taken by a legislative body and is legislative in form. Thus zoning and rezoning are regarded
as legislative acts because done by a city council,
while the granting of special exceptions (by a planning commission) and variances (by a board of adjustment) are treated as administrative. Other courts
reject this approach as too formalistic and look to the
nature and content of the regulation instead; the
rezoning of a small parcel of land, might be held to be
adjudicatory under such an analysis.

In general, the courts seek to avoid being forced
into making substantive zoning decisions, preferring
not to become super-zoning boards who must substitute their judgment for that of experts and local
officials. However, where there are questions of procedural fairness or the protection of basic rights the
courts do not hesitate to intervene.

B. GROUNDS FOR INVALIDATION

Persons aggrieved by a particular land use regulation may institute litigation challenging the propriety of the official action; it may be an owner who has been denied permission to develop his property, a neighbor who is upset because the owner has been granted permission to develop, or a third party representing other land use values. Many of the doctrines which support judicial attacks on regulations have already been discussed and will not be restated here. Examples of these doctrines are lack of authority under the state enabling act, an attack often brought against architectural review, historic preservation, and growth management activities; or improper delegation of authority, an attack often brought against design review boards or neighborhood consent ordinances (requiring block or neighborhood approval as a precondition to granting a permit to engage in an otherwise lawful activity in the area).

1. Arbitrary and Capricious

Local land use regulation, even when it is legislative, is invalid if it is deemed by a court to be arbitrary and capricious. The particular zoning classification applied to an individual parcel of land, or the distinction between the activities excluded and included within a single zoning category are common situations where this issue is raised.

Illustration: The decision of the Village of Lake Success, New York, to reclassify a parcel of property from business to residential was held invalid where the only sensible use of the property was commercial and all the surrounding property was zoned and in fact used commercially.   Udell v. Haas (1968).

Illustration: The ordinance of the city of Newark, New Jersey, was held unreasonable in so far as it prohibited pick-up or delivery service by launderettes in business districts while at the same time permitting such service by bakeries, appliance repair shops, restaurants, cleaners, drug and other retail stores.   Marie's Launderette v. City of Newark (1955).

Illustration: The Zoning Ordinance of James City County, Virginia, was held invalid for making the following distinctions: " 'Hotels, motels, and theatres' are permitted; banks, office buildings, and grocery stores are prohibited. 'Antique shops' are permitted; shops selling antique reproductions are prohibited. 'Restaurants' are permitted; 'fast food' or 'drive-in' restaurants are prohibited. Gift shops are permitted, provided they are 'accessory to hotels or motels having fifty or more dwelling or lodging units' and are 'designed and scaled only to meet the requirements of occupants and their guests'; other retail stores selling identical gifts are prohibited."   Board of Supervisors of James City County v. Rowe (1975).

Invalidation in such cases is not always stated in terms of arbitrary and capricious. The action may be held invalid as failing to be in accordance with the requirement of a comprehensive plan or as being ultra vires. The irrationality of the distinction may also be treated as a constitutional defect on the ground that it denies equal protection or substantive due process to the affected owner.

2. Due Process

Persons whose interest will be affected by a land use proposal are entitled to procedural fairness with regard to its enactment and enforcement. Procedural due process issues are raised in numerous ways in the land use process. In terms of notice, there may be questions as to the form of communication (mailing versus publication or posting), the persons entitled to receive notice (e.g. property owners only or tenants also, local residents or nearby neighbors outside the municipal boundary as well), the adequacy of the information imparted (in terms of property affected or the measure proposed), and the nature of the governmental action (administrative, requiring individual notices to all affected parties, or legislative, requiring only general public notice). In terms of the hearing, there may be questions regarding the relationship of the issues at the hearing to those raised in the notice, the opportunity to speak, the time allowed to present evidence, the right to cross-examine, the taking of unsworn or opinion testimony (including staff reports, field trips and neighbors' opinions), and the completeness of the record kept of the hearing. In terms of reaching a decision there may be questions of conflict of interest (personal involvement, campaign contributions, ex parte contacts) and bias. When the initiative or referendum process is employed an entirely different set of procedural questions is, of course, presented.

Substantive due process considerations are occasionally used by courts to invalidate land use measures which they consider to be excessively arbitrary, inconsistent with the general welfare, or too intrusive upon personal liberty.

3. First Amendment and Associational Rights

Constitutionally protected activities generate special difficulties for land use regulations. The normal presumptions of validity and the attendant judicial deference may not apply when a land use restriction is seen as infringing upon some First Amendment or related right. This is particularly the case with regard to regulation of speech and religious activities or family associations.

a. Speech and Religion

Signs and billboards clearly convey messages to their readers. Communities may regulate their size, shape, illumination and placement, but other restrictions are less enforceable. Restrictions relating to political signs are allowed only when alternative methods of communication are available. Commercial speech is less protected but has not yet been definitively construed; the United States Supreme Court's decision in Metromedia v. City of San Diego (1981) had no majority position and included five separate opinions invalidating an ordinance which prohibited all off-site advertising (i.e., not relating to goods sold on the premises) but did permit on-site signs.

Other forms of protected activity may also require special consideration in being made subject to local land use regulations. In some jurisdictions, churches have a preferred status, and are exempt from many zoning regulations. Schools, bookstores and movie theaters share similar protection in differing degrees, although the validation of special zoning treatment of "adult" theaters and bookstores appears to permit some degree of content dependence in this sphere. On zoning for adult businesses, see p. 421.

Illustration: An ordinance of Mt. Ephraim, New Jersey, which, by virtue of not including it among the enumerated permitted uses, excluded live entertainment throughout the Borough, was held invalid as being an overbroad prohibition against protected forms of expression. As a result, the conviction of an adult bookstore proprietor for permitting nude dancing to occur upon the premises, was set aside by the United States Supreme Court. Schad v. Borough of Mt. Ephraim (1981).

b. Association

Similar protection may be extended to individual living arrangements affected by a single family residential zoning classification. If the ordinance is written in terms of prohibiting certain otherwise lawful social groupings (such as unrelated persons living together), rather than in terms of the residential structure (such as the number of entries or kitchens), it may be held invalid as intruding upon associational or privacy rights.

Illustration: The single family zoning ordinance of Belle Terre, New York, which prohibited more than two unrelated individuals from living together anywhere in the community (although any number of related persons could share a household), was upheld by the United States Supreme Court against charges that it infringed on rights of privacy and travel. Village of Belle Terre v. Boraas (1974).

On the other hand, the definition of a family in the ordinance of East Cleveland, Ohio, which did not permit a grandmother to reside with her son and her two grandsons, who were first cousins rather than brothers, was held invalid by the Supreme Court on the ground that it constituted an improper intrusion into family living arrangements, a violation of substantive due process rights. Moore v. City of East Cleveland, Ohio (1977).

4. Taking

A land use regulation which causes a severe economic burden to the property owner will likely be attacked as constituting a taking of property without the payment of just compensation, in violation of the Fifth Amendment of the United States Constitution or similar provisions in most state constitutions. The courts have never reached a consensus or single theory as to when a regulation amounts to an invalid taking of property.

Illustration: A 1921 Pennsylvania statute prohibiting the mining of anthracite coal when removal would cause residences on the surface to subside was held invalid as taking the coal company's property rights in the coal which it owned but could no longer mine. Pennsylvania Coal Co. v. Mahon (1922).

Illustration: A 1966 Pennsylvania statute prohibiting the mining of bituminous coal when removal would cause residences and public structures to subside was upheld as validly protecting the public interest in health, the environment and "fiscal integrity" and not a taking of property. Keystone Bituminous Coal Ass'n v. DeBenedictis (1987).

A variety of factors appear with some regularity in judicial consideration of this issue. These are discussed below.

a. *The Nature of the Government Activity*

Early cases concentrated on the formal nature of the governmental activity. If government physically took possession or title to property, it was liable to pay just compensation; if governmental activity actually injured property, there might be liability in trespass or nuisance. On the other hand, if property value fell merely as a result of a governmental regulation, there was no unconstitutional taking of property, because title, possession, and the physical condition of the property remained unaffected. Those distinctions are generally rejected today, and it is recognized that a government may take land by oversevere regulation as much as by the institution of formal eminent domain proceedings. It is sometimes said that the more governmental activity resembles the acquisition of resources for itself rather than the regulation of competing private interests, the more likely it is that a taking will be found. Thus, downzoning of property adjacent to the municipal airport may be viewed as an attempt by the community to avoid having to purchase that property or pay its owners nuisance damages, and thus held invalid, whereas the same degree of downzoning might be held valid where it is done in order to protect an adjacent residential neighborhood from industrial intrusion.

Illustration: A New York statute authorizing cable television companies to install lines and boxes on the roofs of apartment buildings was held to constitute a taking of property because it authorized a permanent physical occupation and eliminated the owner's right to exclude even though there was only minimal physical interference with property.   Loretto v. Teleprompter Manhattan CATV Corp. (1982).

Illustration: A New York City landmark preservation ordinance which prohibited a railroad company from constructing a skyscraper over the Grand Central Terminal was held not to constitute a taking of the right to exploit a potential property right (rental income of $3 million yearly) since the owner was earning a reasonable return on the existing structure.

b.   The Nature of the Owner's Property Interest

Not all losses of value are deemed takings of property.   Courts use such phrases as "distinct investment-backed expectations" or "vested rights" to indicate property interests most entitled to protection. The loss of value caused by downzoning an undeveloped parcel of property is not as likely to be declared a taking than the same financial loss when it results from an order for the abatement of an existing nonconforming use or structure.

c.   The Extent of the Loss

The fact that the value of a parcel falls due to the imposition of some new regulation upon it does not automatically mean that part of his property has therefore been taken by the government.   Only when the reduction goes "too far" are the courts likely to hold that a taking has occurred.

Illustration: As a result of imposing an XXX zoning classification on property in Euclid, Ohio, its value fell 75%, from $10,000 to $2,500 per acre.   Nevertheless, in its first case to consider the validity of zoning, the United States Supreme Court upheld the ordinance.   Village of

Euclid v. Ambler Realty (1926). Restrictions causing losses of 87% and 95% have been sustained in other cases (from the Supreme Court and the Ninth Circuit, respectively).

Illustration: Because the state's Beachfront Management Act prohibited the owner of two beachfront lots from building houses on them the state trial court found that he was deprived of all economic use of his property. The state Supreme Court nevertheless upheld the Act, but the United States Supreme Court ruled that such a total deprivation generally constitutes a taking of property unless common law nuisance rules would have led to the same prohibition. Lucas v. South Carolina Coastal Council (1992).

The duration of the loss is often considered relevant. A temporary deprivation of value (such as arises from a temporary moratorium on land development) may be upheld, even though the property may have no economic value whatsoever during the interim. Growth management ordinances which postpone an owner's right to develop for several years are sometimes upheld on the ground that the loss is only temporary.

d. The Public Benefit

Sometimes a balancing test is used, comparing the loss to the owner with the benefit gained by the public. If the benefit is of dubious public value to begin with, or is seen as only favoring a few, it is less likely that a significant economic loss to an owner will be tolerated. Sometimes it is said that property may be regulated in order to eliminate a burden it would otherwise cast upon others but not in order to compel it to confer a benefit upon others; however, critics say that this formula is merely circular.

e.   Sharing the Loss

An ordinance which restricts everyone similarly (such as a uniform height limit over the entire community) is more likely to be upheld than one which singles out one parcel to bear an economic loss for the sake of the others. Landmark designation, by virtue of selecting out individual buildings is sometimes attacked on this basis; when upheld, it is on the basis that the landmark law is part of a comprehensive plan or that the owner of the landmark benefits by the designation of other landmarks within the community. Reverse spot zoning—the downzoning of one parcel out of many for the sake of the others—may be held invalid on this ground.

f.   Mitigation and Compensation Measures

A major purpose of variances is to afford an administrative mechanism for avoiding the taking of property. By virtue of being eligible for a variance in a hardship situation, a property owner may lose his ability to contend that the ordinance constitutes a taking of his property. On variances see p. 429.

Other land use ordinances may give affected property owners offsetting compensation. Tax abatement is common for buildings given landmark status. Some communities have "transferable development right" systems, where an owner of restricted property is permitted to transfer its unused development potential to other land elsewhere in the community.

g.   Relief

An overrestrictive ordinance may always be held invalid by the courts, but owners fear that such relief does little to deter officials from merely enacting a different looking, but similarly repressive alternative. Therefore, aggrieved owners seek to recover damages instead of or in addition to invalidation. In First English Evangelical Lutheran Church v. County of Los Angeles (1987), the United States Supreme Court held the constitution required payment of compensation for the time during which the regulation denied the owner use of his land.

5. Exclusionary Zoning

Many communities enact land use regulations or operate their land use permit processes so as to exclude "undesirable" persons from residing there. Such exclusion is based on racially, etc. discriminatory motives or on the desire to save money by keeping out the poor (who may pay little in taxes but may require extensive social services). Many conventional land use devices, such as minimum lot size, costly building code requirements, and elimination of apartment and mobile home districts can produce this effect while appearing facially innocent and ostensibly justifiable on environmental and public health grounds. Civil rights and welfare organizations often bring actions challenging such activities on the ground that the communities are attempting to avoid housing their fair share of the region's needy.

a. Federal Courts

(1) Constitutional Protection

Nothing in the United States Constitution directly prohibits a community from exercising its land use powers in an exclusionary fashion. However, if the exclusion is directed along racial lines there may be a violation of the Equal Protection or Due Process Clauses of the Fourteenth Amendment.

Illustration: An ordinance adopted by the City of Louisville, Kentucky, making it unlawful for a colored person to reside in any house on a block which was predominantly white, and vice versa, was held unconstitutional by the United States Supreme Court on the ground that it constituted an unconstitutional interference with property rights insofar as it prohibited a person of one race from selling property to one of another race. Buchanan v. Warley (1917).

But even where racial classification is involved, the federal courts require more than a showing of disproportionate impact on one race; it is also required that there be evidence that the activity was undertaken with a discriminatory purpose or intent. A second difficulty in the application of federal constitutional law to exclusionary zoning is the federal position that income level, unlike race, does not constitute a suspect classification. Poverty becomes a suspect class only when the poor are made to suffer an absolute deprivation of a meaningful opportunity to enjoy a desired benefit. Finally, the standing requirement in exclusionary zoning litigation in federal court compels a plaintiff to show some specific housing which would have been available but for the exclusionary community action.

Illustration: The one acre minimum lot size ordinance of the town of Los Altos Hills, California, was held not to deny Mexican–Americans equal protection of the laws even though the requirement tended to exclude them because of their race. Because there was no showing that adequate low-cost housing was unavailable elsewhere in the county, and because wealthy Mexican–Americans were not excluded, the town was not required to show a compelling interest to justify its ordinance. Ybarra v. Los Altos Hills (1974).

Illustration: The refusal of the Village of Arlington Heights, Illinois, to rezone a 15 acre parcel from single-family to multi-family, so as to permit a federally assisted housing project of 190 units for low and moderate income tenants to be constructed there, was held not to violate the Fourteenth Amendment, because there was no showing of a discriminatory intent or purpose. The evidence disclosed that there were typical and legitimate zoning reasons for the governmental action. Under the circumstances, disproportionate racial impact (minorities constituted 18% of the local population but 40% of those eligible for the project) was not enough. Arlington Heights v. Metropolitan Housing Development Corp. (1977).

(2) Statutory Protection

The Federal Fair Housing Act (Title VIII of the Civil Rights Act of 1968) prohibits the refusal to sell or rent housing "to any person because of race, color, religion, sex or national origin." It does not deal with the question of economic discrimination in zoning, but, unlike the constitutional question, a discriminatory intent need not be shown in order to make out a violation. It may be sufficient to show a discriminatory effect resulting from the governmental action.

Illustration: In order to halt the construction of a racially integrated town house development in an unincorporated
area of St. Louis County, Missouri, the residents incorporated the town of Black Jack and immediately created a
planning and zoning commission which enacted a zoning
ordinance barring all further apartment construction. This
ordinance was held to have a racially discriminatory effect
and was found not to have been enacted to promote a
compelling governmental interest. It therefore violated the
Fair Housing Act. United States v. City of Black Jack,
Missouri (1974); Park View Heights Corp. v. City of Black
Jack (1979).

b. State Courts

Several state supreme courts have declined to follow the restrictive federal approach and have held
that exclusionary local land use regulations are invalid even when they are not directed at any particular
racial group nor enacted out of any discriminatory
motive. Such holdings are generally based upon
some provision of the state constitution or zoning
enabling act, but they have in common the principle
that local land use regulation must conform to the
general welfare, which includes the housing needs of
the region for all segments of the community.

Illustration: The zoning ordinances of the Township of
Mt. Laurel, New Jersey, which permitted only single-family
detached dwellings, imposed maximum bedroom requirements and excessive minimum lot area, lot frontage and
building size requirements and allocated too much land for
industrial uses, were held to violate the obligation which
every developing municipality has to make it physically
and economically possible to provide low and moderate
income housing for a "fair share" of the regional housing

needs. Southern Burlington County NAACP v. Township of Mt. Laurel (1975).

Illustration: The Township of Madison, New Jersey, which zoned disproportionate amounts of land for high cost residences, imposed excessively high subdivision and PUD exactions upon developers, and had an extremely expensive permit approval process was held to be "exclusionary, i.e. whether or not so intended, does * * * operate in fact to preclude the opportunity to supply any substantial amounts of new housing for low and moderate income households." With regard to exclusionary developing municipalities, a trial court is not required to "devise specific formulae for estimating their precise fair share of the lower income housing needs of a specifically demarcated region." Instead, the trial court should concentrate on "bona fide efforts toward the elimination or minimization of undue cost-generating requirements. * * * [I]t is incumbent on the governing body to adjust its zoning regulations so as to render possible and feasible the 'least cost' housing, consistent with minimum standards of health and safety, which private industry will undertake, and in amounts sufficient to satisfy the deficit in the hypothesized fair share." Oakwood at Madison, Inc. v. Township of Madison (1977).

*

INDEX

References are to Pages

475

        Bernhardt, Real Prop. 3rd NS—18

†